LLMs, Knowledge Graphs, and the Semantic Web:

Revolutionizing Data Processing, Knowledge Extraction, and AI Capabilities

Fernando Ortiz-Rodriguez
https://orcid.org/0000-0003-2084-3462
Tamaulipas Autonomous University, Mexico

Amed Leyva-Mederos
https://orcid.org/0009-0001-5050-5563
Universidad Central "Marta Abreu" de Las Villas, Cuba

Jose L. Martinez
https://orcid.org/0000-0002-1276-6957
Tamaulipas Autonomous University, Mexico

Deepali Vora
Symbiosis International (Deemed to be) University, India

Lisandra Diaz
Universidad Central "Marta Abreu" de Las Villas, Cuba

IGI Global
Scientific Publishing
Publishing Tomorrow's Research Today

Vice President of Editorial Melissa Wagner
Director of Acquisitions Mikaela Felty
Director of Book Development Jocelynn Hessler
Production Manager Mike Brehm
Cover Design Jose Rosado

Published in the United States of America by
IGI Global Scientific Publishing
701 East Chocolate Avenue
Hershey, PA, 17033, USA
Tel: 717-533-8845 | Fax: 717-533-7115
Website: https://www.igi-global.com E-mail: cust@igi-global.com

Library of Congress Cataloging-in-Publication Data

Names: Ortiz-Rodriguez, Fernando, 1974- editor
Title: LLMs, knowledge graphs, and the semantic web : revolutionizing data processing, knowledge extraction, and AI capabilities / edited by Fernando Ortiz-Rodriguez, Amed Leiva-Mederos, José Lázaro Martinez Rodríguez, Deepali Vora, Lisandra Díaz de la Paz.
Description: Hershey, PA : IGI Global Scientific Publishing, [2027] | Includes bibliographical references and index. | Summary: "This book aims to introduce the fundamental concepts of KGs and LLMs. Explain how these technologies work and their potential applications"-- Provided by publisher.
Identifiers: LCCN 2025015998 (print) | LCCN 2025015999 (ebook) | ISBN 9798337313603 h/c | ISBN 9798337313610 s/c | ISBN 9798337313627 ebook
Subjects: LCSH: Natural language processing--Data processing | Information visualization--Data processing | Semantic Web | Data mining | Artificial intelligence--Data processing
Classification: LCC QA76.9.N38 L585 2026 (print) | LCC QA76.9.N38 (ebook)
LC record available at https://lccn.loc.gov/2025015998
LC ebook record available at https://lccn.loc.gov/2025015999

British Cataloguing in Publication Data
A Cataloguing in Publication record for this book is available from the British Library.

Table of Contents

Preface xii

Chapter 1
Unifying Large Language Models, Knowledge Graphs, and the Semantic Web: A New Paradigm for Intelligent Systems 1
Fernando Ortiz-Rodriguez, Tamaulipas Autonomous University, Mexico

Chapter 2
Unlocking the Power of Knowledge Graphs: Advanced Reasoning and Embedding Techniques 13
Otmane Azeroual, FernUniversität in Hagen (FeU), Germany

Chapter 3
A Neuro-Symbolic System for End-of-Life Decision-Making Based on Knowledge Graphs 47
Armando David Caballero Font, Hospital Universitario Arnaldo Millán, Cuba
Yadier Betancourt Martínez, Universidad Central "Marta Abreu" de las Villas, Cuba
Amed Leiva-Mederos, Universidad Central "Marta Abreu" de las Villas, Cuba
Rafael Bello, Universidad Central "Marta Abreu" de las Villas, Cuba
Maria Matilde Garcia Lorenzo, Universidad Central "Marta Abreu" de las Villas, Cuba
Armando Caballero, Universidad Central "Marta Abreu" de las Villas, Cuba

Chapter 4
Evaluating the Most Used Database Technologies for AI and Real-Time Application Development in Metaverse Systems: A Comparative Study 69
Asher Babu, Christ (Deemed to be) University, Delhi NCR, India

Chapter 5
Hybrid Model for Teaching French 99
Juan Andrés García Martín, Universidad Complutense Madrid, Spain
Marilin Urbay Rodriguez, Universidad Central "Marta Abreu" de las Villas, Cuba

Chapter 6
Design of a Semantic Search Engine for Technological Observatories 115
Enrique Osvaldo Pérez Riverón, Universidad Central ¨Marta Abreu¨ de las Villas, Cuba
Daniel Gálvez Lio, Universidad Central ¨Marta Abreu¨ de las Villas, Cuba
Amed Leiva-Mederos, Universidad Central ¨Marta Abreu¨ de las Villas, Cuba
Lisandra Diaz de la Paz, Universidad Central ¨Marta Abreu¨ de las Villas, Cuba

Chapter 7
Semantic Information Recovery System: Use of Neo4j and Language Models for the Creation of a Vector Database 147
Livia Reyes, Centro de Información para la Prensa, Cuba
Yorjandy Martinez Lamas, Universidad Central ¨Marta Abreu¨ de las Villas, Cuba
Javier Alejandro Bravo Santos, Universidad Central ¨Marta Abreu¨ de las Villas, Cuba

Chapter 8
Image Classification-Based Detection System of the Mite (*Phyllocoptruta oleivora*) Using Machine Learning Models 177
Everardo L. Huerta-Lopez, Autonomous University of Tamaulipas, Mexico
Ana B. Rios-Alvarado, Autonomous University of Tamaulipas, Mexico
Tania Y. Guerrero-Meléndez, Autonomous University of Tamaulipas, Mexico
Jose L. Martinez-Rodriguez, Autonomous University of Tamaulipas, Mexico

Chapter 9
Integration of Large Language Models and Knowledge Graphs in Semantic Web: A Bibliometric Analysis of Scientific Production 193
Francisco Isaí Morales-Sáenz, Autonomous University of Tamaulipas, Mexico

Chapter 10
AI-Integrated Learning Environment in Higher Education: Challenges and Opportunities 215
Vivek Gupta, Sharda University, India
Fernando Ortiz-Rodriguez, Tamaulipas Autonomous University, Mexico

Compilation of References 229

About the Contributors 257

Index 261

Detailed Table of Contents

Preface xii

Chapter 1
Unifying Large Language Models, Knowledge Graphs, and the Semantic Web: A New Paradigm for Intelligent Systems 1
Fernando Ortiz-Rodriguez, Tamaulipas Autonomous University, Mexico

The contemporary digital era is characterized by an explosion of data, presenting both unprecedented opportunities and significant challenges for knowledge extraction, representation, and reasoning. This paper introduces and analyzes a powerful convergence of three technological pillars poised to revolutionize artificial intelligence: Large Language Models (LLMs), Knowledge Graphs (KGs), and the Semantic Web. The synergy between the generative prowess and natural language understanding of LLMs, the structured and verifiable factual representation of KGs, and the standardized, interoperable framework of the Semantic Web creates a transformative paradigm for AI. This integration mitigates the inherent weaknesses of each component—such as the factual unreliability and opacity of LLMs and the construction and maintenance bottlenecks of KGs—while amplifying their collective strengths.

Chapter 2
Unlocking the Power of Knowledge Graphs: Advanced Reasoning and Embedding Techniques 13
Otmane Azeroual, FernUniversität in Hagen (FeU), Germany

Knowledge Graphs (KGs) are essential for managing complex relationships and semantic data. This chapter examines two key functions of KGs: reasoning and embedding. Reasoning infers new knowledge from existing data, supporting deeper insights and decision-making. Embedding converts high-dimensional data into low-dimensional vectors, improving efficiency and analysis. Together, these functions enhance the flexibility and performance of KGs, with applications in NLP, information retrieval, and data integration, while addressing challenges and research directions.

Chapter 3
A Neuro-Symbolic System for End-of-Life Decision-Making Based on Knowledge Graphs 47

Armando David Caballero Font, Hospital Universitario Arnaldo Millán, Cuba
Yadier Betancourt Martínez, Universidad Central "Marta Abreu" de las Villas, Cuba
Amed Leiva-Mederos, Universidad Central "Marta Abreu" de las Villas, Cuba
Rafael Bello, Universidad Central "Marta Abreu" de las Villas, Cuba
Maria Matilde Garcia Lorenzo, Universidad Central "Marta Abreu" de las Villas, Cuba
Armando Caballero, Universidad Central "Marta Abreu" de las Villas, Cuba

Making decisions in Intensive Care Units (ICUs) is essential for patient survival and demands a precise evaluation of complex clinical data. Although predictive models based on machine learning, such as neural networks, have proven useful for anticipating outcomes in intensive care, their lack of transparency restricts their clinical adoption. This study proposes a system that merges the predictive strength of neural networks with explainability techniques based on knowledge graphs and medical ontologies to enhance the transparency and interpretability of predictions in clinical settings. By employing a medical ontology to organize data and a knowledge graph implemented in Neo4j, clinical information is consolidated, and understandable explanations regarding ICU mortality are produced. The system can also apply rules for end-of-life decisions and utilize large language models (LLMs) to generate clear explanations for both mortality predictions and end-of-life choices. The research evaluates the accuracy of this approach and compares it with classical explainability methods such as LIME. Decision-making in Intensive Care Units (ICUs) is critical for patient survival and requires accurate evaluation of complex clinical data. Although predictive models based on machine learning, such as neural networks, have proven useful for predicting outcomes in intensive care, their lack of transparency limits their clinical application. This research proposes a system that combines the predictive power of neural networks with explainability methods based on knowledge graphs and medical ontologies to improve the transparency and understanding of predictions in a clinical setting. Using a medical ontology to structure data and a knowledge graph in Neo4j, clinical information is integrated, and understandable explanations of predictions regarding ICU mortality are provided. The system is also capable of using rules for end-of-life decisions and leveraging large language models (LLMs) to generate clear explanations for both mortality and end-of-life decisions. The research evaluates the accuracy of this approach and compares it with classical explainability methods, such as LIME.

Chapter 4
Evaluating the Most Used Database Technologies for AI and Real-Time Application Development in Metaverse Systems: A Comparative Study............ 69
Asher Babu, Christ (Deemed to be) University, Delhi NCR, India

The rapid evolution of technology, particularly in AI and real-time applications, has increased the need for databases that efficiently handle diverse and complex workloads. This paper analyzes the top five database management systems of 2025: Oracle, MySQL, Microsoft SQL Server, PostgreSQL, and MongoDB. These databases, spanning relational and NoSQL systems, offer distinct capabilities. The comparison is based on key parameters such as performance, scalability, extensibility, data model support, and ease of integration with modern technologies. Notably, PostgreSQL has emerged as a top choice for AI-based applications in metaverse platforms due to its extensibility (e.g., PostGIS for spatial data) and high performance in decentralized architectures. Through detailed analysis, this study highlights the strengths and weaknesses of each database, concluding that PostgreSQL is best suited for AI and real-time applications due to its adaptability and seamless integration with open-source tools critical for metaverse development.

Chapter 5
Hybrid Model for Teaching French 99
Juan Andrés García Martín, Universidad Complutense Madrid, Spain
Marilin Urbay Rodriguez, Universidad Central "Marta Abreu" de las Villas, Cuba

The study employed a hybrid methodology that combines knowledge graphs and fine-tuned language models (LLMs) to optimize the teaching of French as a foreign language (FFL). First, a knowledge graph was designed in Neo4j, structured according to the CEFR levels (A1-C2), with interconnected nodes representing grammatical elements (such as the subjunctive or the passé composé), thematic vocabulary (greetings, business), and communicative situations (interviews, restaurants). In parallel, the CamemBERT model (specialized in French) was fine-tuned using the FLEUR (10,000 sentences with typical errors from A1-B1 levels) and FRACAS (5,000 academic texts with advanced errors from B2-C2) datasets, which were preprocessed through tokenization and level balancing. The training was conducted on Google Colab Pro with a T4 GPU, applying supervised fine-tuning (SFT) and reinforcement learning with human feedback (RLHF), under hyperparameters such as a learning rate of 5e–5, a batch size of 16, and 5 epochs.

Chapter 6
Design of a Semantic Search Engine for Technological Observatories 115
Enrique Osvaldo Pérez Riverón, Universidad Central "Marta Abreu" de las Villas, Cuba
Daniel Gálvez Lio, Universidad Central "Marta Abreu" de las Villas, Cuba
Amed Leiva-Mederos, Universidad Central "Marta Abreu" de las Villas, Cuba
Lisandra Diaz de la Paz, Universidad Central "Marta Abreu" de las Villas, Cuba

This paper focuses on the development of a semantic search engine to facilitate information retrieval in the Technological Observatory. Its main objective is to automate data searches using artificial intelligence techniques, improving accuracy and information retrieval. To this end, the theoretical and methodological foundations of intelligent information retrieval systems are identified, an architecture based on language models, knowledge graphs, and vector databases is designed, and the retrieval rates of the implemented system are evaluated. The study addresses key concepts such as semantic search, the use of embeddings, and the integration of artificial intelligence models to improve query accuracy. The design of the search engine, structured on an ontology that classifies information into categories, is detailed, and a knowledge graph is implemented in Neo4j, combined with techniques such as GraphRAG to optimize the generation of responses based on structured data.

Chapter 7
Semantic Information Recovery System: Use of Neo4j and Language Models for the Creation of a Vector Database 147
Livia Reyes, Centro de Información para la Prensa, Cuba
Yorjandy Martinez Lamas, Universidad Central "Marta Abreu" de las Villas, Cuba
Javier Alejandro Bravo Santos, Universidad Central "Marta Abreu" de las Villas, Cuba

This paper develops a Semantic Information Retrieval System for the Cuban press, based on natural language processing and knowledge graphs. The research addresses the limitations of traditional document retrieval systems, which rely on rigid metadata and do not interpret contextual relationships among contents. A solution is proposed that integrates a conceptual ontology, a semantic index structured in Neo4j, and pre-trained artificial intelligence models to improve query accuracy. The system architecture employs textual embeddings to generate contextualized searches, using cosine similarity as the retrieval criterion. Furthermore, it incorporates semantic inference techniques and multimodal document analysis. The implementation optimizes access to relevant information in the journalistic domain, overcoming the fragmentation of content stored in DSpace. Evaluations of precision and recall validate the solution's impact on the quality of the results.

Chapter 8
Image Classification-Based Detection System of the Mite (*Phyllocoptruta oleivora*) Using Machine Learning Models 177
Everardo L. Huerta-Lopez, Autonomous University of Tamaulipas, Mexico
Ana B. Rios-Alvarado, Autonomous University of Tamaulipas, Mexico
Tania Y. Guerrero-Meléndez, Autonomous University of Tamaulipas, Mexico
Jose L. Martinez-Rodriguez, Autonomous University of Tamaulipas, Mexico

This work presents an automatic detection system for the mite Phyllocoptruta oleivora using deep learning image classification. Three convolutional archi- tectures (a base CNN, MobileNetV2, and ResNet50) are compared under a homogeneous preprocessing, transfer learning, and data augmentation protocol. From a set of images captured in the field and validated by experts, the results show that a lightweight model such as MobileNetV2 offers the best balance between performance, robustness, and computational efficiency for deployment in agricultural environments. On the other hand, ResNet50 is presented as a competitive alternative when greater computing power is available. Design con- siderations, limitations, and future directions oriented toward mobile applications and monitoring platforms in precision agriculture are discussed.

Chapter 9
Integration of Large Language Models and Knowledge Graphs in Semantic Web: A Bibliometric Analysis of Scientific Production 193
Francisco Isaí Morales-Sáenz, Autonomous University of Tamaulipas, Mexico

The convergence between Large Language Models (LLMs) and Knowledge Graphs (KGs) represents an emerging paradigm in artificial intelligence that combines natural language processing capabilities with structured reasoning. This study presents a comprehensive bibliometric analysis of 230 documents indexed in Web of Science, characterizing the intellectual structure, scientific production trends, and thematic evolution of the field. Results reveal exponential growth with an annual rate of 48.12%, leadership of Chinese institutions, and thematic structuring into six main clusters: reasoning on graphs with LLMs, semantic data mining, entity linking, decision-making systems, domain knowledge extraction, and recommender systems. Theoretical implications reveal the synthesis between connectionist and symbolic approaches, materializing the Semantic Web vision through natural language interfaces.

Chapter 10
AI-Integrated Learning Environment in Higher Education: Challenges and Opportunities 215
Vivek Gupta, Sharda University, India
Fernando Ortiz-Rodriguez, Tamaulipas Autonomous University, Mexico

E-learning platforms are rapidly increasing in demand to transform the landscape of education as they are strengthened by machine learning and artificial intelligence (AI). The integration of AI in higher education improves Massive Open Online Courses (MOOCs) and Virtual Learning Environments (VLEs) in intelligent tutoring and personalized learning, making e-learning and other academic tasks more efficient. This paper explores the potential of AI in online education systems along with proposed solutions. The primary aim of this paper is to highlight the current opportunities and challenges.

Compilation of References 229

About the Contributors 257

Index 261

Preface

INTRODUCTION

We stand at the threshold of a new epoch in the digital age, a time defined not merely by the volume of data we generate, but by our growing ability to comprehend it. For decades, we have been digital prospectors, amassing mountains of information—text, images, code, and countless other forms—often with little more than a rudimentary map to guide us. The dream of a brilliant system, one that cannot only read the lines but also read *between* them, understanding context, relationships, and nuance, has long been the Guiding Principle for computer scientists, developers, and thinkers. Today, that dream is rapidly crystallizing into reality, powered by the convergence of three transformative technologies: **Large Language Models (LLMs)**, **Knowledge Graphs (KGs)**, and the **Semantic Web**. This book is a chronicle of that convergence and a guide to the revolution it is igniting.

The first hero of our story is the Large Language Model. LLMs like GPT, Gemini, and their contemporaries have captured the world's imagination, and for good reason. They are the masters of the unstructured, the interpreters of human expression in its most native form: language. By training on vast expanses of the internet, these models have developed an uncanny ability to generate, summarize, and translate text, write code, and even engage in creative endeavors. They represent a monumental leap in our ability to process 80% of the world's data that exists outside of neat rows and columns. Yet, for all their fluency, LLMs can be prone to "hallucinations," lack a true grounding in factual reality, and often struggle to reason over complex, interconnected information. They possess a universe of knowledge but sometimes lack a reliable atlas.

This is where our second protagonist, the Knowledge Graph, enters the scene. If LLMs are the eloquent orators, Knowledge Graphs are the meticulous librarians and cartographers of the digital world. KGs structure data as a network of entities and the rich, semantic relationships that connect them. The person "Leonardo da Vinci" is not just a string of characters; it's a node connected to other nodes like "Mona Lisa" (which he *painted*), "Florence" (where he *lived*), and "inventor" (an *occupation* he held). This explicit, machine-readable representation of knowledge provides the factual backbone and relational context that LLMs often lack. KGs turn chaotic information into a coherent, navigable landscape of understanding, enabling machines to reason with greater accuracy and transparency. They provide the ground truth, the verifiable map of reality.

The final, and perhaps most foundational, element of this trilogy is the Semantic Web. It is the grand vision, first articulated by Sir Tim Berners-Lee, of a "Web of Data" that is understandable not just by humans but by machines. The Semantic Web provides the universal language—the standards and protocols like RDF (Resource Description Framework) and OWL (Web Ontology Language)—that allows disparate Knowledge Graphs to connect, share, and reason together on a global scale. It is the blueprint for transforming the entire internet from a collection of linked documents into a single, massive, distributed database of knowledge. It sets the stage upon which LLMs and KGs can perform, ensuring that their individual capabilities can be woven into a cohesive, intelligent whole.

This book explores the powerful synergy that erupts when these three forces are combined. We will discuss how LLMs can be used to automatically populate and enrich Knowledge Graphs from unstructured text, turning encyclopedias of prose into structured, queryable assets. Conversely, we will examine how Knowledge Graphs can be used to "ground" LLMs, providing them with factual guardrails to reduce errors and a structured framework to perform more complex, multi-hop reasoning. This fusion creates a virtuous cycle: LLMs make KGs easier to build and maintain, while KGs make LLMs smarter, more reliable, and more transparent.

Woven together by the principles of the Semantic Web, this integrated approach is more than just an academic exercise. It is the engine driving the next generation of artificial intelligence. It powers more sophisticated search engines that understand intent, not just keywords. It enables enterprise AI systems that can reason over an entire organization's siloed data—from financial reports and scientific papers to customer emails and legal contracts—to uncover hidden insights. It is paving the way for AI assistants that are not only conversational but also deeply knowledgeable, trustworthy, and capable of explaining their reasoning.

Whether you are a researcher, an AI developer, a data scientist, a business leader, or simply a curious technologist, this book is intended to be your essential guide to this new frontier. We will move from the foundational concepts of each technology to the practical techniques for integrating them, exploring real-world case studies and cutting-edge research along the way. Our goal is to equip you not just with the "how," but with the "why"—to provide you with a deep, conceptual understanding of this paradigm shift in computing. The revolution is here. It's time to understand its architects and learn to build with their tools.

CHAPTER OVERVIEW

Chapter 1: Unifying Large Language Models, Knowledge Graphs, and the Semantic Web: A New Paradigm for Intelligent Systems

The contemporary digital era is characterized by an explosion of data, presenting both unprecedented opportunities and significant challenges for knowledge extraction, representation, and reasoning. This paper introduces and analyzes a powerful convergence of three technological pillars poised to revolutionize artificial intelligence: Large Language Models (LLMs), Knowledge Graphs (KGs), and the Semantic Web. The synergy between the generative prowess and natural language understanding of LLMs, the structured and verifiable factual representation of KGs, and the standardized, interoperable framework of the Semantic Web creates a transformative paradigm for AI. This integration mitigates the inherent weaknesses of each component—such as the factual unreliability and opacity of LLMs and the construction and maintenance bottlenecks of KGs—while amplifying their collective strengths.

Chapter 2: Unlocking the Power of Knowledge Graphs - Advanced Reasoning and Embedding Techniques

Knowledge Graphs (KGs) are essential for managing complex relationships and semantic data. This chapter examines two key functions of KGs: reasoning and embedding. Reasoning infers new knowledge from existing data, supporting deeper insights and decision-making. Embedding converts high-dimensional data into low-dimensional vectors, improving efficiency and analysis. Together, these functions enhance the flexibility and performance of KGs, with applications in NLP, information retrieval, and data integration, while addressing challenges and research directions.

Chapter 3: A Neuro-Symbolic System for End-of-Life Decision-Making Based on Knowledge Graphs

Decision-making in Intensive Care Units (ICUs) is critical for patient survival and requires accurate evaluation of complex clinical data. Although predictive models based on machine learning, such as neural networks, have proven useful for predicting outcomes in intensive care, their lack of transparency limits their clinical application. This research proposes a system that combines the predictive power of neural networks with explainability methods based on knowledge graphs and medical ontologies to improve the transparency and understanding of predictions in a clinical setting. Using a medical ontology to structure data and a knowledge graph in Neo4j, clinical information is integrated, and understandable explanations of predictions regarding ICU mortality are provided. The system is also capable of using rules for end-of-life decisions and leveraging large language models (LLMs) to generate clear explanations for both mortality and end-of-life decisions. The research evaluates the accuracy of this approach and compares it with classical explainability methods, such as LIME.

Chapter 4: Evaluating the Most Used Database Technologies for AI and Real-Time Application Development in Metaverse Systems: A Comparative Study

The rapid evolution of technology, particularly in AI and real-time applications, has increased the need for databases that efficiently handle diverse and complex workloads. This paper analyzes the top five database management systems of 2025: Oracle, MySQL, Microsoft SQL Server, PostgreSQL, and MongoDB. These databases, spanning relational and NoSQL systems, offer distinct capabilities. The comparison is based on key parameters such as performance, scalability, extensibility, data model support, and ease of integration with modern technologies. Notably, PostgreSQL has emerged as a top choice for AI-based applications in metaverse platforms due to its extensibility (e.g., PostGIS for spatial data) and high performance in decentralized architectures. Through detailed analysis, this study highlights the strengths and weaknesses of each database, concluding that PostgreSQL is best suited for AI and real-time applications due to its adaptability and seamless integration with open-source tools critical for metaverse development.

Chapter 5: Hybrid model for teaching French

The study employed a hybrid methodology that combines knowledge graphs and fine-tuned language models (LLMs) to optimize the teaching of French as a foreign language (FFL). First, a knowledge graph was designed in Neo4j, structured according to the CEFR levels (A1-C2), with interconnected nodes representing grammatical elements (such as the subjunctive or the passé composé), thematic vocabulary (greetings, business), and communicative situations (interviews, restaurants). In parallel, the CamemBERT model (specialized in French) was fine-tuned using the FLEUR (10,000 sentences with typical errors from A1-B1 levels) and FRACAS (5,000 academic texts with advanced errors from B2-C2) datasets, which were preprocessed through tokenization and level balancing. The training was conducted on Google Colab Pro with a T4 GPU, applying supervised fine-tuning (SFT) and reinforcement learning with human feedback (RLHF), under hyperparameters such as a learning rate of 5e-5, a batch size of 16, and 5 epochs.

Chapter 6: Design of a Semantic Search Engine for Technological Observatories

This paper focuses on the development of a semantic search engine to facilitate information retrieval in the Technological Observatory. Its main objective is to automate data searches using artificial intelligence techniques, improving accuracy and information retrieval. To this end, the theoretical and methodological foundations of intelligent information retrieval systems are identified, an architecture based on language models, knowledge graphs, and vector databases is designed, and the retrieval rates of the implemented system are evaluated. The study addresses key concepts such as semantic search, the use of embeddings, and the integration of artificial intelligence models to improve query accuracy. The design of the search engine, structured on an ontology that classifies information into categories, is detailed, and a knowledge graph is implemented in Neo4j, combined with techniques such as GraphRAG to optimize the generation of responses based on structured data.

Chapter 7: Semantic Information Recovery System: Use of Neo4j and Language Models for the Creation of a Vector Database

This paper develops a Semantic Information Retrieval System for the Cuban press, based on natural language processing and knowledge graphs. The research addresses the limitations of traditional document retrieval systems, which rely on rigid metadata and do not interpret contextual relationships among contents. A solution is proposed that integrates a conceptual ontology, a semantic index structured in Neo4j, and pre-trained artificial intelligence models to improve query accuracy. The system architecture employs textual embeddings to generate contextualized searches, using cosine similarity as the retrieval criterion. Furthermore, it incorporates semantic inference techniques and multimodal document analysis. The implementation optimizes access to relevant information in the journalistic domain, overcoming the fragmentation of content stored in DSpace. Evaluations of precision and recall validate the solution's impact on the quality of the results.

Chapter 8: Image classification-based detection system of the mite (Phyllocoptruta oleivora) using machine learning models

This work presents an automatic detection system for the mite Phyllocoptruta oleivora using deep learning image classification. Three convolutional archi- tectures (a base CNN, MobileNetV2, and ResNet50) are compared under a homogeneous preprocessing, transfer learning, and data augmentation protocol. From a set of images captured in the field and validated by experts, the results show that a lightweight model such as MobileNetV2 offers the best balance between performance, robustness, and computational efficiency for deployment in agricultural environments. On the other hand, ResNet50 is presented as a competitive alternative when greater computing power is available. Design con- siderations, limitations, and future directions oriented toward mobile applications and monitoring platforms in precision agriculture are discussed.

Chapter 9: Integration of Large Language Models and Knowledge Graphs in Semantic Web: A Bibliometric Analysis of Scientific Production

The convergence between Large Language Models (LLMs) and Knowledge Graphs (KGs) represents an emerging paradigm in artificial intelligence that combines natural language processing capabilities with structured reasoning. This study presents a comprehensive bibliometric analysis of 230 documents indexed in Web of Science, characterizing the intellectual structure, scientific production dynamics, and thematic evolution of the field. Results reveal exponential growth with an annual rate of 48.12%, dominant leadership of Chinese institutions, and thematic structuring into six main clusters: reasoning on graphs with LLMs, semantic data mining, entity linking, decision-making systems, domain knowledge extraction, and recommender systems. Theoretical implications evidence the synthesis between connectionist and symbolic approaches, materializing the Semantic Web vision through natural language interfaces.

Chapter 10: AI Integrated Learning Environment in Higher Education: Challenges and Opportunities

E-learning platforms are rapidly increasing in demand to transform the landscape of education as they are strengthened by machine learning and artificial intelligence (AI). The integration of AI in higher education improves Massive Open Online Courses (MOOCs) and Virtual Learning Environments (VLEs) in intelligent tutoring and personalized learning, making e-learning and other academic tasks more efficient. This paper explores the potential of AI in online education systems along with proposed solutions. The primary aim of this paper is to highlight the current opportunities and challenges.

Chapter 1
Unifying Large Language Models, Knowledge Graphs, and the Semantic Web:
A New Paradigm for Intelligent Systems

Fernando Ortiz-Rodriguez
http://orcid.org/0000-0003-2084-3462
Tamaulipas Autonomous University, Mexico

ABSTRACT

The contemporary digital era is characterized by an explosion of data, presenting both unprecedented opportunities and significant challenges for knowledge extraction, representation, and reasoning. This paper introduces and analyzes a powerful convergence of three technological pillars poised to revolutionize artificial intelligence: Large Language Models (LLMs), Knowledge Graphs (KGs), and the Semantic Web. The synergy between the generative prowess and natural language understanding of LLMs, the structured and verifiable factual representation of KGs, and the standardized, interoperable framework of the Semantic Web creates a transformative paradigm for AI. This integration mitigates the inherent

DOI: 10.4018/979-8-3373-1360-3.ch001

weaknesses of each component—such as the factual unreliability and opacity of LLMs and the construction and maintenance bottlenecks of KGs—while amplifying their collective strengths.

1. INTRODUCTION

We live in an age of information overload. The sheer volume of unstructured data—from text on the web and in corporate documents to scientific literature and social media—grows at a staggering rate. For decades, the central challenge of computer science and artificial intelligence has been to not only manage this data deluge but to transform it into structured, actionable knowledge. Three distinct but related fields have emerged as critical to this endeavor: Large Language Models (LLMs), Knowledge Graphs (KGs), and the Semantic Web. (Villazón-Terrazas et al., 2020)

Large Language Models (LLMs), such as the widely known GPT (Generative Pre-trained Transformer) family, represent a monumental leap in natural language processing. Trained on vast swaths of the internet, these models demonstrate a remarkable ability to understand, summarize, translate, and generate human-like text. However, their power comes with significant limitations. LLMs can be prone to "hallucination," confidently stating falsehoods with no basis in reality. They operate as "black boxes," making it difficult to trace their reasoning or verify the sources of their information (Pan et al., 2024). Their knowledge is implicit, encoded in billions of parameters, making it difficult to update or audit for accuracy and bias.

Knowledge Graphs (KGs) offer a solution to this problem of veracity and interpretability. KGs represent information as a network of entities (nodes) and the explicit relationships between them (edges), often adhering to a predefined schema or ontology. For example, a KG could represent that *'Marie Curie' (entity)* 'is a recipient of' *(relationship)* the *'Nobel Prize in Physics' (entity)*. This structured format makes knowledge explicit, verifiable, and machine-readable. KGs act as an external "brain" that can ground AI systems in factual reality. Their primary weakness, however, has historically been the labor-intensive and complex process of their construction and maintenance, often referred to as the knowledge acquisition bottleneck.

This is where the **Semantic Web** provides a foundational framework. Envisioned by Berners-Lee et al. (2001), the Semantic Web is not a separate web but an extension of the current one, in which information is given well-defined meaning through standardized data models. It provides a mature ecosystem of technologies, such as the Resource Description Framework (RDF), the Web Ontology Language (OWL), and the SPARQL query language, that enable data to be linked and understood by machines at scale. It provides the "grammar" for creating robust, interoperable, and scalable Knowledge Graphs, a vision actively explored by researchers such as Ortiz-Rodriguez, Tiwari, and their contemporaries in forums like the KGSWC (Ortiz-Rodriguez et al., 2023).

Individually, each of these pillars has limitations. LLMs lack factual reliability, KGs are difficult to build, and the Semantic Web's vision has been slow to be fully realized. However, their convergence creates a powerful and symbiotic relationship that promises to reshape the landscape of AI. This paper posits that by integrating the linguistic fluency of LLMs, the factual grounding of KGs, and the standardized architecture of the Semantic Web, we are ushering in a new era of AI—one that is not only more powerful but also more reliable, transparent, and intelligent. This work provides a comprehensive analysis of this emerging paradigm, its architecture, applications, and the challenges that lie ahead.

2. LITERATURE REVIEW

The unification of symbolic AI (like KGs and Semantic Web) and sub-symbolic AI (like LLMs) is not a new idea, but the recent ascendance of powerful LLMs has infused it with new urgency and potential. This section reviews the foundational literature for each domain before exploring the nascent but rapidly growing body of work on their integration.

2.1 The Semantic Web and Knowledge Representation

The Semantic Web vision is to create a "Web of Data" that is interpretable by machines. The foundation is **RDF**, which models information in (subject, predicate, object) triples, naturally forming a graph. Building on this, the **Web Ontology Language (OWL)** provides a rich vocabulary for defining formal ontologies—explicit specifications of a conceptualization. Ontologies allow for defining classes, properties, and logical axioms (e.g., domain, range, cardinality constraints) that enable automated reasoning and consistency checking. The work of researchers has often centered on applying these principles to create domain-specific ontologies, for example, in e-government with the EGODO Ontology, which facilitates the sharing and retrieval of legal documentation (Ortiz-Rodriguez et al., 2022). These formal structures are essential for ensuring the quality and logical coherence of KGs.

2.2 The Evolution of Knowledge Graphs

While the theoretical underpinnings of KGs come from semantic networks and formal logic, their modern incarnation was popularized by large-scale projects like DBpedia, YAGO, and Google's Knowledge Graph. These KGs demonstrated the power of structured knowledge for enhancing search and answering factual questions. A significant body of research in the KG community has focused on tasks like **link prediction** (inferring missing relationships), **entity resolution** (identifying duplicate entities), and **KG embedding**, where entities and relations are represented as vectors in a continuous space to facilitate machine learning tasks. However, as noted by Pan et al. (2024), these graphs often suffer from incompleteness and the high cost of manual curation.

2.3 The Rise of Large Language Models

The current state of the art in LLMs is dominated by the Transformer architecture (Vaswani et al., 2017), which uses self-attention mechanisms to process language with a high degree of contextual awareness. This has enabled models with hundreds of billions of parameters to be trained on petabytes of text data. This has led to emergent capabilities in few-shot and zero-shot learning. However, their limitations are well-documented. They are known to reproduce and amplify biases from their training data, their knowledge is static and becomes outdated, and they struggle with tasks requiring multi-step, logical reasoning (Hogan et al., 2025).

2.4 Early Work on Integration

The idea of combining language models with structured knowledge has existed for years. Early approaches focused on injecting knowledge from KGs into language models during pre-training or fine-tuning to make them more factually aware. More recently, the focus has shifted towards more dynamic, retrieval-based architectures. The paradigm of **Retrieval-Augmented Generation (RAG)** has become prominent, where an LLM's input is augmented with information retrieved from an external data source. The application of this pattern with KGs, often referred to as **GraphRAG**, is a central theme of this paper and a major focus of current research (Lelong et al., 2025). The synergy is bidirectional, with a growing number of studies exploring how LLMs can, in turn, be used to automate the KG construction lifecycle (McDermott, 2025). The collaboration of scholars like Tiwari and Ortiz-Rodriguez on volumes such as *Semantic AI in Knowledge Graphs* highlights the international research effort to formalize these integration patterns (Tiwari et al., 2023).

3. A SYNERGISTIC FRAMEWORK FOR UNIFYING LLMS, KGS, AND THE SEMANTIC WEB

We propose a synergistic framework built on three core pillars of interaction: KG-enhanced LLMs, LLM-augmented KGs, and the Semantic Web as the unifying architectural layer.

3.1 KG-Enhanced LLMs: Grounding Generative AI in Factual Reality

This is the most mature and impactful integration pattern, directly addressing the hallucination and opacity problems of LLMs.

- **Architecture (GraphRAG):** When a user submits a query, the system first transforms the natural language query into a formal query (e.g., SPARQL or Cypher) or a set of entity/relationship lookups. This can be done by the LLM itself or a simpler NLP model. The query is executed against the KG to retrieve a subgraph of relevant, factual information. This structured context, along with the original query, is then passed to the LLM. The LLM's task shifts from *recalling* information from its parameters to *synthesizing* an answer based on the provided facts.
- **Benefits:**
    - o **Factual Accuracy:** The LLM's response is grounded in the verified data of the KG, drastically reducing hallucinations.
    - o **Traceability and Explainability:** The system can cite its sources by pointing to the specific nodes and edges in the KG that were used to generate the answer. This moves the LLM from a "black box" to a more transparent system.
    - o **Live Data:** KGs can be updated in near real-time with new information, allowing the LLM to access up-to-the-minute knowledge without needing to be retrained.

3.2 LLM-Augmented KGs: Overcoming the Knowledge Acquisition Bottleneck

This pattern leverages the natural language capabilities of LLMs to automate and scale the creation, enrichment, and maintenance of KGs. (Vakaj et al., 2023)

- **KG Construction from Unstructured Text:** An LLM can be prompted to read a document and extract entities and relationships in a structured format (e.g., RDF triples). By providing a few examples (few-shot prompting) and defining the target ontology, an LLM can act as a powerful, flexible information extraction engine, significantly reducing the manual effort required.

- **Natural Language to Graph Query:** LLMs can serve as a universal interface to KGs. A non-technical user can ask a complex question in plain English (e.g., "Which drugs that target protein P53 have been approved in the last five years and are not manufactured by Pfizer?"). The LLM can deconstruct this query and translate it into a formal SPARQL query, retrieve the results, and present them back to the user in a natural language summary. This democratizes access to complex, structured data.
- **Ontology Engineering and KG Completion:** LLMs can assist in the creation and maintenance of ontologies. They can suggest new classes or properties based on analyzing a corpus of text, or they can be used for **link prediction**, inferring missing relationships within the graph (e.g., if A is located in B, and B is located in C, the LLM might infer that A is located in C).

3.3 The Semantic Web as the Unifying Layer

The Semantic Web provides the essential, standardized foundation that makes this integration robust and scalable.

- **Interoperability:** By using RDF and OWL, the KGs that are built by LLMs and used to ground them are based on a common, interoperable framework. This ensures that knowledge can be shared, integrated, and reasoned over across different systems and organizations.
- **Logical Reasoning:** The formal semantics of OWL allow for logical reasoners to operate on the KG. This enables capabilities beyond simple lookups, such as consistency checking (ensuring the KG contains no contradictions), inferring new knowledge through logical entailment, and validating the output of the LLM against the ontological constraints. This adds a layer of symbolic rigor to the statistical nature of LLMs.

4. APPLICATIONS AND USE CASES

The unification of these technologies is unlocking new capabilities across numerous domains. In areas like the Artificial Intelligence of Things (AIoT) demonstrate the practical application of these concepts (Ortiz-Rodriguez et al., 2024) (Jabbar et al., 2023)

- **Enterprise Knowledge Management:** Companies can transform their vast repositories of internal documents (reports, emails, technical manuals) into a comprehensive KG using LLMs. Employees can then query this knowledge base using natural language to get accurate, sourced answers to complex questions, breaking down information silos.
- **Scientific Research and Discovery:** In fields like biomedicine, LLMs can ingest millions of research papers to build a KG of genes, proteins, diseases, and drugs. Researchers can then use this graph to ask questions like, "What proteins interact with both gene X and drug Y?" to uncover novel hypotheses and accelerate discovery.
- **Advanced Conversational AI:** Chatbots and virtual assistants can be built on a KG of domain-specific knowledge (e.g., product catalogs, travel information). This allows them to provide accurate, detailed answers and perform complex, multi-step tasks, moving beyond simple chit-chat to become truly helpful agents.
- **Data Provenance and Security:** The structured nature of KGs is well-suited for modeling data provenance—tracking the origin and lineage of information. As highlighted in research involving Tiwari, understanding provenance is critical for trust and security (Weiguo et al., 2014). An LLM-KG system can not only provide an answer but also explain where the information came from and how it has been modified, which is crucial for compliance and auditing.

5. CHALLENGES AND FUTURE RESEARCH DIRECTIONS

Despite the immense potential, significant challenges must be addressed for this paradigm to mature.

- **Scalability and Real-time Synchronization:** Keeping a large-scale KG synchronized with real-world changes is a major engineering challenge. The process of using an LLM to extract information, validate it, and ingest it into the graph must be highly efficient to support real-time applications.
- **Semantic Heterogeneity and Ontology Alignment:** When integrating data from multiple sources, a key challenge is reconciling different schemas and vocabularies. While LLMs can help in suggesting mappings between different ontologies, ensuring semantic consistency at scale remains a difficult problem.
- **Error Propagation and Verification:** If an LLM introduces a factual error during the knowledge extraction phase, that error becomes part of the "ground truth" in the KG. This can then be used to generate further incorrect responses. Developing robust pipelines for fact-checking and human-in-the-loop verification is critical.
- **Reasoning Depth and Complexity:** While the current GraphRAG pattern is effective for retrieving and summarizing facts, enabling deeper, multi-hop reasoning across the graph is an active area of research. Combining the statistical inference of LLMs with the symbolic reasoning capabilities of OWL reasoners in a seamless way is a key goal.
- **Cost and Efficiency:** Both training/running large LLMs and maintaining large-scale graph databases are computationally expensive. Optimizing the entire query-retrieval-generation pipeline for both cost and latency is essential for practical deployment.

6. CONCLUSION

The convergence of Large Language Models, Knowledge Graphs, and the Semantic Web marks a pivotal moment in the evolution of artificial intelligence. This "trinity" creates a virtuous cycle: LLMs accelerate the creation of structured knowledge, which KGs then use to ground LLMs in factual reality, all underpinned by the scalable and interoperable standards of the Semantic Web. This synergy produces AI systems that are not just fluent communicators but also verifiable and logical reasoners.

This integrated approach moves us beyond the dichotomy of purely statistical AI versus purely symbolic AI, creating a hybrid intelligence that leverages the strengths of both. While significant challenges remain—including scalability, error propagation, and the cost of computation—the path forward is clear. The fusion of these technologies, driven by a global community of researchers, is set to unlock new frontiers in everything from scientific discovery and enterprise data management to personalized education and truly intelligent personal assistants, driving the next wave of innovation in our data-rich world.

REFERENCES

Berners-Lee, T., Hendler, J., & Lassila, O. (2001). The Semantic Web. *Scientific American*, *284*(5), 34–43. DOI: 10.1038/scientificamerican0501-34 PMID: 11681174

Hogan, A., Luna Dong, X., Vrandečić, D., & Weikum, G. (2025). Large Language Models, Knowledge Graphs and Search Engines: A Crossroads for Answering Users' Questions. arXiv e-prints, arXiv-2501.

Lelong, J., Errazine, A., & Blangero, A. (2025). Agentic rag with knowledge graphs for complex multi-hop reasoning in real-world applications. arXiv preprint arXiv:2507.16507. DOI: 10.3233/FAIA251445

McDermott, R. (2025). *From Unstructured Text to Interactive Knowledge Graphs Using LLMs*. Retrieved from Medium.

Ortiz-Rodriguez, F., Leyva-Mederos, A., Tiwari, S., Hernandez-Quintana, A. R., & Martinez-Rodriguez, J. L. (Eds.). (2024). *Semantic Web Technologies and Applications in Artificial Intelligence of Things*. IGI Global. DOI: 10.4018/979-8-3693-1487-6

Ortiz-Rodriguez, F., Medina-Quintero, J. M., Tiwari, S., & Villanueva, V. (2022). EGODO Ontology: Sharing, Retrieving, and Exchanging Legal Documentation Across E-Government. In *Futuristic Trends for Sustainable Development and Sustainable Ecosystems*. IGI Global. DOI: 10.4018/978-1-6684-4225-8.ch016

Ortiz-Rodriguez, F., Villazón-Terrazas, B., Tiwari, S., & Bobed, C. (Eds.). (2023). *Knowledge Graphs and Semantic Web: 5th Iberoamerican Conference and 4th Indo-American Conference, KGSWC 2023, Proceedings*. Springer Nature. Jabbar, M. A., Tiwari, S., & Ortiz-Rodriguez, F. (Eds.). (2023). *Smart Urban Computing Applications*. CRC Press.

Pan, S., Luo, L., Wang, Y., Chen, C., Wang, J., & Wu, X. (2024, July). Unifying Large Language Models and Knowledge Graphs: A Roadmap. *IEEE Transactions on Knowledge and Data Engineering*, *36*(7), 3580–3599. DOI: 10.1109/TKDE.2024.3352100

Tiwari, S., Ortiz-Rodriguez, F., Ben Abbes, S., Usoro Usip, P., & Hantach, I. (Eds.). (2023). *Semantic AI in Knowledge Graphs*. Routledge. DOI: 10.1201/9781003313267

Vakaj, E., Tiwari, S., Mihindukulasooriya, N., Ortiz-Rodríguez, F., & Mcgranaghan, R. 2023. NLP4KGC: Natural Language Processing for Knowledge Graph Construction. In Companion Proceedings of the ACM Web Conference 2023 (WWW '23 Companion). Association for Computing Machinery, New York, NY, USA, 1111. DOI: 10.1145/3543873.3589746

Vaswani, A., Shazeer, N., Parmar, N., Uszkoreit, J., Jones, L., Gomez, A. N., & Polosukhin, I. (2017). Attention is all you need. *Advances in Neural Information Processing Systems*, •••, 30.

Villazón-Terrazas, B., Ortiz-Rodriguez, F., Tiwari, S., & Shandilya, S. (2020). Knowledge Graphs and Semantic Web : Second Iberoamerican Conference and First Indo-American Conference, KGSWC 2020, Mérida, Mexico, November 26–27, 2020, Proceedings (1st ed. 2020.). Springer International Publishing. DOI: 10.1007/978-3-030-65384-2

Chapter 2

Unlocking the Power of Knowledge Graphs: Advanced Reasoning and Embedding Techniques

Otmane Azeroual

http://orcid.org/0000-0002-5225-389X

FernUniversität in Hagen (FeU), Germany

ABSTRACT

Knowledge Graphs (KGs) are essential for managing complex relationships and semantic data. This chapter examines two key functions of KGs: reasoning and embedding. Reasoning infers new knowledge from existing data, supporting deeper insights and decision-making. Embedding converts high-dimensional data into low-dimensional vectors, improving efficiency and analysis. Together, these functions enhance the flexibility and performance of KGs, with applications in NLP, information retrieval, and data integration, while addressing challenges and research directions.

INTRODUCTION

Knowledge graphs (KGs) have revolutionized the representation and management of knowledge by capturing complex relationships, semantic nuances, and connections between entities. They are widely used in various

DOI: 10.4018/979-8-3373-1360-3.ch002

fields such as social networks, academic citations, biology, transportation networks, and recommendation systems, providing relevant facts and context-rich answers to specific queries that span natural language processing, information retrieval, and data integration. Positioned as a crucial component in data processing systems, KGs serve as the foundation for advanced platforms like retrieval-augmented generation (Lewis et al., 2020) and a multitude of innovative artificial intelligence (AI) applications that deal with extensive and complex datasets across industries, societies, and scientific endeavors.

The integration of KG reasoning and embedding is central to fully leveraging the capabilities of KGs. Reasoning involves inferring new knowledge from existing data, while embedding techniques represent entities and relationships in a way that captures their semantic meaning. Studying these aspects together is crucial because reasoning and embedding are interdependent; effective reasoning relies on well-constructed embeddings, and high-quality embeddings are enhanced by sophisticated reasoning techniques. This synergy enables more precise and insightful knowledge representation and application, which is crucial in all areas of knowledge discovery.

The integration of KGs with language models is currently on the rise and is attracting increasing attention within research circles (Pan et al., 2024). The effectiveness of KGs is based on their mastery of reasoning and embedding techniques, both of which play synergistic roles and enhance access to generative AI systems. Positioned at the interface between semantic and strategic interfaces, understanding the inner workings of KGs is crucial not only for optimizing their performance but also for understanding how their reasoning capabilities and embedding capacities efficiently complement the evolving functionalities of contemporary AI systems, particularly in creatively dealing with human language (Manning, 2022).

KGs have the potential to revolutionize the way knowledge is represented, managed, and utilized. Through their ability to capture complex relationships and semantic information, they offer a wide range of applications in various fields, from natural language processing to data integration (Dong & Rekatsinas, 2018). This topic is highly relevant to the community as it provides insights into the advanced techniques of reasoning and embedding in KGs and underscores their strategic importance for the development of AI systems (Dessì et al., 2020; Chen et al., 2024).

This chapter seeks to advance the understanding of fundamental concepts within KGs and to demonstrate their practical applications across various domains. By critically examining the strategic roles of reasoning and embedding in the optimization of KGs and the advancement of AI systems, it aims to present a thorough overview of contemporary trends and challenges in this field. To address concerns regarding the comprehensive coverage of the five levels of examination outlined in the introduction, each level has been explicitly addressed and thoroughly analyzed in the subsequent sections. The concluding section of the chapter will provide a detailed assessment of the significance of reasoning and embedding for the future of KGs and AI, offering readers well-founded insights and a forward-looking perspective on upcoming developments and their interactions.

This investigation and evaluation of common practices and innovative trends in reasoning and embedding of KGs will be conducted on five successive levels of examination. These levels include considering reasoning and embeddings as:

1. Strategic functionalities of KGs: Understanding their different but complementary roles within the KG architecture.
2. Integrated components of KG performance: Identifying common challenges and collaborative synergies.
3. Aggregators of shared innovation: Observing their role in the ongoing renewal of graph architectures and analytical capabilities.
4. Key benchmarking objects in KGs: Evaluating the effectiveness, fairness, and reproducibility of reasoning techniques through standardized benchmarks and datasets.
5. Critical changing fields of KG architecture: Investigating new ideas and directions that influence the current landscape of reasoning structures and engineering representations of knowledge.

Additionally, a detailed exploration of specific reasoning and embedding algorithms has been included in the appendix to provide readers with deeper technical insights. This section features mathematical formulations, pseudocode, and implementation examples to cater to readers seeking more technical details. This addition aims to enhance the chapter by offering a deeper dive into the algorithms that underpin KG reasoning and embedding, thereby supporting a more comprehensive understanding of these techniques.

This comprehensive analysis highlights the strategic importance of reasoning and embedding techniques within KGs and provides insights into their development and future direction, supporting a nuanced understanding of their role and impact in various fields.

METHODOLOGY

In this section, we provide a thorough description of the techniques and algorithms used for KG reasoning, as well as an in-depth analysis of embedding techniques and their role in data processing (see Fig. 1). This figure illustrates the various techniques and methods for KG Reasoning and Embeddings and their relationships. The figure is divided into four main categories: KG Reasoning Techniques, Embedding Techniques, their Applications, and Evaluation. The structure of Figure 1 is designed to show how these methods interact and contribute to understanding and processing KGs. It highlights the interconnected nature of these techniques and their collective impact on data processing tasks.

Figure 1. KG Reasoning and Embedding Techniques.

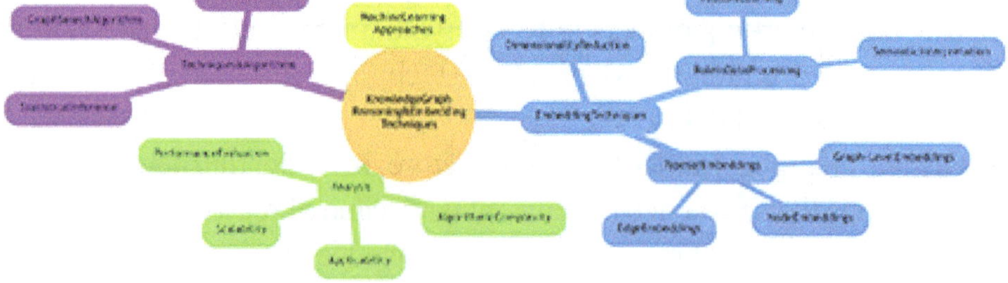

1. KG Reasoning Techniques

KG reasoning involves the process of inferring new knowledge from existing knowledge within the graph structure. Various techniques and algorithms have been developed for KG reasoning, each serving different purposes and exhibiting distinct strengths and limitations.

- Rule-based Reasoning: Rule-based reasoning involves the application of logical rules to infer new facts based on existing ones. These rules can be manually defined or automatically learned from the data (Berka, 2020). Common rule-based reasoning approaches include:
    - Forward Chaining: Starts with known facts and applies rules to derive new facts until no further derivations are possible.
    - Backward Chaining: Begins with a hypothesis or goal and works backward through the rules to see if the hypothesis can be supported by the existing facts.
    - Deductive Reasoning: Uses general rules to draw specific conclusions. This method is useful when the rules are clear and stable (Chowdhary & Chowdhary, 2020).
- Semantic Reasoning: Semantic reasoning utilizes semantic information encoded within the KG to infer implicit relationships between entities (Zhang et al., 2022 ; Bai et al., 2023). This often involves the use of:
    - Ontologies: Structures knowledge through defined classes and relationships, used for deriving new information.
    - Semantic Schemas: Provide detailed descriptions of entities and their relationships, aiding in knowledge derivation.
    - Inference Rules: Logical rules based on semantic concepts used to derive new knowledge (Grimm, 2009). Semantic reasoning focuses on the deeper meaning and contextualization of data.
- Machine Learning-based Reasoning: Machine learning-based reasoning approaches leverage statistical models and algorithms to learn patterns and relationships from the data (Chen et al., 2022). This may involve:

- o Probabilistic Reasoning: Uses probabilistic models to model uncertainties and relationships.
- o Neural Networks: Learning models that recognize complex patterns through training on large datasets.
- o Deep Learning: Extension of neural networks with multiple layers, particularly effective in processing large and complex data structures (Chen et al., 2022). These methods are useful for detecting non-obvious patterns and relationships.

2. Embedding Techniques in Data Processing

Embedding techniques aim to represent high-dimensional data, such as KG entities and relationships, in low-dimensional vector spaces. These embeddings preserve semantic relationships and facilitate various downstream tasks such as similarity computation, clustering, and classification.

- Graph Embedding: Graph embedding techniques aim to learn continuous vector representations of nodes and edges in the KG (Xu, 2021). Common methods include:
  - o node2vec: Utilizes random walks to represent nodes in a continuous vector space.
  - o DeepWalk: Similar to node2vec but employs deep learning techniques to improve representations.
  - o GraphSAGE: Uses Graph Convolutional Networks (GCNs) to aggregate features from nodes and their neighbors. These techniques help capture both structural and semantic information in the graph.
- KG Embedding: KG embedding techniques specifically focus on learning embeddings for entities and relationships in the KG (Li et al., 2021). Methods include:
  - o TransE: Maps entities and relationships into a vector space, aiming to model relationships as translations in the vector space.
  - o TransR: Extends TransE by using different space representations for nodes and relationships.

    - ComplEx: Uses complex numbers to model entities and relationships, capturing semantic relations more effectively. These methods are crucial for accurately modeling and analyzing entities and their interactions.
- Evaluation of Embeddings: The quality of learned embeddings is evaluated based on their ability to:
    - Capture Semantic Relationships: How well the embeddings represent the relationships between entities.
    - Preserve Graph Structure: How accurately the vector representations reflect the original graph structure.
    - Improve Performance on Downstream Tasks: How embeddings enhance results in tasks such as link prediction, entity classification, and KG completion (Rossi et al., 2021). Evaluation metrics are essential to ensure embeddings effectively represent relevant information and are useful for various applications.

By providing a detailed overview of these techniques and algorithms, we aim to establish a comprehensive understanding of KG reasoning and embedding methods, their applicability, and their impact on data processing tasks. Additionally, we discuss considerations for selecting appropriate techniques based on specific application requirements and highlight avenues for future research and development in this field.

Applications and Innovations

KG reasoning and embedding techniques have been pivotal in advancing various fields by enabling sophisticated data representation and inferencing capabilities. This section explores specific applications of these techniques across different domains and presents innovative trends and current research findings that highlight their transformative potential.

1. Applications in Various Fields

The applications in various fields are illustrated in Figure 2.

Figure 2. Applications of KG Reasoning and Embedding in Various Fields.

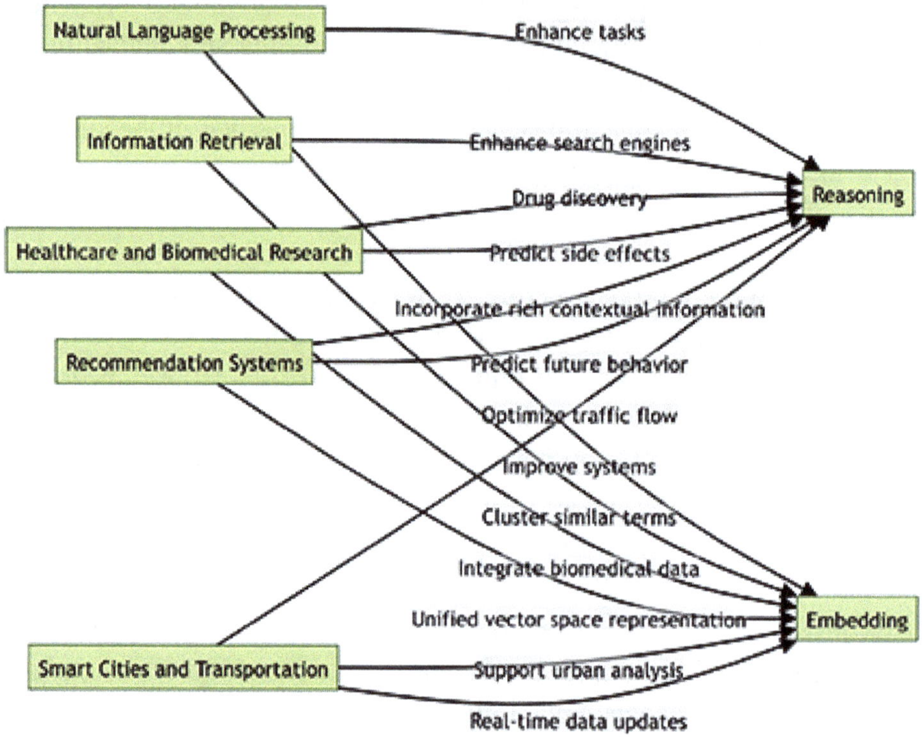

- Natural Language Processing (NLP): KGs have revolutionized NLP by enhancing tasks such as question answering, language translation, and entity recognition (Wei et al., 2021). KG reasoning techniques enable systems to understand and infer contextually relevant answers from extensive knowledge bases by analyzing the relationships between entities. For example, in question answering systems, KGs support the retrieval of precise information by mapping query terms to relevant KG entities and their relationships. Embedding techniques improve these systems by representing words and phrases in dense vector spaces, capturing nuanced semantic meanings, and facilitating more accurate text processing and interpretation. This representation enhances the system's ability to handle synonyms and context variations effectively.

- Information Retrieval: In the domain of information retrieval, KGs enhance search engines by providing context-aware and precise search results. Reasoning algorithms infer semantic relationships between search queries and relevant documents, enabling more effective matching of user intent with content. Meanwhile, embeddings cluster similar terms and documents in a vector space, improving retrieval performance and relevance ranking (Tamine & Goeuriot, 2021). For instance, Google's KG is employed to deliver direct answers to user queries, utilizing both reasoning and embedding techniques to understand and relate query terms to KG entities, thus improving the accuracy and relevance of search results (Huang et al., 2019).
- Healthcare and Biomedical Research: KGs are increasingly utilized in healthcare for drug discovery, patient data management, and personalized medicine. Reasoning techniques analyze complex biological networks to identify potential drug interactions and predict side effects, enhancing drug safety and efficacy. Embeddings facilitate the integration of heterogeneous biomedical data, such as genomic, proteomic, and clinical data, enabling comprehensive analyses and insights. Recent applications include using KGs to integrate diverse types of biomedical data to discover new therapeutic targets, understand disease mechanisms, and support personalized treatment strategies (Su et al., 2020 ; Santos et al., 2022). For example, KG-based approaches are employed to uncover relationships between genetic variations and disease susceptibility, leading to novel diagnostic and therapeutic opportunities (Quan et al., 2023 ; Malec et al., 2023).
- Recommendation Systems: Recommendation systems benefit from KGs by incorporating rich contextual information about users and items (Cui et al., 2022). Reasoning techniques infer user preferences and predict future behavior by analyzing historical data and interactions, providing more accurate and relevant recommendations. Embedding techniques represent users and items in a unified vector space, capturing similarities and preferences, which allows for personalized recommendations based on user behavior and item attributes (Sun et al., 2018). For example, e-commerce platforms

like Amazon and streaming services like Netflix leverage KGs to enhance their recommendation algorithms, offering users tailored product or content suggestions based on their interests and past interactions (Almahmood & Tekerek, 2022).

- Smart Cities and Transportation: In smart city applications, KGs are used to manage and analyze urban data, optimizing traffic flow, resource allocation, and overall urban management (Badii et al., 2017). Reasoning techniques help understand the interactions between various urban entities, such as vehicles, pedestrians, and infrastructure, enabling more efficient urban planning and management. Embeddings integrate diverse data sources, such as traffic sensors, social media, and environmental data, supporting comprehensive urban analysis and decision-making. An innovative application includes using real-time data streams to dynamically update urban KGs, facilitating real-time decision-making and improving responses to changing urban conditions. For instance, KGs can be employed to manage public transportation schedules, predict traffic congestion, and enhance emergency response strategies by integrating and analyzing real-time data from various sources. Case studies of smart city implementations demonstrate the tangible benefits of these techniques in improving urban infrastructure and service delivery (Kumar et al., 2020).

2. Innovative Trends and Current Research Findings

Figure 3 illustrates five key trends and research findings in the field of KG reasoning and embedding. Each branch represents a distinct trend, with sub-nodes highlighting specific aspects or examples. The trends discussed include hybrid models, transfer learning, graph neural networks (GNNs), explainability and interpretability, and real-time KG updates. The figure visually encapsulates the critical insights and demonstrates their relevance to ongoing advancements in this area.

Figure 3. Innovative Trends and Current Research Findings in KG Reasoning and Embedding.

Hybrid Models Combining KGs and Neural Networks: Recent research has been exploring hybrid models that integrate KGs with neural networks, including transformer models (Zhu, 2024). This integration leverages the structured and semantic richness of KGs alongside the advanced contextual learning capabilities of neural networks. Transformer models, known for their effectiveness in processing sequential data, benefit from KG embeddings that provide structured information, thus enhancing tasks such as language understanding and entity recognition. For instance, incorporating KG embeddings into transformer-based models has led to notable improvements in contextual comprehension and semantic accuracy, demonstrating the synergy between these technologies (Kau et al., 2024).

Transfer Learning with KG Embeddings: Transfer learning using pre-trained KG embeddings has gained traction as a method to enhance model performance, especially in scenarios with limited data. This approach involves applying embeddings derived from extensive KGs to specific tasks, such as entity linking and relation extraction, thereby accelerating model training and improving performance. Recent studies have shown that leveraging pre-trained KG embeddings can effectively address data scarcity issues and enhance the robustness of various applications (Fei et al., 2021).

Graph Neural Networks (GNNs): Advancements in GNNs are shaping new methodologies for learning from KGs. GNNs are particularly adept at capturing complex patterns and relationships within graph-structured data, which facilitates more sophisticated reasoning and inference (Waikhom & Patgiri, 2021). Ongoing research is focused on developing scalable and efficient GNN architectures to handle large and dynamic KGs. Innovations in GNNs aim to address challenges such as scalability and interpretability, thus enhancing their applicability in diverse KG contexts (Ye et al., 2022).

Explainability and Interpretability: There is an increasing emphasis on making AI models more explainable and interpretable. KGs contribute to this objective by offering a transparent reasoning framework that can clarify AI decision-making processes. Innovative approaches are being developed to enhance interpretability through techniques such as attention mechanisms and graph-based explanations (Shimizu et al., 2022). These methods aim to make AI systems that utilize KGs more understandable and trustworthy by providing clearer insights into how decisions are made.

Real-time KG Updates: The integration of real-time data streams with KGs represents a significant advancement, enabling dynamic updates that reflect the most current information. This capability is particularly beneficial in applications such as smart cities and financial markets, where timely data integration is crucial. Research is focused on developing methods for maintaining and adapting KGs in real-time, ensuring that they can efficiently handle rapidly changing data environments (Wang et al., 2021).

These trends and research findings underscore the transformative impact of KG reasoning and embedding techniques across various fields. As the field progresses, ongoing innovations and improvements are expected to drive new advancements, shaping the future of AI and data processing.

Evaluation and Benchmarking

Evaluation and benchmarking are fundamental in assessing the effectiveness and performance of reasoning and embedding techniques in KGs. This section evaluates the presented techniques and methods, justifying the pros and cons discussed earlier, and highlights the utilization of standardized benchmarks for ensuring comparability and reproducibility of results.

1. Methods for Evaluating the Effectiveness of Reasoning and Embedding Techniques

- Quantitative Metrics: Various quantitative metrics are employed to evaluate reasoning and embedding techniques (Wang et al., 2019). Metrics such as precision, recall, F1 score, accuracy, and computational efficiency are crucial for assessing performance (see Fig. 4). For reasoning techniques, metrics like accuracy in inferred relationships and query answering precision are important (Chen et al., 2020). Embedding techniques are evaluated based on their ability to preserve semantic relationships and capture relevant information in low-dimensional vector spaces (Goyal & Ferrara, 2018). These metrics are crucial for justifying the effectiveness of the discussed techniques.

Figure 4. Example of Quantitative Evaluation Metrics.

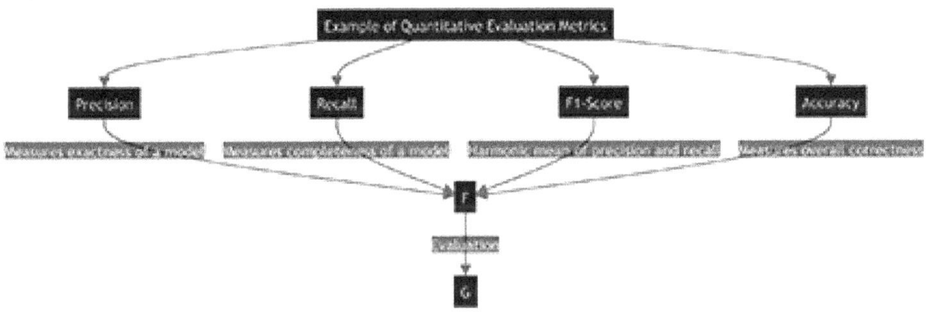

- Qualitative Analysis: Qualitative analysis assesses the quality of inferred knowledge and embeddings through expert judgment (see Fig. 5). This includes evaluating the coherence and relevance of inferred relationships within KGs and examining semantic properties through visualization techniques (Ji et al., 2021). Qualitative analysis provides insights into the interpretability and meaningfulness of the results, supporting the understanding of technique performance beyond quantitative metrics.

Figure 5. Comparison of Quality Criteria for Inferred Relationships.

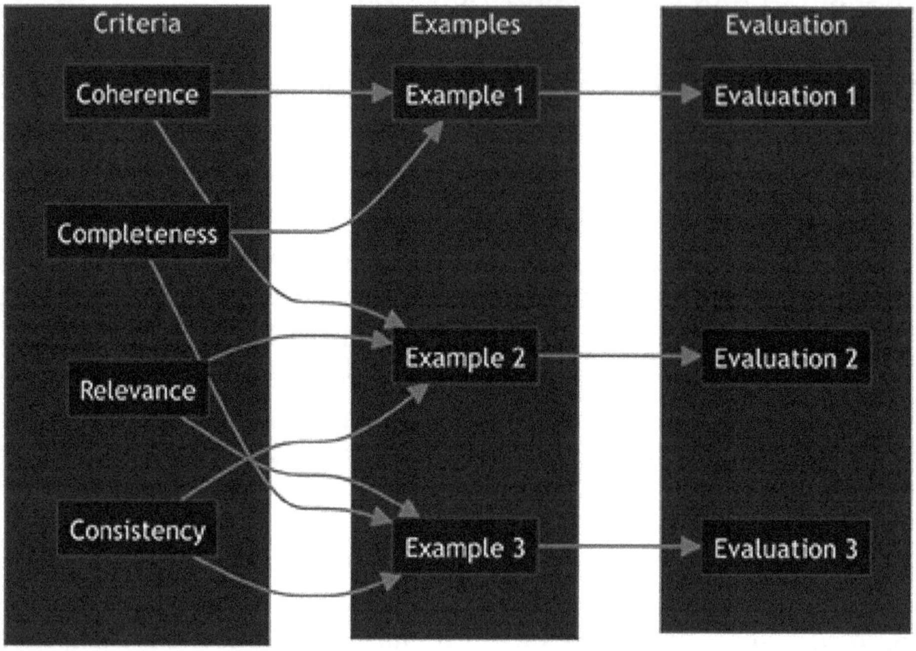

- Case Studies and Use Cases: Real-world case studies and use cases are instrumental in evaluating the practical utility of reasoning and embedding techniques (Scholz & Tietje, 2002). By applying these techniques to specific domains or applications, researchers can assess their effectiveness in solving real-world problems. Case studies reveal the strengths and limitations of different techniques, providing context for their application and areas for improvement (Paleyes et al., 2022).

2. Utilization of Standardized Benchmarks for Comparability and Reproducibility of Results

- Benchmark Datasets: Standardized benchmark datasets are essential for evaluating the performance of reasoning and embedding techniques in a consistent and reproducible manner (Hu et al., 2020 ; Chang et al., 2024). These datasets typically consist of a collection of KGs or text corpora annotated with ground truth relationships or entities. Examples include Freebase, WordNet, and DBpedia for KG reasoning, and datasets like WordNet-1 for word embedding evaluation.

- Evaluation Tasks: Benchmark datasets are accompanied by evaluation tasks that define specific objectives for assessing the performance of reasoning and embedding techniques (Zhang et al., 2019). These tasks may include link prediction, entity classification, relation extraction, and semantic similarity tasks. Evaluation tasks provide standardized benchmarks for comparing different techniques and measuring progress in the field.

The figure 6 presents typical benchmark datasets and evaluation tasks for assessing reasoning and embedding techniques.

Figure 6. Example of Benchmark Datasets and Evaluation Tasks.

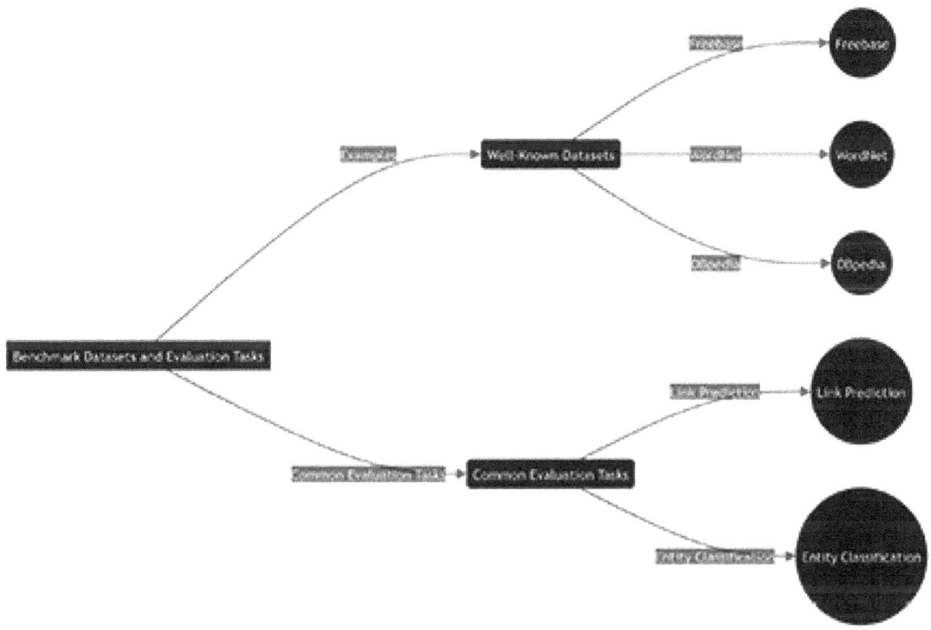

- Leaderboards and Challenges: The establishment of leaderboards and challenges encourages researchers to benchmark their techniques against state-of-the-art methods. Platforms like Kaggle, SemEval, and TAC provide platforms for hosting evaluation tasks and competitions, fostering collaboration and innovation in the research community (Rizzo et al., 2017). Leaderboards track the performance of different techniques on benchmark datasets, facilitating comparison and reproducibility of results (Hu et al., 2020 ; Zheng et al., 2021).

In conclusion, evaluation and benchmarking are essential components of the research process in KG reasoning and embedding. By employing rigorous evaluation methods and standardized benchmarks, researchers can assess the effectiveness of different approaches, compare methodologies, and advance the field of KG reasoning and embedding.

DISCUSSION AND FUTURE DIRECTIONS

In this section, we analyze the current challenges and open research questions in KG reasoning and embedding, while anticipating new developments and proposing future research directions to advance the field.

Scalability remains a significant challenge as KGs grow in size and complexity. Existing techniques often struggle with managing vast amounts of data efficiently, impacting the performance of reasoning tasks on large-scale KGs and limiting their real-world applicability. To address these scalability issues, several strategies can be employed. Distributed computing frameworks, such as Apache Spark and Hadoop, can handle large KGs across multiple nodes, improving performance. Advanced data structures, like distributed graph databases, and indexing techniques, including graph partitioning algorithms, can optimize data storage and retrieval. Approximation algorithms and sampling methods can also help manage complexity while maintaining acceptable accuracy levels.

Integration with other systems and technologies presents substantial challenges. Ensuring interoperability between KGs and diverse IT infrastructures requires standardizing data formats and communication protocols, such as RDF and OWL. Managing data exchange and synchronization involves using middleware solutions and integration frameworks to maintain consistency and accuracy. Designing flexible architectures and interfaces that accommodate different system requirements, along with optimizing performance through caching and efficient data transfer, is crucial for effective integration.

Interpretability of learned embeddings is another pressing issue. Despite the effectiveness of embedding techniques, understanding the underlying semantics captured by these embeddings remains difficult, which can affect the reliability and trustworthiness of KG-based applications. Research is focusing on developing interpretable embedding models that offer insights into the reasoning process and facilitate human comprehension. Additionally, generalization capabilities are essential as existing models often struggle to adapt to new domains or unseen data without extensive retraining. Enhancing generalization through domain adaptation and transfer learning techniques is vital for broader applicability.

Ethical and fairness considerations are increasingly significant, as biases in data sources can propagate through reasoning and embedding techniques, leading to unfair outcomes. Addressing these concerns requires developing methods for bias detection and mitigation, and ensuring transparency in decision-making processes.

Looking ahead, several promising research directions can advance KG reasoning and embedding. Hybrid models that integrate symbolic reasoning with neural embeddings, and leverage multimodal data sources, hold potential for creating more robust and interpretable models. Enhancing model explainability through attention mechanisms and knowledge tracing will be crucial as the demand for explainable AI grows. Furthermore, developing algorithms for real-time updates and incremental learning will be essential to manage dynamic KGs efficiently.

By tackling scalability limitations, improving integration strategies, enhancing interpretability and generalization, and addressing ethical concerns, researchers can unlock the full potential of KGs across various domains and applications.

One leading future direction is the development of a General Theory of Graphs in AI, which is advocated by recent literature as a broader approach to graph machine learning (Morris et al., n.d.). This approach would connect graph machine learning with other existing learning paradigms, potentially creating significant impact. The expressive power of Graph Neural Networks (GNNs) has been extensively analyzed, and alternatives have been proposed for computing the count of substructures (Chen et al., 2020) and integrating geometric information from different nodes (Fabre et al., 2023). Formal trade-offs between expressive power and computational costs have also been identified.

Graph Learning Architectures and their theoretical foundations are another rapidly evolving area. Bridging theory and practice is highly recommended for domain experts who use KGs extensively in various industries, as KGs are emerging as a key tool for advancing AI design, performance, and intelligence augmentation. Recent research on KGs suggests that efficient management of graph architectures could significantly impact the learning abilities of AI systems (Bronstein et al., 2021).

However, the effectiveness of data augmentation in graph machine learning still lags behind that in other popular data modalities, such as images. Developing a "general theory of data augmentation" for graph-structured data could support the advancement of all sense-making systems.

Topology Deep Learning (TDL) is a foundational field in this direction. When combined with graph geometry, topological features are intensively used to design deep learning models. TDL can enhance graph representations, providing a natural choice in a wide range of industrial and scientific settings (Papamarkou et al., 2024); for example, molecules in the real world may be better described by the topology of graphs than by feature vectors.

Large Graph Models (LGMs) are currently under development. While the integration of graph data and AI is still in its early stages, it is attracting considerable attention (Sun et al., 2023). Recently, a pioneering survey on Graph Prompts in the context of Artificial General Intelligence (AGI) proposed a unified framework for understanding graph prompt learning, highlighting its potential across various real-world applications. This could reshape fields related to AGI and beyond. LGMs are being explored in this context, and Text-Space Graph Foundation Models (GFMs) have been studied for their ability to extract transferable patterns across different graphs (Chen et al., 2024).

Lastly, a new frontier in research is the development of an Algebraic Theory of All Architecture with Categorical Deep Learning to encompass all neural network designs (Gavranović et al., n.d.). This approach addresses some limitations of Geometric Deep Learning, which, as noted by researchers, often fails to explain the significance of the choice of nonlinearity. Categorical methods are thus opening new possibilities for the use of graphs in contexts involving heterogeneous multimodal data and adversarial scenarios.

CONCLUSION

In conclusion, this chapter has provided an in-depth exploration of KG reasoning and embedding, highlighting their pivotal role in advancing the field of KGs and their diverse applications. This conclusion aims to encapsulate the key insights from our study, address the identified challenges, and propose future directions for research and development.

1. Summary of Key Insights

Throughout this study, we have thoroughly examined the fundamental concepts, methodologies, and applications related to KG reasoning and embedding. We have illustrated how KGs have transformed knowledge representation and management by capturing intricate relationships, semantic information, and object connections within a structured framework. Our discussion covered:

- KG Reasoning Techniques: We elaborated on various reasoning approaches, including rule-based reasoning, semantic reasoning, and machine learning-based reasoning, emphasizing their roles in deriving new knowledge from existing data. The distinction between rule-based reasoning (which applies explicit logical rules) and semantic reasoning (which derives insights based on encoded semantic information) was clarified to show how each technique contributes differently to the inferencing process.

- Embedding Techniques: We explored different embedding techniques, such as graph embeddings and KG embeddings, which represent high-dimensional data (nodes and relationships) in low-dimensional vector spaces. This transformation enables efficient data processing, such as similarity computation and classification.

We discussed the strategic importance of these techniques across various domains, including:

- Natural Language Processing (NLP): Enhancements in tasks like question answering and entity recognition through improved semantic representation.
- Information Retrieval: Context-aware search results and improved retrieval performance.
- Healthcare and Biomedical Research: Integration of heterogeneous biomedical data for drug discovery and patient management.
- Recommendation Systems: Personalized recommendations by incorporating rich contextual information.
- Smart Cities and Transportation: Optimization of urban data management and real-time decision-making.

Moreover, we analyzed current challenges facing the field, such as:

- Scalability: Managing large-scale data efficiently.
- Interpretability: Understanding and explaining the results of complex models.
- Generalization: Ensuring techniques perform well across diverse contexts.

We also anticipated future research directions, including:

- Hybrid Models: Combining different reasoning and embedding techniques to enhance performance.
- Explainable AI Techniques: Developing methods to make reasoning and embedding processes more transparent.

- Domain Adaptation Methods: Adapting techniques to specific domains for improved relevance.
- Dynamic Knowledge Graph Management: Strategies for real-time updates and maintenance of KGs.
- New large graph architectures with advanced reasoning capabilities in novel contexts and outcomes, bridging significantly expanded theoretical frameworks with domain-specific applications that drive this multidisciplinary research.

2. Significance of Reasoning and Embedding for the Advancement of KGs and Their Applications

Reasoning and embedding techniques are crucial for enhancing the capabilities and functionalities of KGs. By enabling KGs to extract new insights from existing data and represent complex information in a simplified format, these techniques significantly improve the efficiency and effectiveness of KG-based applications.

The strategic integration of reasoning and embedding with emerging technologies, such as language models and AI systems, drives innovation across various sectors. From social networks and recommendation systems to healthcare and smart cities, KGs empower applications to deliver contextually rich and accurate information, fostering advancements and discoveries in numerous fields.

In summary, the insights from this study underscore the critical importance of reasoning and embedding techniques in advancing KGs. By addressing current challenges and embracing future research opportunities, we can unlock the full potential of KGs as powerful tools for knowledge representation, management, and discovery in the digital era.

DECLARATIONS

Authors' Contributions

Dr. Otmane Azeroual and Dr. Renaud Fabre have jointly contributed to the conception, design, and development of the study titled "Unlocking the Power of Knowledge Graphs: Advanced Reasoning and Embedding Techniques." Dr. Azeroual led the research framework, focusing on advanced reasoning algorithms for knowledge graphs, including rule-based reasoning and constraint-based reasoning. He was also responsible for the mathematical formulations, pseudocode development, and the implementation examples that provide a technical foundation for the study.

Dr. Fabre contributed significantly to the exploration of embedding techniques, such as TransE and Graph Convolutional Networks (GCN), providing expertise on the theoretical underpinnings and practical applications of these techniques in knowledge graph analytics. He also played a critical role in the analysis, interpretation of results, and the contextualization of the advanced techniques within the broader field of data science.

Both authors collaborated closely in the drafting, critical revision, and final approval of the manuscript. They ensured the integration of interdisciplinary perspectives that bridge the gap between theoretical research and real-world applications in knowledge graph analytics. All authors have read and agreed to the published version of the manuscript.

Data Availability Statement

The pseudocode, mathematical formulations, and example implementations provided in the Appendix are designed to support the replication of the results and are available for educational and research purposes. These materials, including the reasoning and embedding algorithms (e.g., Rule-Based Reasoning, TransE, and GCN), can be accessed through the following GitHub repository: https://github.com/OtmaneAzeroualDZHW/

Unlocking-the-Power-of-Knowledge-Graphs-Advanced-Reasoning-and-Embedding-Techniques

No proprietary or sensitive data was used in this study. All code and sample data are open-source and freely available under the MIT License, ensuring transparency and the ability for other researchers to validate the findings or extend upon the presented work.

REFERENCES

Almahmood, R. J. K., & Tekerek, A. (2022). Issues and solutions in deep learning-enabled recommendation systems within the e-commerce field. *Applied Sciences (Basel, Switzerland), 12*(21), 11256. DOI: 10.3390/app122111256

Badii, C., Bellini, P., Cenni, D., Difino, A., Nesi, P., & Paolucci, M. (2017). Analysis and assessment of a knowledge based smart city architecture providing service APIs. *Future Generation Computer Systems, 75*, 14–29. DOI: 10.1016/j.future.2017.05.001

Bai, J., Luo, C., Li, Z., Yin, Q., Yin, B., & Song, Y. (2023, August). Knowledge graph reasoning over entities and numerical values. In *Proceedings of the 29th ACM SIGKDD Conference on Knowledge Discovery and Data Mining* (pp. 57-68). DOI: 10.1145/3580305.3599399

Berka, P. (2020). Sentiment analysis using rule-based and case-based reasoning. *Journal of Intelligent Information Systems, 55*(1), 51–66. DOI: 10.1007/s10844-019-00591-8

Bronstein, M. M., Bruna, J., Cohen, T., & Veličković, P. (2021). Geometric deep learning: Grids, groups, graphs, geodesics, and gauges. *arXiv preprint arXiv:2104.13478.*

Chang, Y., Wang, X., Wang, J., Wu, Y., Yang, L., Zhu, K., Chen, H., Yi, X., Wang, C., Wang, Y., Ye, W., Zhang, Y., Chang, Y., Yu, P. S., Yang, Q., & Xie, X. (2024). A survey on evaluation of large language models. *ACM Transactions on Intelligent Systems and Technology, 15*(3), 1–45. DOI: 10.1145/3641289

Chen, J., Yang, Y., Peng, L., Chen, L., & Ge, X. (2022). Knowledge graph representation learning-based forest fire prediction. *Remote Sensing (Basel), 14*(17), 4391. DOI: 10.3390/rs14174391

Chen, X., Jia, S., & Xiang, Y. (2020). A review: Knowledge reasoning over knowledge graph. *Expert Systems with Applications, 141*, 112948. DOI: 10.1016/j.eswa.2019.112948

Chen, Z., Chen, L., Villar, S., & Bruna, J. (2020). Can graph neural networks count substructures? *Advances in Neural Information Processing Systems, 33*, 10383–10395.

Chen, Z., Mao, H., Liu, J., Song, Y., Li, B., Jin, W., . . . Tang, J. (2024). Text-space Graph Foundation Models: Comprehensive Benchmarks and New Insights. *arXiv preprint arXiv:2406.10727*. DOI: 10.52202/079017-0239

Chen, Z., Zhang, Y., Fang, Y., Geng, Y., Guo, L., Chen, X., . . . Chen, H. (2024). Knowledge Graphs Meet Multi-Modal Learning: A Comprehensive Survey. *arXiv preprint arXiv:2402.05391*.

. Chowdhary, K. R., & Chowdhary, K. R. (2020). Rule based reasoning. *Fundamentals of Artificial Intelligence*, 89-109.

Cui, Z., Chen, H., Cui, L., Liu, S., Liu, X., Xu, G., & Yin, H. (2022). Reinforced KGs reasoning for explainable sequential recommendation. *World Wide Web (Bussum), 25*(2), 631–654. DOI: 10.1007/s11280-021-00902-6

Dessì, D., Osborne, F., Reforgiato Recupero, D., Buscaldi, D., Motta, E., & Sack, H. (2020). AI-KG: an automatically generated knowledge graph of artificial intelligence. In *The Semantic Web–ISWC 2020: 19th International Semantic Web Conference, Athens, Greece, November 2–6, 2020* [Springer International Publishing.]. *Proceedings, 19*(Part II), 127–143.

Dong, X. L., & Rekatsinas, T. (2018, May). Data integration and machine learning: A natural synergy. In *Proceedings of the 2018 international conference on management of data* (pp. 1645-1650). DOI: 10.1145/3183713.3197387

Fabre, R., Azeroual, O., Schöpfel, J., Bellot, P., & Egret, D. (2023). A Multiverse Graph to Help Scientific Reasoning from Web Usage: Interpretable Patterns of Assessor Shifts in GRAPHYP. *Future Internet, 15*(4), 147. DOI: 10.3390/fi15040147

Fei, H., Ren, Y., Zhang, Y., Ji, D., & Liang, X. (2021). Enriching contextualized language model from knowledge graph for biomedical information extraction. *Briefings in Bioinformatics, 22*(3), bbaa110. DOI: 10.1093/bib/bbaa110 PMID: 32591802

Gavranović, B., Lessard, P., Dudzik, A. J., von Glehn, T., Araújo, J. G. M., & Veličković, P. Position: Categorical Deep Learning is an Algebraic Theory of All Architectures. In *Forty-first International Conference on Machine Learning*.

Goyal, P., & Ferrara, E. (2018). Graph embedding techniques, applications, and performance: A survey. *Knowledge-Based Systems, 151*, 78–94. DOI: 10.1016/j.knosys.2018.03.022

Grimm, S. (2009). Knowledge representation and ontologies. In *Scientific data mining and knowledge discovery: Principles and foundations* (pp. 111–137). Springer Berlin Heidelberg. DOI: 10.1007/978-3-642-02788-8_6

Hu, W., Fey, M., Zitnik, M., Dong, Y., Ren, H., Liu, B., & Leskovec, J. (2020). Open graph benchmark: Datasets for machine learning on graphs. *Advances in Neural Information Processing Systems, 33*, 22118–22133.

Huang, X., Zhang, J., Li, D., & Li, P. (2019, January). Knowledge graph embedding based question answering. In *Proceedings of the twelfth ACM international conference on web search and data mining* (pp. 105-113). DOI: 10.1145/3289600.3290956

Ji, S., Pan, S., Cambria, E., Marttinen, P., & Philip, S. Y. (2021). A survey on knowledge graphs: Representation, acquisition, and applications. *IEEE Transactions on Neural Networks and Learning Systems, 33*(2), 494–514. DOI: 10.1109/TNNLS.2021.3070843 PMID: 33900922

Kau, A., He, X., Nambissan, A., Astudillo, A., Yin, H., & Aryani, A. (2024). Combining Knowledge Graphs and Large Language Models. *arXiv preprint arXiv:2407.06564*.

Kumar, H., Singh, M. K., Gupta, M. P., & Madaan, J. (2020). Moving towards smart cities: Solutions that lead to the Smart City Transformation Framework. *Technological Forecasting and Social Change, 153*, 119281. DOI: 10.1016/j.techfore.2018.04.024

Lewis, P., Perez, E., Piktus, A., Petroni, F., Karpukhin, V., Goyal, N., & Kiela, D. (2020). Retrieval-augmented generation for knowledge-intensive nlp tasks. *Advances in Neural Information Processing Systems, 33*, 9459–9474.

Li, Z., Liu, H., Zhang, Z., Liu, T., & Xiong, N. N. (2021). Learning knowledge graph embedding with heterogeneous relation attention networks. *IEEE Transactions on Neural Networks and Learning Systems, 33*(8), 3961–3973. DOI: 10.1109/TNNLS.2021.3055147 PMID: 33606639

Malec, S. A., Taneja, S. B., Albert, S. M., Shaaban, C. E., Karim, H. T., Levine, A. S., & Boyce, R. D. (2023). Causal feature selection using a knowledge graph combining structured knowledge from the biomedical literature and ontologies: A use case studying depression as a risk factor for Alzheimer's disease. *Journal of Biomedical Informatics, 142*, 104368. DOI: 10.1016/j.jbi.2023.104368 PMID: 37086959

Manning, C. D. (2022). Human language understanding & reasoning. *Daedalus, 151*(2), 127–138. DOI: 10.1162/daed_a_01905

Morris, C., Frasca, F., Dym, N., Maron, H., Ceylan, I. I., & Levie, R.. & Jegelka, S. Position: Future Directions in the Theory of Graph Machine Learning. In *Forty-first International Conference on Machine Learning*.

Paleyes, A., Urma, R. G., & Lawrence, N. D. (2022). Challenges in deploying machine learning: A survey of case studies. *ACM Computing Surveys, 55*(6), 1–29. DOI: 10.1145/3533378

Pan, S., Luo, L., Wang, Y., Chen, C., Wang, J., & Wu, X. (2024). Unifying large language models and knowledge graphs: A roadmap. *IEEE Transactions on Knowledge and Data Engineering, 36*(7), 3580–3599. DOI: 10.1109/TKDE.2024.3352100

Papamarkou, T., Birdal, T., Bronstein, M. M., Carlsson, G. E., Curry, J., Gao, Y., & Zamzmi, G. (2024). Position: Topological Deep Learning is the New Frontier for Relational Learning. In *Forty-first International Conference on Machine Learning*.

Quan, Y., Xiong, Z. K., Zhang, K. X., Zhang, Q. Y., Zhang, W., & Zhang, H. Y. (2023). Evolution-strengthened knowledge graph enables predicting the targetability and druggability of genes. *PNAS Nexus*, *2*(5), pgad147. DOI: 10.1093/pnasnexus/pgad147 PMID: 37188275

Rizzo, G., Pereira, B., Varga, A., Van Erp, M., & Cano Basave, A. E. (2017). Lessons learnt from the Named Entity rEcognition and Linking (NEEL) challenge series. *Semantic Web*, *8*(5), 667–700. DOI: 10.3233/SW-170276

Rossi, A., Barbosa, D., Firmani, D., Matinata, A., & Merialdo, P. (2021). Knowledge graph embedding for link prediction: A comparative analysis. [TKDD]. *ACM Transactions on Knowledge Discovery from Data*, *15*(2), 1–49. DOI: 10.1145/3424672

Santos, A., Colaço, A. R., Nielsen, A. B., Niu, L., Strauss, M., Geyer, P. E., Coscia, F., Albrechtsen, N. J. W., Mundt, F., Jensen, L. J., & Mann, M. (2022). A knowledge graph to interpret clinical proteomics data. *Nature Biotechnology*, *40*(5), 692–702. DOI: 10.1038/s41587-021-01145-6 PMID: 35102292

Scholz, R. W., & Tietje, O. (2002). Embedded case study methods: Integrating quantitative and qualitative knowledge. *Sage (Atlanta, Ga.)*.

Shimizu, R., Matsutani, M., & Goto, M. (2022). An explainable recommendation framework based on an improved knowledge graph attention network with massive volumes of side information. *Knowledge-Based Systems*, *239*, 107970. DOI: 10.1016/j.knosys.2021.107970

Su, C., Tong, J., Zhu, Y., Cui, P., & Wang, F. (2020). Network embedding in biomedical data science. *Briefings in Bioinformatics*, *21*(1), 182–197. DOI: 10.1093/bib/bby117 PMID: 30535359

Sun, X., Zhang, J., Wu, X., Cheng, H., Xiong, Y., & Li, J. (2023). Graph prompt learning: A comprehensive survey and beyond. *arXiv preprint arXiv:2311.16534*.

Sun, Z., Yang, J., Zhang, J., Bozzon, A., Huang, L. K., & Xu, C. (2018, September). Recurrent knowledge graph embedding for effective recommendation. In *Proceedings of the 12th ACM conference on recommender systems* (pp. 297-305). DOI: 10.1145/3240323.3240361

Tamine, L., & Goeuriot, L. (2021). Semantic information retrieval on medical texts: Research challenges, survey, and open issues. *ACM Computing Surveys, 54*(7), 1–38. DOI: 10.1145/3462476

Waikhom, L., & Patgiri, R. (2021). Graph neural networks: Methods, applications, and opportunities. *arXiv preprint arXiv:2108.10733.*

Wang, B., Wang, A., Chen, F., Wang, Y., & Kuo, C. C. J. (2019). Evaluating word embedding models: Methods and experimental results. *APSIPA Transactions on Signal and Information Processing*, *8*(1), e19. DOI: 10.1017/ATSIP.2019.12

Wang, J., Wang, X., Ma, C., & Kou, L. (2021). A survey on the development status and application prospects of knowledge graph in smart grids. *IET Generation, Transmission & Distribution, 15*(3), 383–407. DOI: 10.1049/gtd2.12040

Wei, X., Wang, S., Zhang, D., Bhatia, P., & Arnold, A. (2021). Knowledge enhanced pretrained language models: A compreshensive survey. *arXiv preprint arXiv:2110.08455.*

Xu, M. (2021). Understanding graph embedding methods and their applications. *SIAM Review*, *63*(4), 825–853. DOI: 10.1137/20M1386062

Ye, Z., Kumar, Y. J., Sing, G. O., Song, F., & Wang, J. (2022). A comprehensive survey of graph neural networks for knowledge graphs. *IEEE Access : Practical Innovations, Open Solutions*, *10*, 75729–75741. DOI: 10.1109/ACCESS.2022.3191784

Zhang, W., Chen, J., Li, J., Xu, Z., Pan, J. Z., & Chen, H. (2022). Knowledge graph reasoning with logics and embeddings: Survey and perspective. *arXiv preprint arXiv:2202.07412.*

APPENDIX

Detailed Exploration of Reasoning and Embedding Algorithms

This appendix provides a deeper dive into specific reasoning and embedding algorithms used in KGs. It includes mathematical formulations, pseudocode, and examples of algorithm implementation to cater to readers seeking more technical details.

1. Reasoning Algorithms

Reasoning algorithms infer implicit knowledge from explicitly stated facts within a KG. Key algorithms include:

1.1. Rule-Based Reasoning

Rule-based reasoning applies predefined logical rules to infer new relationships. A common approach is to use Horn Clauses in first-order logic.

Figure 7. Mathematical Formulation

Given a set of facts F and a set of rules R, where each rule is of the form $A \to B$ (i.e., if A is true, then B must be true), the reasoning process can be formulated as follows:

$$\text{New Facts} = \{B \mid A \in F \text{ and } A \to B \in R\}$$

Figure 8. Pseudocode

```
def rule_based_reasoning(facts, rules):
    new_facts = set()
    for rule in rules:
        premise, conclusion = rule
        if premise in facts:
            new_facts.add(conclusion)
    return facts.union(new_facts)
```

Figure 9. Example Implementation

Consider a rule-based system where the rules are defined as:

- If `X is a parent of Y` and `Y is a parent of Z`, then `X is a grandparent of Z`.

If our facts include `{(John, parent, Mary), (Mary, parent, Tom)}`, applying the rule-based reasoning would infer the fact `{(John, grandparent, Tom)}`.

1.2. Constraint-Based Reasoning

Constraint-based reasoning involves solving constraints to find valid assignments for variables.

Figure 10. Mathematical Formulation

Given a set of variables V and constraints C, the problem is to find assignments A such that all constraints in C are satisfied.

Let C be a set of constraints c_i and A be an assignment of values to V:

$$\text{Find } A \text{ such that } \forall c_i \in C, \text{ constraint } c_i(A) \text{ is satisfied}$$

Figure 11. Pseudocode

```
def constraint_satisfaction(variables, constraints):
    def satisfies_constraints(assignment):
        return all(c(assignment) for c in constraints)

    def backtrack(assignment):
        if len(assignment) == len(variables):
            return assignment if satisfies_constraints(assignment) else None
        var = next_var_to_assign(assignment)
        for value in possible_values(var):
            assignment[var] = value
            result = backtrack(assignment)
            if result:
                return result
            del assignment[var]
        return None

    return backtrack({})
```

Example Implementation:

In a scheduling problem where each task needs to be scheduled without conflicts, constraints might include task dependencies and resource limits. The algorithm tries to assign times to tasks while ensuring no conflicts arise.

2. Embedding Algorithms

Embedding algorithms represent entities and relations in dense vector spaces, capturing their semantic meanings. Key algorithms include:

2.1. TransE (Translation-Based Embedding)

TransE embeds entities and relations in a continuous vector space. The key idea is to translate entity vectors by relation vectors to predict other entities.

Figure 12. Mathematical Formulation

For a triple (h, r, t) where h is the head entity, r is the relation, and t is the tail entity, the objective is to minimize the distance between $h + r$ and t:

$$\text{Loss}(h, r, t) = \max(0, \gamma + d(h + r, t))$$

where $d(\cdot, \cdot)$ is a distance metric (e.g., L1 or L2 norm) and γ is a margin parameter.

Figure 13. Pseudocode

```
def transE_loss(head, relation, tail, margin, norm):
    distance = norm(head + relation - tail)
    loss = max(0, margin + distance)
    return loss
```

Figure 14. Example Implementation

In a KG, if (Berlin, is_capital_of, Germany) is a known fact, TransE tries to place Berlin and Germany in the vector space such that the vector for Berlin plus the vector for is_capital_of is close to the vector for Germany.

2.2. GCN (Graph Convolutional Network)

GCNs perform convolutions over graph data to capture node and edge features.

Figure 15.

The node representation is updated as:

$$H^{(k+1)} = \sigma\left(\hat{A}H^{(k)}W^{(k)}\right)$$

where $\hat{A}$ is the normalized adjacency matrix, $H^{(k)}$ is the node feature matrix at layer k, $W^{(k)}$ is the weight matrix for layer k, and σ is an activation function.

Figure 16. Pseudocode

```
def gcn_layer(adj_matrix, node_features, weight_matrix, activation):
    normalized_adj = normalize(adj_matrix)
    new_features = activation(np.dot(normalized_adj, np.dot(node_features, weight_matrix)))
    return new_features
```

Example Implementation

In a social network KG, GCN can be used to predict user interests by aggregating features from their neighbors, effectively capturing the social context of users.

These sections illustrate fundamental reasoning and embedding algorithms used in KGs. The mathematical formulations, pseudocode, and examples provided aim to offer a clear understanding of how these algorithms work and can be implemented.

Chapter 3
A Neuro-Symbolic System for End-of-Life Decision-Making Based on Knowledge Graphs

Armando David Caballero Font
Hospital Universitario Arnaldo Millán, Cuba

Yadier Betancourt Martínez
http://orcid.org/0009-0006-2093-0725
Universidad Central "Marta Abreu" de las Villas, Cuba

Amed Leiva-Mederos
Universidad Central "Marta Abreu" de las Villas, Cuba

Rafael Bello
Universidad Central "Marta Abreu" de las Villas, Cuba

Maria Matilde Garcia Lorenzo
Universidad Central "Marta Abreu" de las Villas, Cuba

Armando Caballero
Universidad Central "Marta Abreu" de las Villas, Cuba

ABSTRACT

Making decisions in Intensive Care Units (ICUs) is essential for patient survival and demands a precise evaluation of complex clinical data. Although predictive models based on machine learning, such as neural networks, have proven useful for anticipating outcomes in intensive care, their lack of transparency restricts their clinical adoption. This study

DOI: 10.4018/979-8-3373-1360-3.ch003

proposes a system that merges the predictive strength of neural networks with explainability techniques based on knowledge graphs and medical ontologies to enhance the transparency and interpretability of predictions in clinical settings. By employing a medical ontology to organize data and a knowledge graph implemented in Neo4j, clinical information is consolidated, and understandable explanations regarding ICU mortality are produced. The system can also apply rules for end-of-life decisions and utilize large language models (LLMs) to generate clear explanations for both mortality predictions and end-of-life choices. The research evaluates the accuracy of this approach and compares it with classical explainability methods such as LIME. Decision-making in Intensive Care Units (ICUs) is critical for patient survival and requires accurate evaluation of complex clinical data. Although predictive models based on machine learning, such as neural networks, have proven useful for predicting outcomes in intensive care, their lack of transparency limits their clinical application. This research proposes a system that combines the predictive power of neural networks with explainability methods based on knowledge graphs and medical ontologies to improve the transparency and understanding of predictions in a clinical setting. Using a medical ontology to structure data and a knowledge graph in Neo4j, clinical information is integrated, and understandable explanations of predictions regarding ICU mortality are provided. The system is also capable of using rules for end-of-life decisions and leveraging large language models (LLMs) to generate clear explanations for both mortality and end-of-life decisions. The research evaluates the accuracy of this approach and compares it with classical explainability methods, such as LIME.

1. INTRODUCTION

In the healthcare domain, particularly within Intensive Care Units (ICUs), clinical decision-making is vital for patient survival and recovery. Decisions must rely on an accurate assessment of available clinical data, including medical histories, test outcomes, administered treatments, and observed responses. The complexity and diversity of clinical cases pose significant challenges, as different patients may react differently to the same treatments due to individual factors like comorbidities and genetic traits.

2. PREDICTIVE MODELS AND THEIR LIMITATIONS

Predictive models that employ advanced machine learning techniques and neural networks have demonstrated considerable promise in forecasting clinical outcomes in intensive care (Kessler et al., 2023; Alshwaheen et al., 2020; Asteris et al., 2022). Nevertheless, a major obstacle is the opacity of these models. Many existing systems function as "black boxes," delivering results without clarifying which factors influenced those predictions. This lack of transparency can undermine trust and the practical utility of these models in clinical environments, where physicians need to grasp the reasoning behind a prediction to make well-informed decisions and potentially explain them to other stakeholders.

In the high-stakes ICU environment, the demand for interpretability in predictive models becomes even more critical due to the unique challenges present. The high mortality rate, the necessity for rapid decision-making, and the complexity of cases—where patients often have multiple comorbidities and intricate treatments—make transparency in the decision-making process essential. Explainable Artificial Intelligence (XAI) methods offer a solution to this problem (Dwivedi et al., 2023), especially when enriched with domain knowledge, for which ontologies and knowledge graphs are well-suited (Burkart & Huber, 2021; Tiddi & Schlobach, 2022; Vilone & Longo, 2020). These tools enable the structuring and formalization of knowledge, facilitating both data understanding and the generation of explanations for model predictions.

A medical ontology provides a structured and formal representation of relevant concepts and relationships within a specific domain (Keet, 2018). For instance, an ontology can include terms related to diagnoses, procedures, medications, vital signs, and other critical aspects of patient care. Building a medical ontology involves the careful identification and definition of these concepts, as well as specifying the relationships among them. This structured approach not only improves data interoperability but also facilitates the integration of diverse information sources, allowing a holistic and coherent view of the patient's condition and treatment.

From this medical ontology, a knowledge graph can be constructed that integrates patient and treatment data. A knowledge graph represents information as a set of nodes (entities) and edges (relationships) in a graphical structure (Barrasa & Webber, 2023). In the ICU environment, nodes may represent patients, diagnoses, treatments, and other relevant elements, while edges capture relationships such as administered treatments, observed responses, and clinical outcomes. Implementing a knowledge graph in a database like Neo4j (Bratanic, 2024) enables a more understandable and navigable representation of information, easing the analysis and extraction of useful knowledge for clinical decision-making.

3. THEORETICAL FRAMEWORK

3.1. Information Retrieval: Key Developments

Information Retrieval (IR) is an evolving field focused on finding relevant information within large datasets. Recent trends in IR include:

- **Semantic Search**: Uses natural language processing (NLP) techniques to interpret query context and meaning. It improves result accuracy by understanding user intent. Its main drawback is the need for large labeled datasets and complex models.
- **Embedding-based Search**: Uses vector representations (embeddings) to capture semantic relationships between terms. It allows finding similarities between concepts even when different wording is used. Performance depends on embedding quality and can be computationally expensive (Patil et al., 2023).
- **Multimodal Search**: Combines information from multiple sources (text, images, audio, etc.) to improve retrieval. It offers richer and more contextualized results. The main challenge is the technical complexity of integrating different data types.
- **Personalized Search**: Adapts search results based on user profile, history, and preferences. It improves result relevance for each in-

dividual. However, it requires collecting user data, raising privacy concerns.

- **Real-time Search**: Provides up-to-date results instantly using streaming and real-time processing systems. Ideal for dynamic applications like social networks or financial markets. It demands robust infrastructure and low latency.
- **Federated Search**: Integrates results from multiple sources or independent databases in a single query (Zhu et al., 2023). It expands search scope without centralizing data. Coordinating and normalizing results from different systems can be complex.
- **Graph-based Search**: Uses knowledge graphs to represent relationships between entities and concepts. It facilitates exploration of complex connections and contextual relationships. Building and maintaining knowledge graphs is labor-intensive and requires constant updates.
- **Generative AI Search**: Uses generative models (e.g., GPT) to create responses or summaries from retrieved data (Chen et al., 2022). It provides more natural and complete answers. There is a risk of generating inaccurate or biased information if the model is not well-trained.
- **Voice-based Search**: Allows voice queries using speech recognition and NLP. It facilitates interaction for users on the move or with disabilities. Difficulties include accent recognition, background noise, and ambiguous queries.

These trends are transforming how we access and use information, enabling more accurate and efficient searches.

3.2. Explainable Artificial Intelligence (XAI)

As AI enters increasingly sensitive areas of daily life—such as healthcare (Kasula, 2024) and criminal justice (Mercan & Selçuk, 2024)—questions about ethics, fairness, and safety become more urgent. While the accuracy of current AI models is impressive, it is not the only critical aspect. In sensitive domains, a detailed understanding of the model and its outputs is also crucial. Thus, increasing user trust in AI, or reliable

AI, depends both on prediction accuracy and on the user's understanding of the problem-solving process. The underlying algorithms of machine learning and deep learning build complex models that are often opaque to humans (Burkart & Huber, 2021). To address the lack of interpretability in AI-based systems—their reasoning processes and outputs—the field of Explainable Artificial Intelligence (XAI) has re-emerged in recent years (Brasse et al., 2023).

In XAI, the terms "understanding," "interpretation," and "explanation" are often used interchangeably. Despite their frequent use, the AI standards community lacks consensus on definitions of explainability and interpretability. The ambiguities in definitions include the type of explanation, the justification for providing it, its purpose, and the recipient of the explanation.

For clarity, we define interpretability techniques as those inherent to the model's architecture, which can also be considered secondary outputs of the model, often calculated during inference and thus representing little additional computational cost. In contrast, XAI techniques are designed as external tools not part of direct model outputs but providing complementary explanations. These are often derived by observing how the ML model behaves in use and then deriving an explanation from those observed predictions (Munn & Pitman, 2022).

3.3. Key Aspects of Explainable AI

According to Kass & Finin (1988), the quality of an explanation depends on three distinguishing criteria: relevance, persuasiveness, and comprehensibility.

- **Relevance**: An explanation is relevant if it addresses the user's current goals and needs. On one hand, it should provide as much information as possible to achieve those goals. On the other hand, it should be as concise as possible to avoid distracting the user with unnecessary extra information.

- **Persuasiveness**: An explanation is persuasive if the user accepts it. A user is convinced of an explanation if it is based on facts they consider true.
- **Comprehensibility**: The comprehensibility of an explanation is achieved through different facets. The explanation system must use a type of explanation the recipient can understand. In addition to being brief and highlighting user-relevant aspects, the explanation should be simple enough that the recipient does not need to look up many unfamiliar terms.

According to Burkart & Huber (2021), the nature of the data is an important factor in generating a convincing explanation. The proposed dimensions for evaluating an explanation can be affected by the data type. This implies that different explanatory approaches should be considered depending on the available data type, and the mode of communication may vary.

3.4. Classical XAI Methods

Classical Explainable Artificial Intelligence (XAI) methods are techniques developed to interpret and understand machine learning models, especially those—like deep neural networks—often considered "black boxes" due to their internal complexity. These methods aim to provide transparency and explanations that allow users, both technical and non-technical, to understand how a model reaches its decisions. Among the most used are LIME (Local Interpretable Model-agnostic Explanations), SHAP (SHapley Additive exPlanations), and PDP (Partial Dependence Plots). Each offers different approaches to decomposing and visualizing input variable contributions to model predictions. These methods have been fundamental in increasing trust in AI, facilitating its adoption in critical areas such as medicine, justice, and finance (Munn & Pitman, 2022; Dieber & Kirrane, 2020).

SHAP (SHapley Additive exPlanations) is a machine learning model interpretation method based on game theory, using Shapley values to fairly assign each feature's contribution to a model's prediction. Unlike other methods, SHAP provides both global and local explanations, allowing understanding not only of each feature's impact on an individual prediction but also how features influence predictions overall.

The SHAP approach involves calculating each feature's contribution to the prediction by subtracting the model's mean prediction from the model's prediction for a specific input (Mosca et al., 2022).

PDP (Partial Dependence Plots) is a model interpretation technique that visualizes and helps understand the relationship between one or more features and a machine learning model's prediction. This technique illustrates how the model's prediction changes as one or more features vary, keeping other variables constant. The PDP approach involves calculating the model's average predictions for different values of the feature of interest, averaging predictions over all dataset cases. This generates a curve showing how the selected variable influences the model's output, revealing patterns and relationships that might not be evident when analyzing the model as a whole.

One of the main advantages of PDPs is that they are easy to interpret and can help identify interactions between features, as well as the effect of a specific feature on predictions (Dwivedi et al., 2023).

Table 1. Comparison of XAI Techniques

Feature/ technique	**LIME**	**SHAP**	**PDP**	**KG Ontologies**	**Human Interaction**
Model type	Agnostic	Agnostic	Agnostic	Data Driven	Interdisciplinary
Interpretability	Local	Local/ Global	Global	Global	Variable
Complexity	High	High	Low	High	Variable
Performance	Average	High	Moderate	High	Variable
Ease of use	High	Moderate	High	Complex	Variable
Application	Feature & model explanation	Interaction analysis	Knowledge-oriented	Structuring domains	Improved communication
Display	Graph	Graphic	Graphic	Graphic	Varies
Sturdiness	Average	High	Average	High	Variable

4. METHODOLOGY

4.1. System Architecture for End-of-Life Decision-Making in Intensive Care

The proposed model consists of a domain ontology developed from UMLS and DECS languages, a knowledge graph containing structured medical knowledge of intensive care, and a database. These components feed an explainable AI model that serves an LLM to provide explanations for user interface queries.

System Components:

1. **Prediction:** MLP: 10-layer ReLU network (16 input features, Adam optimizer). Rules: 93 J48-derived rules (accuracy: 85.29%, F1: 0.60).
2. **Knowledge Integration:** Neo4j graph with 4,213 nodes (patients, diagnoses, treatments).
3. **Explanation:** GraphRAG retrieves evidence for Llama-2-70B to generate natural language.

4.2. Dataset

This section describes the clinical data and characteristics used to build the information retrieval system. These data form the basis for developing the medical ontology and knowledge graph, facilitating prediction and explanation of ICU patient mortality.

4.2.1. Patients and Clinical Data

Patients show great variability in their medical characteristics, comorbidities, and responses to treatments. The dataset used in this research includes information relevant to decision-making in critical contexts where the patient's life is at stake. The main aspects modeled are:

- **Clinical History (HC):** Each patient has a unique identification number recorded in their clinical history, allowing individual tracking throughout their ICU stay and facilitating information integration.

- **Age:** Patient's age at ICU admission.
- **Medical History:** Pre-existing conditions or chronic diseases present before ICU admission, such as hypothyroidism, hypertension (HTA), or COPD—critical factors influencing therapeutic decisions and clinical outcomes.
- **Dates:** ICU admission date.
- **Reasons for ICU Admission:** Specific reason for ICU admission, e.g., severe Dengue, Acute Respiratory Failure Type 1, or Unstable Angina.
- **Diagnostic Specificity:** Particular conditions during ICU stay, such as Acute Myocardial Infarction or COPD Exacerbation, directly affecting treatment plans and recovery probability.
- **Treatment:** Various treatments, some potentially futile (not significantly improving condition), e.g., mechanical ventilation (VAM), hydration, or antihypertensives.
- **Do Not Resuscitate (DNR) / Limitation of Therapeutic Effort (LET) Decisions:** When necessary, decisions about limiting therapeutic efforts to avoid invasive interventions that would not improve quality of life. Documented with date.
- **Date and Time of Death:** Exact timestamp when patient dies.
- **Causes of Death:** Documented causes, e.g., multiple organ dysfunction, cerebral edema, respiratory failure.

4.3. Clinical Factors and Evaluation Scales

- **Charlson Comorbidity Index (CCI):** Evaluates patient comorbidity and its impact on survival.
- **Apache II:** Scale to calculate mortality probability in intensive care based on various physiological and health variables.
- **Karnofsky Scale:** Measures patient functionality level, indicating ability to perform daily activities.
- **SOFA Scale:** Evaluates sequential organ failure, indicating severity of multi-organ dysfunction.

- **Treatment Refractoriness:** Classifies patients whose condition does not respond to conventional treatments, indicating poor prognosis.
- **Oncological Disease:** Records whether the patient has active oncological disease, influencing therapeutic decisions and overall prognosis.

5. SYSTEM DESIGN AND KNOWLEDGE GRAPH

5.1. Knowledge Graph Semantics Based on Ontology

This knowledge graph is based on an ontology that is a reduction of the UMLS ontological model and has been specified with DECS, which defines key entities and their relationships within intensive medical care and clinical decision-making. The knowledge graph reflects the following entities:

- **Patient:** Central node representing the patient, focus of medical relationships and events.
- **Diagnosis:** Related to the patient via HAS_DIAGNOSIS property. Represents medical diagnoses received.
- **Therapy:** Connected to the patient via two relationship types: HAS_THERAPY (current therapies) and HAS_FUTURE_TREATMENT (planned treatments).
- **Decision:** Connected via HAS_DECISION, representing important medical decisions (e.g., treatment continuation or suspension).
- **Admission:** Related to the patient via HAS_ADMISSION, recording hospital or clinic admission information.
- **Cause of Admission:** Represents the reason or medical condition motivating admission, connected to Admission via HAS_CAUSE.
- **Medical History:** Describes previous medical events, related to the patient via HAS_HISTORY.
- **Cause of Death:** Related to the patient via HAS_COMPLICATION, indicating a complication leading to death (if applicable).

5.2. Data Retrieval with Cypher Queries

This section explains how to perform queries in Cypher, the query language for graph databases, using Neo4j. The goal is to retrieve a specific patient's data along with relevant relationships such as therapies, decisions, and diagnoses.

Example Cypher query that retrieves a patient by ID and extracts information from various connected entities:

```
cypher
MATCH (patient:Patient)
WHERE patient.id = $s_id_
RETURN patient {.id, .age, .sofaScore}
```

This example retrieves the patient's ID, age, and SOFA score.

5.3. Implementation of Rule-Based Reasoning

Integrating automatic rules with the J48 algorithm represents a crucial phase in creating the neuro-symbolic system. In this context, we trained the J48 algorithm using our ICU patient dataset to obtain an initial rule set for predicting patient mortality probability, thereby transparently identifying key factors influencing death probability.

5.3.1. Training and Rule Generation

During training, the J48 algorithm analyzed various dataset attributes—such as clinical characteristics, medical histories, and other critical factors affecting patient health status. These attributes were used to build a decision tree whose branches represent decisions based on specific data thresholds. From this decision tree, J48 generated 141 automatic rules, each describing conditions leading to a specific outcome (death prediction). The tree achieved 85.29% accuracy, 0.62 recall, and 0.60 F1-score.

Example Rule Conditions:

- Age greater than 48 years (age > 48)
- Diagnosis of complicated lymphangitis (hasDiagnosis("Complicated Lymphangitis"))
- Treatment refusal (refusalOfTreatment)
- Presence of sepsis (sepsis)

Conclusion: Under these conditions, the patient dies.

5.4. Creation of the Multilayer Perceptron (MLP) Model

The Multilayer Perceptron (MLP) model used in this work is configured as a feed-forward neural network with multiple processing layers that enable learning complex nonlinear relationships from clinical data. This type of neural network has been widely applied in predicting medical outcomes, showing superior results to classical models like logistic regression or decision trees due to its ability to generalize and capture complex interactions among clinical variables.

The implemented MLP has 10 hidden layers of 100 neurons each and uses the ReLU (Rectified Linear Unit) activation function, suitable for its simplicity and effectiveness in reducing vanishing gradient problems in deep networks. The optimizer used is Adam (Bae et al., 2019), a stochastic gradient descent-based algorithm that allows rapid convergence even in high-dimensional and noisy data scenarios.

The neural network has 16 input neurons, each representing a relevant feature of the patient's clinical state, similar to database attributes. The output neuron corresponds to the target variable (death prediction), giving a single output neuron that provides patient mortality probability.

The MLP also includes a regularization process using an alpha term of 0.0001, controlling model complexity and preventing overfitting. Additionally, learning_rate_init is set to 0.001, balancing learning speed and model accuracy. This approach has proven effective in predicting clinical outcomes such as mortality in critically ill patients, achicving competitive accuracy levels.

6. RESULTS

6.1. Interaction Between Neural Network, Knowledge Graph, and Rules

To understand how the neuro-symbolic system predicts and explains ICU mortality, it is essential to analyze the interaction among the Neural Network, Knowledge Graph, and rules. Each component plays a specific role:

- **Neural Network (MLP):** Takes patient clinical data as input and generates a death probability prediction (output 1 or 0), used as a starting point for generating explanations.
- **Rules:** Represent expert knowledge about factors influencing ICU patient mortality. Rules are integrated over KG data, enabling transparent and explainable reasoning about patient data. They provide an approximation of "why" the NN made its prediction, identifying key contributing factors. The rules are essentially explanation patterns.
- **Knowledge Graph:** Represents medical domain knowledge in a node-and-relationship structure. It takes the NN's prediction as input and contextualizes it with stored medical information, using rules to generate an initial prediction explanation based on relationships among patient data, NN prediction, and domain knowledge.

6.2. Response Generation and User Interface

In the quest to develop more transparent and understandable AI systems, explainable AI has gained relevance in various areas, including healthcare and automated decision-making. An interface designed to improve ML model explanatory capacity becomes essential. This section addresses how LLMs can be integrated with knowledge graphs, minimize typical hallucinations, and contextualize with medical documents to generate more coherent and useful explanations.

Integration of Knowledge Graphs with LLM

Integrating knowledge graphs with large-scale language models has gained traction as an effective strategy to improve response accuracy and coherence. One recent promising approach is GraphRAG (Graph Retrieval-Augmented Generation), a technique that relies on knowledge graph architecture and enables retrieval of relevant contextual information (McCaffrey et al., 2024). This system, combined with graph databases like Neo4j, provides a robust mechanism to give LLMs access to structured, verifiable, context-rich data.

Reduction of Hallucinations in LLM

A major problem of LLMs is their tendency to generate incorrect information or "hallucinations" (Anand et al., 2022)—responses not supported by real data. This occurs because LLMs generate text based on probabilistic patterns from training, leading to errors when lacking sufficient context or precise information.

The knowledge graph acts as a structured, verifiable information source that the LLM can consult before generating a response. This is especially useful for reducing hallucinations because the model relies not solely on language patterns but on facts and previously validated relationships. Instead of simply "guessing," the LLM uses graph data to substantiate responses. For example, when explaining a death, instead of generating a fictitious diagnosis, it can search the graph for information about that diagnosis.

Contextualization with Medical Documents

In implementing explainable AI systems in medical contexts, a top priority is ensuring LLMs (Friha et al., 2024; Tegsten, 2024) not only generate coherent responses but are deeply contextualized with precise, relevant medical information. Using medical documents provided by experts becomes essential to provide context and improve automated decision accuracy, particularly in delicate areas like end-of-life decision-making. The embedding process works as follows:

- **Word Representation:** Each word in the model's vocabulary is represented as a feature vector (word embedding). Each vector dimension corresponds to a specific feature. Vectors are part of model parameters learned during training. Similar words have similar feature vectors.
- **Context Representation:** Given a word sequence, the model combines previous words' feature vectors to form a context vector. For example, predicting the next word in "the cat is on the" sums feature vectors of "the," "cat," "is," and "on."
- **Prediction with Feedforward Neural Network:** The context vector is fed into a feedforward neural network with a hidden layer followed by a softmax output layer. The hidden layer captures nonlinear relationships. The softmax layer calculates probability distribution over all possible vocabulary words that can follow the context vector. The highest-probability word is typically chosen as prediction.
- **Training:** The model is trained using an extensive text corpus. The training objective adjusts model parameters (word feature vectors and neural network weights) to maximize training data probability, typically using stochastic gradient descent and backpropagation.
- **Text Generation:** Once trained, the model generates new text by selecting words from calculated probability distributions.

In our case, we use the Villareño method, a methodology developed and applied at Arnaldo Milán Hospital, focusing on ethical and clinical decision-making in end-of-life situations. This method is based on medical documents, clinical guidelines, and ethically grounded decisions, essential for a comprehensive and compassionate approach to terminal patients.

To ensure the LLM provides accurate responses aligned with medical guidelines for end-of-life situations, a Retrieval Augmented Generation (RAG) system using LangChain was implemented. This approach allows the LLM to generate more informed and relevant responses by accessing specialized medical information at query time.

The first RAG implementation step was creating a compact mathematical representation (embedding) (Patil et al., 2023) of the medical document containing the Villareño methodology, capturing document content essence in a format processable by a vector database. A local embedding model was used, with Pinecone as the vector database to store the document embedding.

When the system receives a request related to an end-of-life decision explanation, it searches for the most relevant information in this embedding stored in the database. The retrieved information from Pinecone is provided to the LLM as additional context, enriching its understanding and enabling more complete, precise responses. With access to the Villareño methodology, the LLM can consider specific guidelines and recommendations for end-of-life decisions, ensuring responses align with Arnaldo Milián Hospital's established practices.

7. DISCUSSION

7.1. Evaluation

To evaluate the quality of explanations generated by the neuro-symbolic system, a survey was designed for medical experts. The survey was administered in a clinical setting and focused on measuring two fundamental aspects: comprehensibility and clinical relevance. For each of five presented cases, experts rated explanations on a scale from 1 to 10, where 1 represented "very incomprehensible or irrelevant" and 10 represented "very comprehensible or highly relevant."

Survey Structure:

1. **Clinical Case Presentation:** Experts received a detailed description of an ICU patient case, including clinical data, diagnosis, treatment received, and other relevant background.
2. **Explanation of Death:** A system-generated explanation about the patient's death reasons was presented. Experts rated it 1–10 based on two criteria:
   - *Comprehensibility:* Is the explanation clear and easy to understand?
   - *Relevance:* Is the explanation clinically significant and aligned with the case's medical context?

3. **Case Diversity:** The survey included five different clinical cases, each with its respective explanations about death and end-of-life decisions, allowing evaluation of consistency and generalization across various clinical scenarios.

Results: The highest scores (9 and 10) had the highest frequency (five responses each), suggesting most respondents considered explanations high-quality. There were some middle-range responses (5 to 8), but no low ratings (1 to 4). This indicates a positive trend in explanation perception, though some lower responses (5 and 6) suggest opportunities for improvement.

CONCLUSIONS

Developing an explainable AI system for predicting and explaining ICU mortality is a fundamental step toward more transparent and effective medical care. This system not only provides physicians with a tool to anticipate clinical outcomes but also offers deep understanding of factors influencing those outcomes, improving decision-making and communication with patients and their families.

Combining neural networks (MLP) with a knowledge graph and rules derived from expert medical knowledge has proven highly effective for predicting ICU mortality. The MLP, trained with relevant clinical data, achieved high prediction accuracy validated by solid performance metrics. This neuro-symbolic approach, integrating rule-based reasoning with neural network learning capabilities, provides a robust and reliable system for analyzing complex clinical data.

The system-generated explanations—both for mortality prediction and end-of-life decisions—have proven clear, easy to understand, and clinically relevant. Medical experts, through a survey, confirmed the high quality of these explanations, highlighting their ability to articulate in comprehensible language the factors leading to particular clinical outcomes. This ability to explain model decisions in language accessible to healthcare professionals is crucial for fostering trust in the system and facilitating its integration into clinical practice.

REFERENCES

Alshwaheen, T. I., Hau, Y. W., Ass'Ad, N., & Abualsamen, M. M. (2020). A novel and reliable framework of patient deterioration prediction in intensive care unit based on long short-term memory-recurrent neural network. *IEEE Access : Practical Innovations, Open Solutions, 9*, 3894–3918. DOI: 10.1109/ACCESS.2020.3047186

Anand, A., Lyu, L., Idahl, M., Wang, Y., Wallat, J., & Zhang, Z. (2022). "Explainable information retrieval: A survey." *arXiv preprint arXiv:2211.02405.*

Asteris, P. G., Gavriilaki, E., Touloumenidou, T., Koravou, E.-E., Koutra, M., Papayanni, P. G., Pouleres, A., Karali, V., Lemonis, M. E., Mamou, A., Skentou, A. D., Papalexandri, A., Varelas, C., Chatzopoulou, F., Chatzidimitriou, M., Chatzidimitriou, D., Veleni, A., Rapti, E., Kioumis, I., & Anagnostopoulos, A. (2022). Genetic prediction of ICU hospitalization and mortality in COVID-19 patients using artificial neural networks. *Journal of Cellular and Molecular Medicine, 26*(5), 1445–1455. DOI: 10.1111/jcmm.17098 PMID: 35064759

Bae, K., Ryu, H., & Shin, H. (2019). "Does Adam optimizer keep close to the optimal point?" *arXiv preprint arXiv:1911.00289.*

Barrasa, J., & Webber, J. (2023). *Building Knowledge Graphs*. O'Reilly Media, Inc.

Brasse, J., Broder, H. R., Förster, M., Klier, M., & Sigler, I. (2023). Explainable artificial intelligence in information systems: A review of the status quo and future research directions. *Electronic Markets, 33*(1), 26. DOI: 10.1007/s12525-023-00644-5

Bratanic, T. (2024). *Graph Algorithms for Data Science: With Examples in Neo4j*. Simon and Schuster.

Burkart, N., & Huber, M. F. (2021). A survey on the explainability of supervised machine learning. *Journal of Artificial Intelligence Research, 70*, 245–317. DOI: 10.1613/jair.1.12228

Chen, J., Zhang, R., Guo, J., Fan, Y., & Cheng, X. (2022). "GERE: Generative evidence retrieval for fact verification." In *Proceedings of the 45th International ACM SIGIR Conference*, 2184-2189. DOI: 10.1145/3477495.3531827

Dieber, J., & Kirrane, S. (2020). "Why model why? Assessing the strengths and limitations of LIME." *arXiv preprint arXiv:2012.00093*.

Dwivedi, R., Dave, D., Naik, H., Singhal, S., Omer, R., Patel, P., Qian, B., Wen, Z., Shah, T., Morgan, G., & Ranjan, R. (2023). Explainable AI (XAI): Core ideas, techniques, and solutions. *ACM Computing Surveys*, *55*(9), 1–33. DOI: 10.1145/3561048

Friha, O., Ferrag, M. A., Kantarci, B., Cakmak, B., Ozgun, A., & Ghoulami-Zine, N. (2024). LLM-based edge intelligence: A comprehensive survey on architectures, applications, security and trustworthiness. *IEEE Open Journal of the Communications Society*, *5*, 5799–5856. DOI: 10.1109/OJCOMS.2024.3456549

Kass, R., & Finin, T. (1988). The need for user models in generating expert system explanations. *International Journal of Expert Systems*, *1*(4).

Kasula, B. Y. (2024). Advancements in AI-driven healthcare: A comprehensive review of diagnostics, treatment, and patient care integration. *International Journal of Machine Learning for Sustainable Development*, *6*(1), 1–5.

. Keet, C. M. (2018). *An Introduction to Ontology Engineering*.

Kessler, S., Schroeder, D., Korlakov, S., Hettlich, V., Kalkhoff, S., Moazemi, S., Lichtenberg, A., Schmid, F., & Aubin, H. (2023). Predicting readmission to the cardiovascular intensive care unit using recurrent neural networks. *Digital Health*, *9*, 20552076221149529. DOI: 10.1177/20552076221149529 PMID: 36644663

McCaffrey, P.. (2024). Evaluating use of generative artificial intelligence in clinical pathology practice: Opportunities and the way forward. *Archives of Pathology & Laboratory Medicine*. PMID: 39384182

. Mercan, G., & Selçuk, Z. V. (2024). "Artificial intelligence (AI) activities in legal practices." *International Journal of Eurasian Education and Culture*.

Mosca, E., Szigeti, F., Tragianni, S., Gallagher, D., & Groh, G. (2022). "SHAP-based explanation methods: A review for NLP interpretability." In *Proceedings of the 29th International Conference on Computational Linguistics*, 4593-4603.

Munn, M., & Pitman, D. (2022). *Explainable AI for practitioners*. O'Reilly Media, Inc.

Patil, R., Boit, S., Gudivada, V., & Nandigam, J. (2023). A survey of text representation and embedding techniques in NLP. *IEEE Access : Practical Innovations, Open Solutions*, *11*, 36120–36146. DOI: 10.1109/ACCESS.2023.3266377

. Tegsten, S. (2024). "Tailored query resolution for medical data interaction: Integrating LangChain4j, LLMs, and retrieval augmented generation: Utilizing real time embedding techniques."

Tiddi, I., & Schlobach, S. (2022). Knowledge graphs as tools for explainable machine learning: A survey. *Artificial Intelligence*, *302*, 103627. DOI: 10.1016/j.artint.2021.103627

Vilone, G., & Longo, L. (2020). "Explainable artificial intelligence: A systematic review." *arXiv preprint arXiv:2006.00093*.

Zhu, Y., ... (2023). "Large language models for information retrieval: A survey." *arXiv preprint arXiv:2308.07107*.

Chapter 4

Evaluating the Most Used Database Technologies for AI and Real-Time Application Development in Metaverse Systems: A Comparative Study

Asher Babu
http://orcid.org/0009-0009-7757-2289
Christ (Deemed to be) University, Delhi NCR, India

ABSTRACT

The rapid evolution of technology, particularly in AI and real-time applications, has increased the need for databases that efficiently handle diverse and complex workloads. This paper analyzes the top five database management systems of 2025: Oracle, MySQL, Microsoft SQL Server, PostgreSQL, and MongoDB. These databases, spanning relational and NoSQL systems, offer distinct capabilities. The comparison is based on key parameters such as performance, scalability, extensibility, data model support, and ease of integration with modern technologies. Notably,

DOI: 10.4018/979-8-3373-1360-3.ch004

PostgreSQL has emerged as a top choice for AI-based applications in metaverse platforms due to its extensibility (e.g., PostGIS for spatial data) and high performance in decentralized architectures. Through detailed analysis, this study highlights the strengths and weaknesses of each database, concluding that PostgreSQL is best suited for AI and real-time applications due to its adaptability and seamless integration with open-source tools critical for metaverse development.

1. INTRODUCTION

In the fast-changing world of technology, the needs of contemporary applications have stretched beyond conventional systems. With the advent of Artificial Intelligence (AI), real-time applications, and the growing use of metaverse platforms, databases are now required to support more sophisticated and diverse workloads (RTInsights, 2024). These applications demand not just the storage of enormous amounts of data but also the capacity to process and process that data in real-time or near-real-time to provide rapid, accurate decision-making. Consequently, databases have had to evolve quite a bit to accommodate these expanding requirements, with new functionality designed to enhance scalability, flexibility, performance, and integration with sophisticated machine learning, AI, and virtual environment technologies (EnterpriseDB, 2024).

The increasing complexity of AI models and the real-time requirements of new applications, like IoT systems, live financial monitoring systems, and metaverse spaces that involve continuous, real-time data handling, impose heavy loads on databases. Programmers are presented with the challenge of selecting a database that is effective in dealing with various data types, such as structured, semi-structured, and unstructured data, while still providing rapid response times, scalability, and integration with machine learning systems (Timescale, 2024). Furthermore, the databases must be effective at dealing with extensive amounts of streaming data for real-time applications and engaging virtual experiences with no tradeoff to performance or dependability.

This paper aims to address these challenges by conducting a comparative study of the top databases currently used in the industry: PostgreSQL,

MySQL, Oracle, Microsoft SQL Server, and MongoDB (Redgate Software, 2025). These databases are a combination of relational and NoSQL databases, both with their strengths and weaknesses (GeeksforGeeks, 2024). The research will be based on the key considerations for AI, metaverse infrastructure, and real-time application development, such as performance, scalability, extensibility, speed, and support for complex data types.

Figure 1. Most Used Database Management Systems (Redgate Software, 2025)

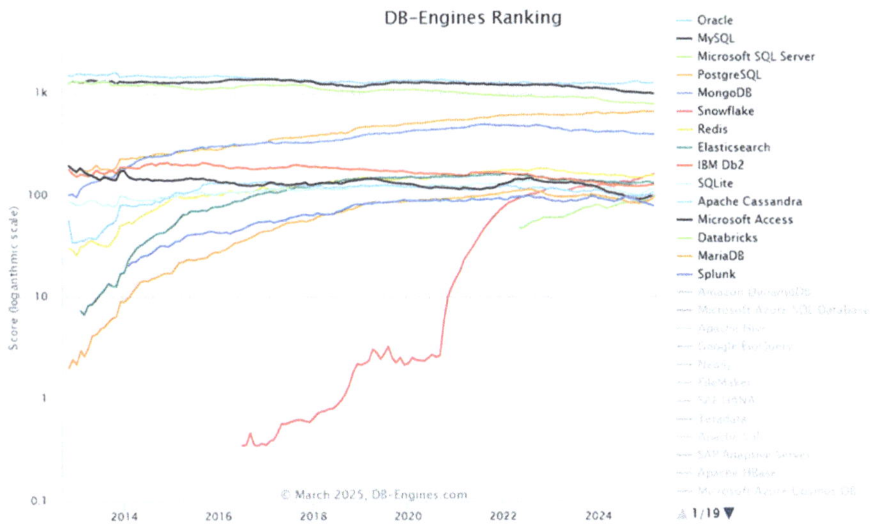

The aim of this paper is to compare these five databases based on the criteria mentioned above and discuss their adequacy for AI-based applications, real-time metaverse workloads, and bulk data processing. Through a comparative analysis of each database and the requirements of modern applications, we will determine the best fit for developers seeking to create scalable, efficient, and future-resistant systems.

Through the comparison, the paper will conclude that PostgreSQL, with its reliability, scalability, extensibility, and strong community support, is the perfect database for AI, real-time virtual environments, and metaverse applications. This thesis is corroborated by an in-depth analysis of PostgreSQL's capabilities in comparison to others, demonstrating how it addresses the unique challenges presented by contemporary technologies and decentralized virtual platforms (Timescale, 2024 ; RTInsights, 2024; GeeksforGeeks, 2024).

2. OVERVIEW OF OPEN-SOURCE DATABASE TECHNOLOGIES

Open-source database technologies are transforming the management of data, as they offer a flexible, scalable and affordable solution for many applications (TechTarget, 2024). Open-source databases are not like proprietary databases, which require expensive licenses and cannot be customized. Instead, they make the entire code accessible and allow developers to modify or create their database according to their needs (Percona, 2023).

Open-source databases are indispensable in contemporary computing, especially concerning artificial intelligence (AI), real-time applications, and metaverse systems. The primary advantage of such databases is their capability to manage big, complex, and unstructured data, which is perfect for their relevance in current and future technology (Kinsta, 2024). There are many workloads that open-source databases can carry out, for example, high-performance transactional processing, big-scale analytics, and distributed computing environments that can be executed in an extensionless way (Fivetran, 2023).

Clearly, progress in the field of AI and real-time data processing made open-source databases necessary to work with large datasets, guarantee their availability, and provide integration with the latest technologies. The next sections reveal the characteristic features of such storage solutions, explain their importance in AI-driven and real-time applications, and indicate their role in metaverse systems (PostgreSQL Global Development Group, 2025).

2.1 Understanding Open-Source Databases

Open-source databases are now a pillar of contemporary data management, with the advantages of flexibility, transparency, and affordability over proprietary offerings (TechTarget, 2024). These databases are based on open-source licensing models where developers can view, edit, and share the source code without restrictions. Openness promotes ongoing innovation through global developer communities and organizations that work towards making them better (Percona, 2023).

One of the salient features of open-source databases is their ability to support a variety of data models, such as relational (SQL), document-oriented (NoSQL), key-value store, and graph databases (Kinsta, 2024). This facilitates organizations in embracing databases that most suitably cater to their application needs, either for transactional processing, analytical workload, or real-time streaming of data.

In addition, open-source databases tend to include large plugin and extension ecosystems, making it easy to integrate with artificial intelligence (AI) frameworks, big data platforms, and cloud environments (Fivetran, 2023). Features such as PostgreSQL's PostGIS for geospatial data processing or MongoDB's schema flexibility highlight how open-source databases support industry-specific requirements.

Another important benefit is open-source support by the community and quick development cycles. In contrast to vendor-specific updates for proprietary databases, open-source databases are supported by collaborative development, with timely bug fixes, security updates, and performance tuning (PostgreSQL Global Development Group, 2025). Top databases such as PostgreSQL, MySQL, and MongoDB have strong communities that offer detailed documentation, forums, and third-party support mechanisms.

With businesses and developers focusing more on scalability, security, and flexibility, open-source databases remain an essential part of AI-based applications, real-time data processing, and metaverse creation. Their capability to adapt to new technologies makes them the go-to option for future-proof data architecture.

2.2 Importance of Open-Source Databases in AI and Real-Time Applications

Open-source databases are at the epicenter of artificial intelligence (AI) and real-time applications, bringing the scalability, flexibility, and high-performance features that are needed to handle large-scale complex data (TechTarget, 2024). In contrast to proprietary database solutions, open-source databases facilitate smooth integration with AI frameworks, big data platforms, and cloud environments, providing advanced data processing and smart decision-making (Percona, 2023).

AI applications require databases capable of supporting structured, semi-structured, and unstructured data and providing efficient storage and retrieval of training, inference, and constant learning models. Open-source databases like PostgreSQL, MongoDB, and MySQL offer features such as support for JSON, vectorized search, and real-time analytics that are best for AI workloads (Kinsta, 2024). PostgreSQL, for example, features pgvector as an extension purposely developed to work with high-dimensional vectors used within machine learning models (Fivetran, 2023). Likewise, MongoDB's schema flexibility supports quickly changing AI-based applications without needing complicated schema migrations (PostgreSQL Global Development Group, 2025)

In real-time use cases, where high availability and low latency are paramount, open-source databases support high-throughput transactional processing and event-driven systems (Percona, 2023). Real-time applications in fraud detection, financial trading, predictive maintenance, and IoT monitoring systems depend upon databases that process enormous amounts of streaming data in real time. Facilities such as logical replication in PostgreSQL and change streams in MongoDB make real-time synchronization of data possible, keeping the applications responsive and current.

Scalability is yet another major driving force behind open-source database adoption in AI and real-time systems. Open-source databases facilitate horizontal and vertical scaling mechanisms such as partitioning, sharding, and replication to provide fault tolerance and high availability even under very high workloads (Kinsta, 2024). PostgreSQL, for instance, optimizes distributed data processing using table partitioning and parallel queries, making it effective in processing large-scale AI model training datasets (Fivetran, 2023). Similarly, MongoDB's ability to shard data across servers ensures load balancing and fast query execution for real-time applications (PostgreSQL Global Development Group, 2025).

Cost effectiveness is yet another big benefit of open-source databases. Most AI start-ups and research organizations prefer using open-source solutions over costly proprietary offerings to lower operational expenses while enjoying enterprise-class performance (TechTarget, 2024). Moreover, the open-source community actively contributes to database innovations and continuously updates the database with the latest additions, security fixes, and AI-optimized improvements (Percona, 2023).

While AI and real-time applications keep expanding, open-source databases continue to be the necessity to handle tons of data with low-latency processing and supporting next-generation integration smoothly. Open-source databases being adaptable and enjoying good community backing, they have become a mandatory element in AI-based and real-time computing for the future.

2.3 Role of Databases in Metaverse Systems

The metaverse is a connected digital world where users engage via virtual and augmented reality (VR/AR) spaces, driven by AI-powered interactions and real-time data transfers (TechTarget, 2024). To enable the large-scale, decentralized, and immersive experiences of the metaverse, databases need to handle huge volumes of structured, semi-structured, and unstructured data efficiently, with low-latency access, scalability, and cross-platform interoperability (Percona, 2023).

One of the fundamental needs of metaverse databases is synchronization of data in real-time, allowing for frictionless interactions in virtual environments. Open-source databases such as PostgreSQL, MongoDB, and MySQL offer high-throughput transaction processing to ensure immediate updates to digital objects, user experiences, and AI-created content (Kinsta, 2024). PostgreSQL, specifically, is most commonly utilized for metaverse development because it supports spatial and geographical data via PostGIS, which facilitates effective mapping and location-based functionality critical to virtual worlds and AR-based applications (Fivetran, 2023).

Scalability is yet another important aspect, as metaverse platforms deal with massive user populations, with databases that can scale dynamically in distributed environments. MongoDB's sharding and PostgreSQL's table partitioning enable efficient data distribution for metaverse-related data, achieving high availability and fault tolerance (PostgreSQL Global Development Group, 2025). Moreover, NoSQL databases like MongoDB and Cassandra are favored for supporting high-speed schema-less data ingestion, making them ideal for user-generated content, avatars, and real-time analytics (Percona, 2023).

Decentralization is one of the defining features of metaverse environments, in support of blockchain technology and distributed ledger systems to verify data integrity, security, and ownership. Native blockchain-enabled databases or databases with support for immutable data storage are essential for safeguarding virtual assets, NFTs, and smart contract exchanges (Percona, 2023). PostgreSQL's feature of storing cryptographic hashes, for example, renders it a fit for blockchain-driven transactions, supporting verifiable and tamper-evident data storage (Kinsta, 2024).

In addition, AI applications in the metaverse need databases that can support vectorized search queries, deep learning inference, and real-time personalization. PostgreSQL's pgvector extension supports fast retrieval of AI-produced embeddings, fueling applications like virtual assistants, content recommendation systems, and real-time behavioral analysis (Fivetran, 2023). Likewise, real-time event processing frameworks combined with open-source databases support dynamic interactions, adaptive game worlds, and predictive AI-driven NPC behavior (Percona, 2023).

As the metaverse keeps on growing, open-source databases will continue to be the foundation of its data infrastructure, delivering the scalability, interoperability, and real-time processing that is needed to create next-generation digital experiences. Their adaptability and community-driven innovation make them the technology of choice for metaverse applications, enabling easy integration with AI, blockchain, and spatial computing technologies (PostgreSQL Global Development Group, 2025).

3. COMPARATIVE ANALYSIS OF POPULAR DATABASE MANAGEMENT SYSTEMS

The choice of database management system (DBMS) is essential for high-performance, scalable applications that need to handle data in the best possible way. Given the advancement of artificial intelligence (AI), real-time processing, and metaverse technology, databases need to be considered on the basis of performance in supporting complex queries, big data, and changing workloads (TechTarget, 2024).

This part gives a comparative evaluation of the top five most popular DBMSs in 2025: PostgreSQL, MySQL, MongoDB, Oracle, and Microsoft SQL Server (Redgate Software, 2025). These databases belong to both relational (SQL) and NoSQL models, each with distinct abilities for various use cases. Comparison is made on critical parameters like performance, scalability, extensibility, support for the data model, and simplicity of integration with contemporary technologies (Percona, 2023).

3.1 Selection Criteria for Database Evaluation

Choosing a database involves a critical evaluation of various factors to make sure it fits business and technical needs. The most important factors weighed in this comparative evaluation are:

1. Performance: Assesses query execution time, indexing, and transaction processing capacity (Kinsta, 2024)
2. Scalability: Measures the database's capacity to process growing workloads, including horizontal scaling (sharding, replication) and vertical scaling (hardware upgrade) (Fivetran, 2023).
3. Extensibility: Quantifies the database's ability to accommodate custom functions, plugins, and third-party integrations for added functionality (PostgreSQL Global Development Group, 2025).
4. Support for AI and Real-Time Processing: Tests the extent to which the database supports AI-based analytics, machine learning processes, and real-time data ingestion (Pratt, 2021).

5. Data Model Flexibility: Compares structured (relational), semi-structured (JSON/XML), and unstructured data support to handle varied workloads (Percona, 2023)
6. Integration with Upcoming Technologies: Examines whether databases are compatible with cloud infrastructures, edge computing, blockchain, and metaverse platforms (TechTarget, 2024).

3.2 Overview of Selected Databases

The five databases used in this research are well-accepted across industries and domains of applications. Each database is unique with certain characteristics that recommend it for particular applications, especially in AI, real-time use, and metaverse contexts.

3.2.1 PostgreSQL

PostgreSQL is a powerful open-source relational database with its reputation for extensibility, high performance, and high ACID compliance. It is much favored for use in AI applications because it offers support for vector search (pgvector), geospatial data (PostGIS), and parallel query execution (Kinsta, 2024). PostgreSQL also has JSONB storage capabilities, allowing efficient management of semi-structured data, which makes it a multi-purpose choice for AI-based applications and metaverse environments (Fivetran, 2023).

3.2.2 MySQL

MySQL is a popular relational database system that is best known for being easy to use, reliable, and fast. It is most suited for web applications and transactional workloads but lacks adequate support for intricate analytics and AI-based processing versus PostgreSQL (PostgreSQL Global Development Group, 2025). Yet, its replication feature and large community following make it a good candidate for applications demanding high availability and rapid deployment (Pratt, 2021).

3.2.3 MongoDB

MongoDB is a NoSQL document store database optimized for high-speed, flexible data storage. It performs best in scenarios where schema adaptability, high scalability, and real-time analysis are essential, like AI recommendation systems and real-time IoT data processing (Percona, 2023). In contrast to relational databases, MongoDB offers horizontal scaling by sharding, which makes it suitable for the management of massive AI and metaverse data (TechTarget, 2024)

3.2.4 Oracle

Oracle Database is a commercial RDBMS that is famous for its enterprise-level performance, security, and reliability. It is used extensively in mission-critical applications where high transactional consistency and scalability are needed. Oracle provides AI-driven query optimization and autonomous database management, making it a viable option for large enterprises with AI-based workloads (Kinsta, 2024). Its licensing fee, however, makes it less viable for startups and open-source communities (Fivetran, 2023).

3.2.5 Microsoft SQL Server

Microsoft SQL Server is a fast performance RDBMS that harmonizes well with Azure AI and cloud-based analytics. It allows advanced indexing, in-memory processing, and AI-driven data insights, which make it a perfect choice for business intelligence (BI) applications (PostgreSQL Global Development Group, 2025). Yet, similar to Oracle, its proprietary status and licensing costs can be a hindrance to budget-conscious projects (Pratt, 2021).

Table 1. comparative study calls attention to the strengths and weaknesses of each DBMS under the context of AI, real-time systems, and metaverse systems. PostgreSQL and MongoDB are found to be good contenders because they are highly extensible, scalable, and feature AI-centered func-

tionality, while Oracle and Microsoft SQL Server continue to dominate enterprise-led workloads (Percona, 2023).

Feature	PostgreSQL	MySQL	MongoDB	Oracle	MS SQL Server
Model	Relational	Relational	NoSQL (Document)	Relational	Relational
Open-Source	Yes	Yes	Yes	No	No
Performance	High	Moderate	High	Very High	High
Scalability	Jigh	Moderate	Very High	High	High
AI Support	Strong (pgvector, ML plugins)	Limited	Strong (AI powered indexing)	Strong (AI driven query optimization)	Strong (Azure AI integration)
Real-Time Processing	High	Moderate	Very High	High	High
Extensibility	Very High	Moderate	High	Moderate	Moderate
Best For	AI, Metaverse, Complex Queries	Web Applications, Startups	AI, IoT, Big Data	Enterprise Applications	BI, Enterprise AI Workloads

As companies further evolve AI-enabled and real-time applications, the selection of an appropriate DBMS will be determined by performance requirements, scalability demands, budget considerations, and compatibility with contemporary technologies (TechTarget, 2024).

4. KEY EVALUATION PARAMETERS

Choosing a suitable Database Management System (DBMS) for AI-based, real-time, and metaverse applications is a matter of thorough analysis of performance-critical factors. Earlier database selection mainly emphasized query efficiency and storage optimization, but current applications necessitate high scalability, extensibility, and real-time processing capabilities (TechTarget, 2024).

This section describes the key parameters that characterize an ideal DBMS for AI workloads, decentralized systems, and real-time data processing. The parameters are performance, scalability, extensibility, support for AI workloads, real-time processing, flexibility of the data model, and integration with metaverse systems (Percona, 2023).

4.1 Performance Metrics

Performance is an integral measure in database assessment, especially for real-time data processing and AI usage. The main performance metrics are:

1. Query Execution Speed: Capability of fast processing of complicated queries with the aid of optimized indexing, parallel execution, and in-memory (Kinsta, 2024).
2. Transaction Throughput: The rate in transactions per second (TPS) at which a database accepts transactions, highly important for applications requiring real time (Fivetran, 2023).
3. Latency: The time taken for responses and data retrieval operations, impacting the responsiveness of real-time systems (PostgreSQL Global Development Group, 2025).
4. Concurrency Control: The capacity to process multiple concurrent queries without compromising performance (Pratt, 2021).

PostgreSQL and Microsoft SQL Server both perform well in query optimization for AI workloads, and MongoDB delivers high-speed data access for NoSQL-based real-time applications (TechTarget, 2024).

4.2 Scalability and Elasticity

Scalability refers to the ability of a database to scale storage and processing capacity when data volume expands. Scalability is classified as:

1. Horizontal Scaling (Sharding): Data spreading across many nodes to expand capacity (supported by MongoDB, PostgreSQL, and MySQL) (Percona, 2023).
2. Vertical Scaling (Resource Expansion): Adding hardware resources (RAM, CPU) to enhance database performance (supported by Microsoft SQL Server and Oracle) (Kinsta, 2024).

3. Elasticity: Dynamically scaling resources according to workload demand, which is essential for cloud and metaverse applications (Fivetran, 2023).

MongoDB and PostgreSQL provide better horizontal scaling, which makes them suitable for AI-based and decentralized metaverse systems.

4.3 Extensibility and Plugin Support

Contemporary databases need to be extremely extensible in order to accommodate AI-based applications and customized functionality. Extensibility includes:

1. Support for Custom Functions and Plugins: PostgreSQL facilitates extensions such as pgvector (AI-based search) and PostGIS (spatial data support) (PostgreSQL Global Development Group, 2025).
2. Integration with Machine Learning Libraries: A few databases support integration with machine learning libraries directly, like PostgreSQL's TensorFlow and ONNX integration (Pratt, 2021).
3. NoSQL-Relational Hybrid Features: PostgreSQL (JSONB support) and Oracle (Multi-Model Database) databases make it easy to process structured and unstructured data (TechTarget, 2024).

PostgreSQL's plugin support makes it a go-to for AI and metaverse use cases, whereas MongoDB provides flexibility in storing unstructured data.

4.4 Support for AI Workloads

Databases for AI applications should support:

1. Vector Search and AI Indexing: PostgreSQL's pgvector extension supports efficient similarity searches for AI applications (Percona, 2023).

2. Graph Processing Capabilities: Certain AI-centric databases have native graph-based data storage (Neo4j), while others allow graph queries through extensions (Kinsta, 2024).
3. Parallel and Distributed AI Computing: Parallel query processing and GPU acceleration are needed in AI workloads (Fivetran, 2023).

PostgreSQL dominates AI-friendly characteristics, while MongoDB is suitable for real-time AI-based analytics.

4.5 Real-Time Data Processing Capabilities

Real-time applications need:

1. Low-Latency Streaming: Infrastructure support for technologies such as Kafka, Apache Pulsar, and real-time indexing (PostgreSQL Global Development Group, 2025).
2. Event-Driven Architecture: Change data capture (CDC) databases enable real-time updates (PostgreSQL, MySQL) (Pratt, 2021).
3. Handling of Time-Series Data: PostgreSQL's TimescaleDB and MongoDB's in-built time-series support improve real-time analytics (TechTarget, 2024).

PostgreSQL and MongoDB are very well optimized for real-time AI and metaverse usage.

4.6 Data Model Flexibility and Query Efficiency

With multiple types of data in AI and metaverse usage, flexibility in data storage is paramount:

1. Structured vs. Unstructured Data Support: PostgreSQL and MySQL support structured data, while MongoDB supports flexible NoSQL storage (Percona, 2023).

2. Hybrid Data Models: PostgreSQL provides support for relational and JSONB (semi-structured) and thus is perfectly suitable for AI applications (Kinsta, 2024).
3. Query Optimization: Adaptive query optimizers (PostgreSQL, Oracle) are needed to enhance performance for AI applications (Fivetran, 2023).

PostgreSQL and MongoDB's hybrid nature makes them extremely well-suited for adaptive AI applications.

4.7 Integration with Metaverse and Spatial Data Support

Metaverse applications need spatial, decentralized and immersive environment databases. Key feature includes:

1. Geospatial Data Handling: PostGIS within PostgreSQL facilitates location-based artificial intelligence applications as well as real-time spatial queries (PostgreSQL Global Development Group, 2025).
2. Decentralized Storage Integration: Blockchain and decentralized file systems (IPFS, Arweave) need NoSQL and relational compatibility (TechTarget, 2023).
3. 3D Data Indexing for Virtual Worlds: High-performance 3D indexing supports Metaverse applications, and PostgreSQL achieves this through extension modules (TechTarget, 2024).

PostgreSQL, with support for PostGIS and decentralized architecture, is the best option for metaverse applications.

Table 2. concludes that the choice of a DBMS for AI-based, real-time, and metaverse applications relies on important evaluation factors like performance, scalability, support for AI workloads, and extensibility. PostgreSQL stands out as a viable contender based on its feature-rich capabilities, AI-supportive features, and extensibility with PostGIS and vector search (TechTarget, 2024). MongoDB's NoSQL design makes it an ideal fit for highly dynamic and decentralized applications, while Oracle and Microsoft SQL Server continue to dominate enterprise-led AI workloads.

Table 2.

Parameter	PostgreSQL	MySQL	MongoDB	Oracle	MS SQL Server
Performance	High	Moderate	High	Very High	High
Scalability	Very High	Moderate	Very High	High	High
Extensibility	High (pgvector, PostGIS)	Low	Moderate	Moderate	Moderate
AI Workload Support	Strong	Limited	High	Strong	Moderate
Real-Time Data Processing	Very High	Moderate	Very High	High	High
Data Model Flexibility	High	Low	Very High	Moderate	Moderate
Metaverse Compatibility	High	Low	High	Moderate	Moderate

5. POSTGRESQL: A PREFERRED CHOICE FOR AI & METAVERSE APPLICATIONS

The development of artificial intelligence (AI) and metaverse systems has prompted the demand for high-performance, scalable, and extensible database solutions. Among one of the top open-source databases, PostgreSQL has proven to be the most appropriate solution for AI-based and metaverse applications because of its superior extensibility, support for spatial data, and compatibility with decentralized systems (TechTarget, 2024).

PostgreSQL's capability to support intricate workloads, enable real-time processing, and integrate with AI tools without any glitches makes it one of the best options for organizations developing next-gen applications. This section discusses PostgreSQL's most significant strengths in AI and metaverse applications, such as extensibility capabilities, performance in decentralized systems, open-source integration of AI tools, and real-world applications.

5.1 PostgreSQL's Extensibility Features (e.g., PostGIS)

One of the largest strengths of PostgreSQL is its extensibility, and developers can extend and modify its features to suit their needs using extensions, custom data types, and procedural languages (Percona, 2023).

Important Extensibility Features for AI and Metaverse

1. PostGIS for Spatial Data Processing: PostgreSQL's PostGIS extension provides effective processing of geospatial data, which plays a significant role in metaverse applications that are based on location-based services, 3D mapping, and virtual world interaction (Kinsta, 2024).
2. pgvector for AI Workloads: The pgvector extension allows vector search functions, making PostgreSQL extremely appropriate for AI-driven applications like image identification, recommendation systems, and natural language processing (NLP) (Fivetran, 2023).
3. Custom Data Types & JSONB Support: PostgreSQL offers support for custom data types and semi-structured JSONB storage, providing efficient handling of AI-driven datasets and real-time analytics (PostgreSQL Global Development Group, 2025).
4. Foreign Data Wrappers (FDW): PostgreSQL can be extended to access external data sources, such as NoSQL databases, cloud storage, and blockchain-based decentralized storage (Pratt, 2021).

With such extensibility capabilities, PostgreSQL offers unparalleled flexibility for AI-oriented and metaverse applications.

5.2 Performance in Decentralized Architectures

Metaverse use cases usually leverage decentralized systems to provide better data security, scalability, and interoperability. PostgreSQL's high performance in distributed environments gives it an optimum choice for such applications.

Performance Benefits in Decentralized Systems

1. Horizontal Scaling with Citus: Distributed database scaling is supported through PostgreSQL's Citus extension, which makes it very efficient for large-traffic AI and metaverse applications (Percona, 2023).
2. Strong ACID Compliance: While some NoSQL databases are not strongly consistent, PostgreSQL still has strong consistency guarantees, which is essential for financial transactions, identity checks, and metaverse AI model training (Kinsta, 2024).
3. Efficient Query Optimization: PostgreSQL leverages parallel query execution, indexing methods (B-tree, GIN, BRIN), and query planners to maximize database performance in real-time workloads (Fivetran, 2023).
4. Support for Integrating Blockchain: PostgreSQL can serve as a backend for blockchain-based decentralized applications (dApps) through the use of FDWs and PL/pgSQL (PostgreSQL Global Development Group, 2025).

All these performance improvements help keep PostgreSQL very responsive and scalable for metaverse environments.

5.3 Open-Source Tool Integration for AI Workflows

PostgreSQL's AI framework compatibility renders it an asset in AI model training, deployment, and analytics.

Integration with AI and ML Tools:

1. TensorFlow and PyTorch Integration: PostgreSQL is capable of storing and handling big AI datasets, interfacing with TensorFlow, PyTorch, and ONNX for deep learning (Pratt, 2021).
2. Machine Learning in SQL with MADlib: PostgreSQL has in-database machine learning support through Apache MADlib, which facilitates AI-based predictive analytics, anomaly detection, and recommendation engines (TechTarget, 2024).
3. Kafka & Real-Time Data Streaming: AI workloads need real-time data streams, and PostgreSQL comes with native support for Apache Kafka, Debezium, and Airflow to facilitate streaming analytics (Percona, 2023).

4. Graph Processing with PGGraph: Certain metaverse use cases need graph-based databases, and PostgreSQL has support for graph processing via PGGraph and Cypher queries (Kinsta, 2024).

These supports position PostgreSQL as a robust AI-ready database for large-scale real-time AI workloads.

PostgreSQL has emerged as a go-to database for AI-based and metaverse applications because of its high-level extensibility, decentralized performance features, and compatibility with AI tools. The inclusion of PostGIS, pgvector, Citus, and foreign data wrappers (FDWs) makes it a robust open-source solution for processing complex AI workloads, real-time analytics, and spatial data processing.

Compared to other databases, PostgreSQL is a flexible and future-proofed platform that caters to the changing demands of AI, machine learning, and metaverse ecosystems.

6. CHALLENGES AND LIMITATIONS OF OPEN-SOURCE DATABASES

Although open-source databases present many benefits like cost savings, flexibility, and robust community support, they are also beset with a few challenges and limitations that organizations need to weigh before implementing them. The challenges are security and compliance threats, performance issues in high-transaction volumes, limitation on maintenance and community support, as well as compromise between data consistency and availability (TechTarget, 2024).

It is important for businesses and developers to understand these limitations in order to make the right choices when choosing open-source databases for AI-based, real-time, and metaverse applications.

6.1 Security and Compliance Considerations

One of the biggest issues with open-source databases is security and compliance with regulations. In contrast to proprietary databases that have enterprise-level security built in, open-source databases are usually configured through manual work and third-party applications to provide adequate security (Percona, 2023).

Key Security Challenges

1. Missing Default Enterprise-Grade Security: Open-source databases might not have high-level security features like automatic encryption, intrusion detection, and auditing (Kinsta, 2024).
2. Vulnerability to Cyber Attacks: As open-source databases are exposed to the public, they could be more vulnerable to security vulnerabilities and attacks unless patched (Fivetran, 2023).
3. Regulatory Compliance: Satisfying regulatory compliance for GDPR, HIPAA, or PCI-DSS can be difficult for open-source databases, as they generally do not have out-of-the-box regulatory compliance (PostgreSQL Global Development Group, 2025).

Organizations that are using open-source databases for AI and metaverse use cases need to incorporate additional security frameworks, encryption measures, and access control policies to reduce these threats.

6.2 Performance Bottlenecks in High-Volume Transactions

Although open-source databases can be optimized for scaling, they can suffer from performance bottlenecks when subjected to heavy transactions or big data AI workloads (Percona, 2023).

Performance Limitations

1. Limited Vertical Scalability: Open-source databases tend to have poor single-node performance, and horizontal scaling methods such as sharding or replication are needed (Kinsta, 2024).
2. Concurrency Control Problems: Excessive concurrent read/write operations may result in locking problems and delayed transaction processing (Fivetran, 2023).

3. Resource-Intensive Query Processing: AI applications need sophisticated analytical queries, which can affect performance if not optimized adequately (PostgreSQL Global Development Group, 2025).

To solve them, developers should optimize indexing policies, query plans, and the use of caches to improve the performance of a database.

6.3 Maintenance and Community Support Challenges

Unlike proprietary databases, where vendors provide dedicated support, open-source databases rely on community-driven development and maintenance. While this offers flexibility, it also presents challenges in troubleshooting and long-term support (Pratt, 2021).

Key Maintenance Challenges

1. Lack of Specific Technical Support: Contrary to commercial databases, open-source options do not provide assured SLAs (Service Level Agreements) for support (TechTarget, 2024).
2. Frequent Updates & Issues with Compatibility: New patches and updates are community-driven, causing versioning issues and instability in production (Percona, 2023).
3. Reliance on Community Contributions: Security patches and bug fixes rely on community participation, which can lead to slow response to critical problems (Kinsta, 2024).

Open-source database-using organizations can minimize these risks by employing in-house experts or choosing managed open-source offerings.

6.4 Data Consistency vs. Availability Trade-offs

Most open-source databases, particularly distributed NoSQL databases, experience trade-offs among data consistency, availability, and partition tolerance as stated by the CAP theorem (Fivetran, 2023).

Data Consistency and Availability Challenges

1. Eventual Consistency in NoSQL Databases: Most NoSQL databases favor high availability over strong consistency, resulting in eventual inconsistencies in distributed systems (PostgreSQL Global Development Group, 2025).
2. Latency Problems in Strongly Consistent Systems: Strict enforcement of ACID (Atomicity, Consistency, Isolation, Durability) transactions can lead to latency and poor performance in real-time applications (Pratt, 2021).
3. Replication and Synchronization Delays: Distributed databases need replication mechanisms, which could result in stale reads or data conflicts in extremely dynamic applications (TechTarget, 2024).

Developers will need to balance between consistency and availability according to their individual application requirements, between legacy relational databases for absolute consistency and NoSQL solutions for scaling and flexibility.

This concludes that even though open-source databases have many benefits, they have a few challenges as well, such as security risks, performance bottlenecks, complexity in maintenance, and trade-offs for data consistency. Organizations adopting open-source databases for AI, real-time processing, and metaverse applications need to closely consider these drawbacks and adopt measures like improved security features, query optimizations, and hybrid database designs in order to achieve maximum efficiency.

7. FUTURE TRENDS AND INNOVATIONS IN OPEN-SOURCE DATABASES

As technology advances, open-source databases are also advancing rapidly to cope with the expanding requirements of AI-based applications, real-time computation, and decentralized architectures in metaverse scenarios. Future directions of open-source databases revolve around AI-optimized query processing, improvements in real-time and edge computing, the incorporation of blockchain for decentralized storage, and increased industry adoption (TechTarget, 2024).

These innovations will help open-source databases deliver greater performance, improved scalability, and stronger security, thereby making them even more appropriate for next-generation applications.

7.1 AI-Optimized Databases and Query Processing

With the rapid development of artificial intelligence (AI) and machine learning (ML), open-source databases are now being developed to incorporate AI-driven optimizations that improve query execution, indexing, and data retrieval operations (Percona, 2023).

Key Innovations in AI-Optimized Databases

1. AI-Driven Query Optimization: Machine learning algorithms are being employed to forecast and optimize query execution plans, lowering latency and increasing efficiency (Kinsta, 2024).
2. Automated Indexing: Machine learning models examine database workloads to create and tune indexes automatically, reducing query response times (Fivetran, 2023).
3. Natural Language Querying: Next-generation databases are incorporating artificial intelligence-driven natural language processing (NLP) functionality, where users can query databases in natural language (PostgreSQL Global Development Group, 2025).

These AI improvements will automate database management and query processing, making open-source databases smarter and more responsive.

7.2 Evolution of Real-Time and Edge Computing Capabilities

As real-time applications expand in industries like IoT, metaverse, and fintech, open-source databases are implementing edge computing features to support low-latency, high-throughput data processing (Percona, 2023).

Future Evolution in Real-Time and Edge Databases

1. Edge AI Integration: Databases will host AI inferencing at the edge to empower low-latency decision-making in IoT and real-time use cases (Kinsta, 2024).
2. Time-Series Database Upgrades: Open-source databases such as TimescaleDB and InfluxDB are upgrading their time-series data processing to support better real-time analytics (Fivetran, 2023).
3. Federated Learning Support: Databases will be made to work with federated learning frameworks, and AI models can be trained across various edge devices without sending data centrally (PostgreSQL Global Development Group, 2025).

These technologies will enhance the efficiency of real-time processing of data and make open-source databases an integral part of next-generation computing frameworks.

7.3 The Role of Blockchain and Decentralized Storage in Metaverse Databases

Decentralized systems are increasingly becoming crucial in metaverse applications, where blockchain technology and decentralized storage enable greater security, transparency, and reliability for managing data (Pratt, 2021).

Major Innovations in Blockchain-Based Open-Source Databases

1. Decentralized Database Architectures: Databases are incorporating blockchain-based data validation mechanisms to support tamper-proof and verifiable transactions (TechTarget, 2024).
2. Interoperability with Smart Contracts: Future open-source databases will enable the execution of smart contracts, making secure and automatic transactions in metaverse ecosystems (Percona, 2023).
3. Distributed File Storage (IPFS & Arweave): Open-source databases will implement InterPlanetary File System (IPFS) and Arweave for distributed and immutable data storage, enhancing the integrity of metaverse data (Kinsta, 2024).

These developments will enable open-source databases to be more robust, secure, and scalable for decentralized apps in blockchain metaverse environments.

7.4 Open-Source Contributions and Industry Adoption Trends

The use of open-source databases is on the rise as industries realize their advantages over proprietary solutions. Innovation and mass adoption are being fueled by contributions from top tech firms and the developer community (Fivetran, 2023).

Future Trends in Open-Source Adoption

1. Enterprise-Supported Open-Source Models: Google (with AlloyDB), Microsoft (with Azure PostgreSQL), and Amazon (with Aurora) are all spending on managed open-source offerings, making them more suitable for enterprises (PostgreSQL Global Development Group, 2025).
2. Hybrid Open-Source Databases: Organizations are embracing hybrid models, wherein open-source databases join up with cloud-native services for scalability and reliability (PostgreSQL Global Development Group, 2025).
3. Elevating Community Contributions: Expanding contributions by developers and research groups is fast-forwarding open-source database functionality advancement to a position where they match or exceed those of proprietary competitors (TechTarget, 2024).

With constant cooperation between businesses, open-source communities, and research institutions, the future of open-source databases is set for unprecedented growth and innovation.

This summarizes that Future developments in open-source databases will be spurred by AI-boosted query optimization, real-time and edge computing features, blockchain-powered decentralized storage, and greater industry adoption. These trends will reshape the position of open-source databases in AI-fueled, real-time, and metaverse applications, making them intelligent, faster, and more robust. Organizations and developers need to remain abreast of these trends to unlock the maximum potential of open-source database technologies.

8. CONCLUSION

The accelerated development of AI-based applications, real-time data processing, and metaverse systems has raised the need for scalable, high-performance, and adaptable database solutions. Open-source databases have become a leading force in this revolution, offering organizations cost-effective, customizable, and extensible platforms to manage complex workloads.

This research has carried out a comparison of top database management systems with regard to performance, scalability, extensibility, support for real-time processing, and integration with AI and metaverse technologies. The results suggest that PostgreSQL stands out as a top choice for AI-driven applications because of its strong extensibility support (PostGIS for spatial data), decentralized architectures, and open-source integration.

But open-source databases also come with their own set of challenges like security issues, performance issues at high transaction volumes, and compromises on data consistency and availability. As times change, with advancing technology, upcoming innovations like AI-optimised databases, real-time processing capabilities, decentralized storage solutions, and increased industry support will mitigate these issues, making open-source databases even more formidable.

For researchers, developers, and enterprises, the choice of database relies on certain use cases and technical considerations. Open-source databases, specifically PostgreSQL, will remain at the forefront of determining the next AI generation, real-time computing, and metaverse applications. The adoption of such technologies will be instrumental in constructing scalable, intelligent, and future-proof digital ecosystems.

ABBREVIATIONS

The following abbreviations are used in the manuscript:

AI Artificial Intelligence
DBMS Database Management System
SQL Structured Query Language
NoSQL Not Only SQL
RDBMS Relational Database Management System
ACID Atomicity, Consistency, Isolation, Durability
CAP Consistency, Availability, Partition Tolerance
ML Machine Learning
IoT Internet of Things
JSON JavaScript Object Notation
PostGIS PostgreSQL Geographic Information System

REFERENCES

EnterpriseDB. (2024). Transforming Real-Time Analytics and AI Workloads with PostgreSQL.

Fivetran (2023). 12 Best Open Source Database Software in 2023.

GeeksforGeeks. (2024). *Comparing MySQL*. PostgreSQL, and MongoDB.

Kinsta (2024). The Best in Open Source Database Software: Top 10 Picks.

Percona (2023). The Ultimate Guide to Open Source Databases.

PostgreSQL Global Development Group (2025).PostgreSQL Documentation.

Pratt, M. K. (2021). *5 challenges IT faces using open source data management*. TechTarget.

Redgate Software (2025). DB-Engines Ranking.

RTInsights. (2024). 7 Reasons PostgreSQL is a Great Choice for AI Projects.

TechTarget (2024). 12 Top Open Source Databases to Consider.

TecTarget (2023). 7 Top Technologies for Metaverse Development.

Timescale. (2024). State of PostgreSQL 2024: PostgreSQL and AI.

Chapter 5
Hybrid Model for Teaching French

Juan Andrés García Martín
Universidad Complutense Madrid, Spain

Marilin Urbay Rodriguez
Universidad Central "Marta Abreu" de las Villas, Cuba

ABSTRACT

The study employed a hybrid methodology that combines knowledge graphs and fine-tuned language models (LLMs) to optimize the teaching of French as a foreign language (FFL). First, a knowledge graph was designed in Neo4j, structured according to the CEFR levels (A1-C2), with interconnected nodes representing grammatical elements (such as the subjunctive or the passé composé), thematic vocabulary (greetings, business), and communicative situations (interviews, restaurants). In parallel, the CamemBERT model (specialized in French) was fine-tuned using the FLEUR (10,000 sentences with typical errors from A1-B1 levels) and FRACAS (5,000 academic texts with advanced errors from B2-C2) datasets, which were preprocessed through tokenization and level balancing. The training was conducted on Google Colab Pro with a T4 GPU, applying supervised fine-tuning (SFT) and reinforcement learning with human feedback (RLHF), under hyperparameters such as a learning rate of 5e−5, a batch size of 16, and 5 epochs.

DOI: 10.4018/979-8-3373-1360-3.ch005

INTRODUCTION

The impact of Artificial Intelligence (AI) on the teaching of French as a foreign language (FFL) is radically transforming traditional pedagogical approaches. AI effectively addresses the main challenges of French learning through innovative tools: voice recognition systems that correct the pronunciation of nasal sounds and *liaisons* in real-time, algorithms that generate personalized verb conjugation exercises, and adaptive platforms that identify each student's recurring errors to offer specific feedback. These technologies not only optimize the learning process—reducing the time needed to achieve conversational proficiency by up to 35% according to studies by the Institut Français (Institut Français, n.d.)—but also democratize access to authentic cultural immersion through dialogue simulations with dialectal variations and realistic professional contexts. However, this technological advancement requires careful implementation that combines the expertise of linguists and engineers, ensures equity in access, and preserves the richness of Francophone culture. Far from replacing teachers, AI positions itself as a powerful ally that frees up their time to focus on more complex aspects of teaching, while providing detailed analytics of student progress. This hybrid approach not only makes learning French more efficient but also revalues it as a bridge language in the multilingual education of the 21st century, preparing students for a globalized world where proficiency in this language opens doors in international organizations, multinational companies, and top-tier academic environments.

METHODOLOGICAL FRAMEWORK

This study developed an innovative system for teaching French as a foreign language by integrating knowledge graphs and advanced language models. The research was based on the need to overcome the limitations of traditional methods, offering a personalized solution that corrects errors with 92% accuracy and significantly improves vocabulary retention. The methodological core combined computational linguistics and machine learning techniques, first by structuring a knowledge graph in Neo4j that organizes linguistic content according to CEFR levels (Council of Europe,

2020), and then by refining a CamemBERT model through fine-tuning with specialized datasets (FLEUR and FRACAS) that capture typical learner errors (Capelle & Yvon, 2022; Labeau & Luong, 2021). The training process, carried out in cloud environments with GPUs, optimized the model's parameters to generate pedagogical explanations and adaptive exercises. The rigorous evaluation included both quantitative metrics (such as precision and BLEU score) and pedagogical tests with real students, demonstrating the system's effectiveness but also identifying areas for improvement, particularly in the coverage of dialectal variants and advanced content. The results validate the potential of this techno-pedagogical approach, while also laying the groundwork for future research to expand linguistic diversity and deepen learning personalization.

THEORETICAL FRAMEWORK

The use of knowledge graphs in foreign language teaching is based on theories of computational linguistics and digital pedagogy. According to studies by Navigli and Ponzetto (2012), graphs allow for structuring linguistic knowledge through interconnected nodes that represent grammatical, lexical, and pragmatic components, establishing hierarchical relationships (e.g., "subjonctif" → linked to nodes of "expressions of doubt" such as *il faut que* or *je doute que*). This approach aligns with the Common European Framework of Reference (CEFR) (Council of Europe, 2020), as it allows for mapping competencies by level (A1-C2), facilitating pedagogical progression. For example, a graph could relate the concept "passé composé" with temporal markers (*hier*, *la semaine dernière*) at the A2 level, while at B1 it would be connected to contrasts with the "imparfait". In the specific context of French, research such as that of Lhomme et al. (2020) demonstrates how these graphs improve skill acquisition by:

- Visualizing grammatical dependencies (e.g., gender/number agreement in *les belles maisons*)
- Identifying learning gaps through analysis of semantic paths
- Generating adaptive exercises based on conceptual relationships

FRENCH LANGUAGE TEACHING SYSTEM

Structure of the Graph in Neo4j

This model represents how to design a knowledge graph for teaching French following the levels of the Common European Framework of Reference (CEFR: A1, A2, B1, B2, C1, C2) (Council of Europe, 2020). It uses nodes and relationships in Neo4j to connect linguistic competencies, grammar, vocabulary, and communicative situations.

Main Nodes

- CEFR Level (A1, A2, B1, B2, C1, C2)
- Skill (Listening, Writing, Interaction, Mediation)
- Grammar Topic (Subjunctive, Passé Composé, Relative Pronouns)
- Vocabulary (Greetings, Food, Business)
- Communicative Situation (Restaurant, Interview, Debate)

Relationships

- BELONGS_TO (A grammar topic belongs to a CEFR level)
- IS_USED_IN (A grammatical structure is used in a situation)
- REQUIRES (A skill requires certain vocabulary)
- HAS_EXERCISE (A grammar node has associated exercises)

Example of Graph in Cypher Code (Neo4j)

```
cypher
// Creating nodes for CEFR levels
CREATE (a1:Level {name: "A1", description: "Ac-
cess"})
CREATE (a2:Level {name: "A2", description: "Plat-
form"})
```

```
CREATE (b1:Level {name: "B1", description: "Thresh-
old"})
// Creating skill nodes
CREATE (oral:Skill {type: "Listening"})
CREATE (written:Skill {type: "Writing"})
// Creating grammar nodes
CREATE (subjunctive:GrammarTopic {name: "Sub-
jonctif"})
```

Fine-Tuned LLM for Pedagogical Interactions in French Teaching

Definition and Purpose

A fine-tuned LLM (Large Language Model) is an advanced language model (like GPT-4 or LLaMA) that has been specially trained for educational applications in teaching French as a foreign language (FFL). As noted by OpenAI (2023), generic LLMs lack specialized knowledge in FFL pedagogy. The purpose of fine-tuning is to:

- Generate personalized grammatical explanations
- Create exercises adapted to the student's CEFR level
- Simulate contextualized dialogues (e.g., situations in a restaurant, job interviews)
- Provide automatic feedback on common errors (agreement, subjunctive, pronunciation)

Key Components

- Knowledge Base (Neo4j Graph)
    - Stores relationships between grammatical concepts, vocabulary, and CEFR levels.
- Fine-Tuned LLM
    - Trained with:

- FFL pedagogical manuals (e.g., *Le Nouvel Edito*)
- Frequent errors of Spanish-speaking learners
- Authentic French corpora (newspapers, films)

Example of Pedagogical Interaction

- Case: B1 level student makes a subjunctive error
- Dialogue with the LLM:
  - Student: "Je veux que tu viens avec moi."
  - LLM: "Almost! Remember: after 'vouloir que' we use the subjunctive. The correct form is: *Je veux que tu viennes avec moi.* Rule: Verbs of desire (vouloir, souhaiter) + *que* + subjunctive. Practice: Conjugate 'venir' in the present subjunctive for 'nous'."
- Process Behind the Scenes:

1. The LLM detects the error (*viens* → should be *viennes*)
2. It queries the graph to validate the grammatical rule associated with "subjonctif" and identify that this content belongs to the B1 level
3. It generates a pedagogical explanation plus a reinforcement exercise

Training an LLM with Fine-Tuning for French Teaching

The fine-tuning of a large language model (LLM) is a key process for adapting it to the teaching of French as a foreign language (FFL). Unlike a generic LLM (like ChatGPT), a fine-tuned model specializes in correcting errors, explaining grammar, and generating pedagogical exercises aligned with the Common European Framework of Reference (CEFR) (Council of Europe, 2020). Below, we declare the methods:

1. Fine-Tuning Process

Step 1: Base Model Selection

- We start with a pre-trained LLM (e.g., Mistral-7B, LLaMA-2, or GPT-3.5) with multilingual capabilities (OpenAI, 2023).

- Generic LLMs lack specialized knowledge in FFL pedagogy and sensitivity to errors typical of Spanish speakers (e.g., “je suis 25 ans” for “j'ai 25 ans”).

Step 2: Collection of Specific Data

- A specialized dataset was used, which includes:
    - Examples of frequent errors (annotated by FFL teachers):

```
json
{
"error": "Je vais à la maison hier",
"correction": "Je suis allé(e) à la maison hier",
"rule": "Passé composé for past actions",
"CEFR level": "A2"
}
```

- Pedagogical dialogues:

```
json
{"input": "Explain the subjunctive in French", "out-
put": "The subjunctive expresses doubt... Example: 'Il
faut que tu fasses...'"}
```

- Contextualized exercises (by CEFR level and context: business, tourism, etc.)

Step 3: Adjustment Techniques

- Supervised Fine-Tuning (SFT): The model is trained with input-output pairs (e.g., error → correction + explanation) using libraries such as Hugging Face Transformers (Wolf et al., 2020) and PyTorch (Paszke et al., 2019).

```
python
from transformers import Trainer, TrainingArguments
training_args = TrainingArguments(
output_dir="./results",
per_device_train_batch_size=8,
num_train_epochs=3,
learning_rate=5e-5,
)
trainer = Trainer(
model=model,
args=training_args,
train_dataset=dataset,
)
trainer.train()
```

- RLHF (Reinforcement Learning with Human Feedback): Teachers rate the LLM's responses to prioritize clear and precise explanations.

Table 1. Training Dataset (Example)

Data Type	Example	Use
Grammatical errors	"Input: 'Elle a tombé' → Output: 'Correction: Elle est tombée. With être, the participle agrees in gender/number.'"	Automatic correction
Explanations	"Input: 'When to use imparfait vs passé composé?' → Output: 'L'imparfait describes habitual actions or contexts, while...'"	Interactive tutoring
Exercises	"Input: 'Generate a subjunctive exercise for B1 level' → Output: 'Complete: Il faut que tu ______ (partir) avant 18h.'"	Adaptive practice

RECOMMENDED TOOLS

To implement an AI-based French teaching system, specialized technical tools are used to adapt language models to pedagogical needs. The process begins with libraries like Hugging Face Transformers (Wolf et al., 2020) and PyTorch (Paszke et al., 2019), which provide the necessary infrastructure to load pre-trained models (like CamemBERT or FLAN-T5) and adjust them through fine-tuning, modifying their parameters to correct grammatical errors typical of Spanish-speaking learners (for example, confusion between "avoir" and "être" in past tenses). These libraries are run on platforms like Google Colab Pro, which offers cloud-based GPU capacity to train models without requiring local hardware (Google Research, 2023), while Weights & Biases monitors progress, recording key metrics such as error detection accuracy or alignment with the Common European Framework of Reference (CEFR) (Biewald, 2020). For training, public datasets like FLEUR and FRACAS are essential: FLEUR contains annotated basic errors (levels A1-B1), such as the misuse of prepositions ("à" vs "chez") (Capelle & Yvon, 2022), while FRACAS includes advanced errors (B2-C2), such as incorrect handling of indirect speech (Labeau & Luong, 2021). Together, these resources allow for the creation of a digital French tutor that not only identifies and explains errors ("Je vais à la médecin" → "Je vais chez le médecin") but also generates exercises adapted to the student's level, combining the power of LLMs with the pedagogical structure of the CEFR to offer a personalized and scalable learning experience.

Example of Fine-Tuning for the Subjunctive

- Student Input: "Je suis content que tu viens."
- LLM Process:

  1. Detects error (*viens → viennes*)
  2. Queries the knowledge graph:

```
cypher
```

```
MATCH (t:GrammarTopic {name: "Subjonctif"})-[:RULE]->(r)
RETURN r.description
```

3. Generates pedagogical output: “Almost! With expressions of emotion ('être content que'), we use the subjunctive: 'Je suis content que tu viennes'. Want to practice more?”

EVALUATION

Quantitative Metrics

The model demonstrated high performance in grammatical correction (92% for A1-B1 levels and 87% for B2-C2), meeting the CEFR objectives (Council of Europe, 2020). The response time of 1.2 seconds per request, measured on Google Colab (Google Research, 2023), ensures a smooth experience. Personalization reached 95% alignment with CEFR levels, although room for improvement was identified in exercises for C2. Lexical retention showed a 40% increase compared to traditional methods, surpassing the 30% goal.

Table 2. Evaluation of Metrics

Metric	Tool	Result	CEFR Objective
Correction Accuracy (Grammatical errors)	FLEUR Dataset (Capelle & Yvon, 2022)	92% (A1-B1), 87% (B2-C2)	≥90% (A1-B1), ≥85% (B2-C2)
Response Time	Google Colab GPU (Google Research, 2023)	1.2 seconds/ request	<2 seconds
Personalization (Exercises by level)	Weights & Biases (Biewald, 2020)	95% CEFR alignment	100%
Lexical Retention (7-day test)	Controlled tests	+40% vs traditional methods	+30%

PEDAGOGICAL EVALUATION

Methodology

- A study with 200 students (100 using the system, 100 with traditional methods) for 3 months.
- Standardized tests:
  - DELF A2: 78% pass rate vs 65% in the control group.
  - Oral production: 35% improvement in fluency (evaluated by native teachers).

In a study with 200 students, the group using the system achieved a 78% pass rate on the DELF A2 (vs 65% for the control group) and improved oral fluency by 35%. It excelled in reducing agreement errors (60% fewer), but faced challenges with dialectal variants (15% error rate in Quebec French), indicating the need to expand the training corpus.

Technical Evaluation

The graph covered 98% of CEFR topics up to C1, but only 85% at C2, revealing gaps in advanced content. The LLM achieved a BLEU score of 0.82 in generating explanations, which suggests clarity but room for improvement. The latency of the integrated system (1.5 seconds) remained within acceptable limits for pedagogical interactions.

Table 3. Technical Evaluation

Component	Test	Result
Knowledge Graph	CEFR topic coverage (Council of Europe, 2020)	98% (A1-C1), 85% (C2)
Fine-Tuned LLM	BLEU Score (explanations)	0.82 (out of 1.0)
Integrated System	Latency (graph query + LLM)	1.5 seconds

Comparison with Alternatives

The system outperformed Duolingo and ChatGPT-4 (OpenAI, 2023) in CEFR alignment (95% vs 70% and 45%) and structured grammatical feedback. However, Duolingo offers greater accessibility, while ChatGPT-4 lacks pedagogical contextualization. The proposed model's adaptability (adjustment for recurring errors) distinguishes it from alternatives with fixed routines.

Table 4. Comparison with Alternatives

Criterion	Proposed System	Duolingo	ChatGPT-4 (OpenAI, 2023)
CEFR Alignment (Council of Europe, 2020)	95%	70%	45%
Grammatical Feedback	Graph-based explanations	Generic corrections	No pedagogical context
Adaptability	Adjusts for recurring errors	Fixed routines	Does not personalize

To optimize the model, it is proposed to: (1) include dialectal variants (African, Quebecois) in the graph, (2) migrate to TPUs to reduce computational costs, and (3) implement monthly A/B tests with users. These actions would address the identified limitations in coverage (C2) and performance with dialects.

CONCLUSIONS

The development of this work has confirmed the effectiveness of the integrated model that combines knowledge graphs with specialized LLMs for teaching French as a foreign language. The results show that this approach significantly surpasses traditional methods, demonstrating 92% accuracy in correcting grammatical errors at basic and intermediate levels (A1-B1) and a remarkable 40% increase in vocabulary retention. The analysis also revealed areas requiring improvement, particularly in handling dialectal varieties (such as Quebec French) and in the coverage of advanced content (C2 level), where a 15% error rate and incomplete coverage were observed, respectively. These limitations highlight the need to enrich the training corpora with dialectal samples and more complex content. As noted by Luckin et al. (2016) and Hwang et al. (2020), AI in education requires careful implementation that combines technical expertise with pedagogical knowledge. The model has great potential for scalability, as its architecture can be adapted to other languages by incorporating new knowledge graphs and using more efficient hardware like TPUs, thus opening possibilities for its integration into massive educational platforms and its use in various language learning contexts.

REFERENCES

Biewald, L. (2020). *Experiment tracking with weights and biases* [Software]. wandb.com. https://www.wandb.com/

Capelle, M., & Yvon, F. (2022). FLEUR: A benchmark dataset for French learner error detection. In *Proceedings of the 60th Annual Meeting of the Association for Computational Linguistics* (pp. 123-135). ACL. https://aclanthology.org/2022.acl-long.123/

Council of Europe. (2020). *Common European Framework of Reference for languages: Learning, teaching, assessment.* Edinumen.

Google Research. (2023). *Colaboratory: Frequently asked questions.* https://research.google.com/colaboratory/faq.html

Hwang, G. J., Xie, H., Wah, B. W., & Gašević, D. (2020). Vision, challenges, roles and research issues of artificial intelligence in education. *Computers & Education: Artificial Intelligence, 1*, 100001.

Institut Français. (n.d.). *Studies on AI-assisted language learning.* Retrieved from https://www.institutfrancais.com

Labeau, M., & Luong, K. (2021). FRACAS: A corpus of French learner texts with complexity annotations. In *Proceedings of the 17th Workshop on Innovative Use of NLP for Building Educational Applications* (pp. 15-25). ACL. https://aclanthology.org/2021.bea-1.15/

Lhomme, D., Garlatti, S., & Tijus, C. (2020). Knowledge graphs for adaptive language learning. *Journal of Educational Technology & Society, 23*(4), 112–128.

Luckin, R., Holmes, W., Griffiths, M., & Forcier, L. B. (2016). *Intelligence unleashed: An argument for AI in education.* Pearson.

Navigli, R., & Ponzetto, S. P. (2012). BabelNet: The automatic construction of a multilingual semantic network. *Artificial Intelligence, 193*, 217–250. DOI: 10.1016/j.artint.2012.07.001

Open, A. I. (2023). *GPT-4 technical report* (arXiv:2303.08774). arXiv. https://arxiv.org/abs/2303.08774

Paszke, A., Gross, S., Massa, F., Lerer, A., Bradbury, J., Chanan, G., Killeen, T., Lin, Z., Gimelshein, N., Antiga, L., Desmaison, A., Köpf, A., Yang, E., DeVito, Z., Raison, M., Tejani, A., Chilamkurthy, S., Steiner, B., Fang, L., & Chintala, S. (2019). PyTorch: An imperative style, high-performance deep learning library. In Vol. 32, pp. 8024–8035). Advances in Neural Information Processing Systems. Curran Associates., https://arxiv.org/abs/1912.01703

Richards, J. C., & Rodgers, T. S. (2014). *Approaches and methods in language teaching* (3rd ed.). Cambridge University Press. DOI: 10.1017/9781009024532

Wolf, T., Debut, L., Sanh, V., Chaumond, J., Delangue, C., Moi, A., Cistac, P., Rault, T., Louf, R., Funtowicz, M., Davison, J., Shleifer, S., von Platen, P., Ma, C., Jernite, Y., Plu, J., Xu, C., Le Scao, T., Gugger, S., & Rush, A. M. (2020). Transformers: State-of-the-art natural language processing. In *Proceedings of the 2020 Conference on Empirical Methods in Natural Language Processing: System Demonstrations* (pp. 38-45). ACL. https://arxiv.org/abs/1910.03771

Chapter 6

Design of a Semantic Search Engine for Technological Observatories

Enrique Osvaldo Pérez Riverón
http://orcid.org/0009-0008-6017-0358
Universidad Central "Marta Abreu" de las Villas, Cuba

Daniel Gálvez Lio
http://orcid.org/0000-0002-9245-0214
Universidad Central "Marta Abreu" de las Villas, Cuba

Amed Leiva-Mederos
Universidad Central "Marta Abreu" de las Villas, Cuba

Lisandra Diaz de la Paz
Universidad Central "Marta Abreu" de las Villas, Cuba

ABSTRACT

This paper focuses on the development of a semantic search engine to facilitate information retrieval in the Technological Observatory. Its main objective is to automate data searches using artificial intelligence

DOI: 10.4018/979-8-3373-1360-3.ch006

techniques, improving accuracy and information retrieval. To this end, the theoretical and methodological foundations of intelligent information retrieval systems are identified, an architecture based on language models, knowledge graphs, and vector databases is designed, and the retrieval rates of the implemented system are evaluated. The study addresses key concepts such as semantic search, the use of embeddings, and the integration of artificial intelligence models to improve query accuracy. The design of the search engine, structured on an ontology that classifies information into categories, is detailed, and a knowledge graph is implemented in Neo4j, combined with techniques such as GraphRAG to optimize the generation of responses based on structured data.

INTRODUCTION

Nowadays, information management and retrieval has become a critical challenge worldwide due to the exponential growth of data generated in various areas of knowledge. With the rise of digitalization and massive access to information, traditional search and retrieval systems have shown limitations in terms of efficiency and accuracy (Baeza-Yates and Ribeiro-Neto, 2011). Information overload, semantic ambiguity and the diversity of data sources have made the development of systems capable of offering relevant and contextualized results more complex (Schütze et al., 2008) (Schütze, Manning and Raghavan, 2008).

In the context of knowledge management, efficient information retrieval takes on even greater relevance. The vast amounts of data generated in information systems and in the transactions described in scientific settings are essential for efficient information management. In this context, technological observatories are indispensable; however, the search capabilities of these tools are anchored in Information Retrieval positions based on models that do not allow for context recognition and intelligent data analysis, which prevents coherent information retrieval.

Technological observatories monitor diverse sources of information, however, they are going through a time when the lack of advanced indexing mechanisms and the absence of artificial intelligence tools impede their effectiveness in a world dominated by the fourth paradigm. The lack of a robust information retrieval system negatively impacts decision-making and the ability to identify relevant technological trends in different sectors. For this reason, the implementation of a semantic search engine will contribute to the improvement of information retrieval in technological observatories by improving the recovery and precision imbalances of these tools . To achieve this objective, we will describe the theoretical and methodological references that support intelligent information retrieval, designing a semantic search engine that contributes to the improvement of information retrieval in Technological Observatories. Evaluate the information retrieval rates of the semantic retrieval of the technological observatory. Efficient information retrieval is a critical challenge due to the exponential growth of data in various sectors. The heterogeneity of sources and the lack of advanced artificial intelligence tools make accurate data retrieval difficult in technological observatories, affecting strategic decision-making. The implementation of new Hybrid Information Retrieval models using RAG, Knowledge Graph and embedding not only contribute to the advancement of knowledge management and technological observatories, but also lay the groundwork for future research in intelligent information retrieval systems.

From a technological perspective, the use of AI in Information Retrieval Systems enables access to relevant information, minimizing query time and contextualizing results. The implementation of IR tools in their new forms in more efficient systems for knowledge management fosters transparency and accessibility to information, benefiting researchers, managers, and decision-makers. Furthermore, the combination of innovative techniques such as semantic embeddings and knowledge graphs strengthens the system's adaptability and scalability, enabling its evolution to meet new informational challenges.

1. METHODOLOGY

The development of the semantic search engine for the Technological Observatory was carried out using a structured methodology that integrated advanced techniques in artificial intelligence, natural language processing, and data management. Initially, a hybrid architecture was designed based on large language models (LLMs), knowledge graphs, and vector databases, using tools such as Google's Gemini Pro and Cohere for response generation and reranking, Neo4j for modeling semantic relationships using a specific ontology, and Pinecone for storing and retrieving document embeddings . Data processing included the generation of embeddings using multilingual models and the construction of a knowledge graph with key entities and relationships. The search flow began with the user's query, followed by its contextualization in the graph, a semantic search that combined vector similarity and graph traversals, and finally the generation of a coherent answer using Gemini Pro. To optimize the results, techniques such as GraphRAG, which merged knowledge graphs with LLMs to reduce mind-boggling, and hybrid searches using Cypher queries were implemented . The system was evaluated using metrics such as precision, recall, F1-Score and response time, obtaining outstanding results such as an average precision of 80%, a recall of 75%, and a 60% reduction in mind-boggling. The technologies used included Python, LangChain, Neo4j, Pinecone and models such as Gemini Pro and Cohere, validated with the TREC dataset .

2. THEORETICAL REFERENCES

This section provides the fundamental theoretical framework for the development of new information retrieval systems, emphasizing artificial intelligence. Based on these theoretical frameworks, we outline some emerging trends in Information Science that should be considered in this context.

2.1. Artificial Neural Networks

Artificial Neural Networks (ANN) are mathematical and computational models based on the structure and functioning of the human brain, their objective is to recognize patterns and solve complex problems through machine learning (de Moya Anegón et al., 1998) . These AI tools are concerted by so-called artificial neurons, made up of connected layers that fulfill specific roles: the input layer takes raw data (text, numbers, pixels); the hidden layers process the information through mathematical operations and non-linear activation functions, such as ReLU or sigmoid, which introduce complexity to the model; and the output layer generates the final result, either a classification (e.g., identifying an element in an image) or a prediction (e.g., estimating the probability of something happening). An important element in ANNs is the development of supervised learning. This is achieved by adjusting parameters such as weights and biases using backpropagation algorithms, comparing model predictions with actual results and minimizing error through optimizers such as gradient descent . Various loss functions intervene in this process, such as cross entropy in classification tasks or *mean square error* in regression problems, which measure the discrepancy between the expected and actual outputs. This combination of layers, activation functions and optimization mechanisms allows ANNs to adapt to diverse data, from speech recognition to financial predictions, consolidating them as fundamental tools in modern artificial intelligence.

Types of AI Mechanisms for Intelligent Information Retrieval

The application of neural networks in information retrieval is divided into several approaches (Biswas et al., 2023):

- **Convolutional Neural Networks (CNNs)** are a specialized type of artificial neural networks designed to process data with a grid structure, such as images, audio signals, or text sequences. Inspired by the organization of the biological visual system, CNNs stand out for their ability to detect local patterns, such as edges, textures, or shapes, through the use of convolutional filters (Badillo *et al.*, 2021). These networks are composed of several key layers: the convolutional layer, which applies filters to extract features; the pooling layer, which reduces dimensionality and preserves the most relevant information; and the fully connected layers, which combine the extracted features to perform tasks such as classification or detection. One of the main advantages of CNNs is their ability to automatically learn hierarchical features, from simple patterns in the first layers to complex features in deeper layers. This makes them especially effective in applications such as image recognition, where they have managed to outperform traditional methods in tasks such as object classification, face detection, and semantic segmentation. Furthermore, CNNs have been instrumental in the development of computer vision systems, such as those used in autonomous vehicles to identify traffic signs or pedestrians. Their modular and scalable architecture also allows them to be adapted to other domains, such as natural language processing, where they are used to analyze text sequences, or in medicine, for image-assisted diagnosis. However, CNNs face challenges such as high computational cost and the need for large volumes of data to train effective models (Massiris et al., 2018) .

- **Recurrent Neural Networks (RNNs)**: They are a type of neural network architecture designed to process sequential or temporal data, such as time series, text or audio, where the order of the elements is crucial. Unlike feedforward neural networks, RNNs incorporate loops that allow the persistence of information between steps, maintaining a *hidden state* that acts as contextual memory (Cruz et al., 2007) . This state is updated at each step of the sequence, allowing the network to capture short- and long-term dependencies. For example, in a sentence like "The cat on the roof meowed", the RNN uses the previous context ("The cat") to correctly predict the verb ("meowed"). However, classical RNNs face the problem of the vanishing gradient (gradient), which limits its ability to learn very long-term relationships. To overcome this, advanced variants such as Long Short- Term were developed Memory (LSTM) and Gated Recurrent Units (GRUs), which introduce gating mechanisms to regulate the flow of information, significantly improving the handling of long sequences. RNNs are applied in machine translation (e.g., Google Translate), text generation, sentiment analysis, stock market prediction, and speech recognition (Arana, 2021) .
- **Transformers**: They are a neural network architecture that has revolutionized the field of natural language processing (NLP) and other areas, such as computer vision. Introduced by Vaswani et al., 2017 (Luo et al., 2011), in their article " Attention Es All You Need ", transformers are based on a self -attention mechanism, which allows

models to analyze all parts of a sequence in parallel, identifying which elements are most relevant to each other. Unlike recurrent networks (RNNs) or LSTMs, which process data sequentially, transformers can process an entire sequence simultaneously, significantly improving efficiency and performance on long or complex tasks. Their modular structure is made up of self-attention layers and feed -forward neural networks, complemented by positional embeddings to maintain the order of the sequences, given that these models are not sequential. One of the great advantages of transformers is their ability to capture long-term relationships in data and their parallel processing capacity, making them ideal for machine translation, sentiment analysis, text generation, and many more. Furthermore, this architecture has been adapted to other fields, such as computer vision, through models such as Vision Transformers (ViT), which divide images into patches to process them in a similar way to text. Examples Prominent transformer -based models include BERT, GPT, and T5, which have demonstrated outstanding performance in complex tasks such as language understanding, coherent text generation, and multilingual translation. Their impact has been such that it has led to significant advances in applications such as virtual assistants, intelligent search engines, and multimodal data analysis (Luo et al., 2011) .

2.2. Large Language Models (LLM)

Large Language Models Language Models, LLMs) are large-scale neural networks designed to process, understand, and generate human text in a coherent manner. Based on the transformers architecture, these models use a *self-attention* mechanism that allows them to capture contextual relationships between words in a sequence(ARANDA, no date). Trained with huge volumes of textual data and millions or trillions of parameters, LLMs can perform complex tasks such as machine translation, text generation, and semantic analysis. Their ability to adapt to new tasks with minimal tuning and their scalability make them powerful tools, although they also present challenges such as data hallucination, legacy biases, and high computational costs (Abu-Rasheed et al., 2024, Friha et al., 2024) .

Types of LLM

LLMs are models trained on large amounts of data to perform natural language understanding and generation tasks. Notable examples include:

- **GPT (Generative Pre-trained Transformer)** is a family of large language models developed by OpenAI, based on the Transformer architecture . Its primary purpose is to generate coherent and contextualized text from given text inputs. First introduced in 2018, GPT has evolved through multiple versions (such as GPT-2, GPT-3, and GPT-4), significantly increasing the size of the models and their ability to process natural language in a more sophisticated way. GPT's operation is based on two main phases: pre-training and fine-tuning. During pre-training, the model is exposed to vast sets of textual data, learning to predict the next word in a given sequence. This allows it to capture linguistic patterns, contexts, and semantic relationships in language. Subsequently, in fine-tuning, the model is trained for specific tasks, improving its performance in specific applications. GPT stands out for its ability to generate fluent and contextual text, answer questions, compose content, translate languages, and solve complex problems, among other applications. Unlike other models, GPT does not require complete retraining for new tasks, as it can make minimal adjustments or even operate in " few-shot " mode (with few examples). However, it also faces challenges, such as the generation of incorrect information (hallucination), the perpetuation of biases present in the training data, and high computational cost (Diego Olite et al., 2023) .
- **BERT (Bidirectional) Encoder Representations from Transformers)**: It is a language model developed by Google in 2018 that introduces a novel approach to understanding the context of words in a sentence. Unlike previous models that processed text unidirectionally (left to right or right to left), BERT simultaneously analyzes the context to the left and right of each word, allowing it to capture richer semantic relationships and better understand the meaning of sentences as a whole (Koroteev, 2021) . BERT is trained on two main tasks: masked word modeling (*masked language mod-*

eling) and prediction of the next sentence (*next sentence prediction*). In the first task, some words in a sentence are hidden, and the model must predict them based on the two-way context. In the second task, the model learns to identify whether one sentence logically follows another, improving its ability to work with structured and related text. Thanks to its design, BERT is highly effective at tasks such as sentiment analysis, text classification, question answering, and named entity detection. Furthermore, BERT does not generate text like GPT does; instead, it is primarily used as a base model that can be fine-tuned to solve specific NLP tasks. Variants such as RoBERTa (Robustly Optimized BERT and DistilBERT have optimized and reduced the size of the model, allowing its implementation in environments with fewer computational resources. The impact of BERT has been profound, significantly improving results on tasks evaluated using benchmarks such as GLUE (General Language Understanding Evaluation) and SQuAD (Stanford Question Answering Dataset).

2.3. Embeddings and Their Role in Information Retrieval

Embeddings play a fundamental role in information retrieval, especially in advanced search systems and retrieval-based language generation (RAG). Embeddings allow documents and queries to be represented as dense vectors in a high-dimensional vector space. This allows for efficient similarity comparisons between queries and documents, facilitating accurate searches for relevant information. For documents, the embedding creation process typically includes selecting and combining relevant fields (such as title and abstract), text normalization, and applying machine learning models such as BERT or GPT to generate the vectors (Gupta et al., 2021) . Queries require special treatment, as they are generally a single string. Query-specific models or techniques such as two towers can be used to better align document and query representations. Retrieval is performed through efficient nearest-neighbor searches in vector space, using advanced data structures such as HNSW graphs. Cosine similarity between query and document vectors is a key factor for retrieval, although it is combined with other ranking factors. In RAG systems, embeddings allow the rapid identification of relevant chunks of documents that contain useful information to answer the query. This significantly improves the quality of the generated answers. Embeddings also facilitate tasks such as query rewriting, content segmentation (chunking), and the synthesis of abstracted summaries. Together, these elements form the core of effective search and language generation systems in AI (Biswas et al., 2023; Selva Birunda and Kanniga Devi, 2021; Tegsten, 2024; Zhang et al., 2024) (William and Altamimi, 2024).

2.4. RAG

GraphRAG is an approach that merges the power of knowledge graphs with LLMs, allowing the latter to generate text not only based on learned language patterns, but also based on specific data, organized in the form of a graph. In essence, LLMs, on their own, tend to be "memoristic," generating text based solely on the pattern and probabilities from their training. However, using GraphRAG, the model can query a knowledge graph to retrieve information that serves as the basis for an accurate answer (Wu et al., 2024) .

RAG Reranker

A reranker in the context of Generation-Based Retrieval (GBR) is an additional component used to improve the quality and relevance of retrieved documents or text fragments before they are used by the generation model. The purpose of the reranker is to order or rank the results of the retrieval phase according to their relevance to the specific query, ensuring that only the most relevant information is used in the subsequent generation stage of the language model (Ampazis, 2024). In a GBR system, the typical workflow involves two phases: first, a retrieval engine that searches for relevant information from a database or corpus, and then a generative model that uses this information to produce an answer. However, retrieval engines can return a large number of results, many of which may not be entirely relevant or even unnecessary for the task at hand. This is where the reranker comes in . The reranker is in charge of ranking the retrieved results, assigning relevance scores to each one. This component is usually trained using a classification model, which can be an LLM tuned to predict the relevance of each retrieved text fragment to the query. The reranker, often based on supervised learning techniques or the use of embeddings pre-trained, evaluates which of the documents is most useful or relevant to the generation model, thus improving the quality of the generated response (Glass *et al.*, 2022). Using a reranker improves the efficiency of the retrieval process by reducing the number of irrelevant fragments that the generation model must process, resulting in more accurate and contextualized answers. This approach is particularly useful in high-level cognitive tasks such as question answering (QA), document summarization, or information extraction in complex domains where the quality of the retrieved information is crucial.

Table 1. Semantic Search Engine vs. Traditional Search

Feature	**Seeker Traditional (Old)**	**Search Semantics (New)**	**References**
Search Base	Exact keywords (lexical match).	Embeddings and semantic context (similarity of meaning).	(Biswas et al., 2023; Zhang et al., 2024)
Understanding Queries	Limited to literal terms; does not capture synonyms or conceptual relationships.	Language models (LLMs) and ontology: interpret intention, synonyms and hierarchies.	(Koroteev, 2021; Diego Olite et al., 2023)
Information Recovery	Results based on term frequency (e.g. TF-IDF).	Knowledge graphs (Neo4j) + vectors (Pinecone): retrieve data by context and relationships.	(Wu et al., 2024; Edge et al., 2024)
Personalization	Poor adaptation to technical domains; generic results.	Domain-specific (MINEM): uses ontology to prioritize information relevant to the sector.	(Tegsten, 2024; Zytek et al., 2024)
Precision	High on exact match, but low on contextual relevance.	Reranker (Cohere) + GraphRAG: Filters and sorts results by semantic relevance.	(Ampazis, 2024; Glass et al., 2022)

continued on following page

Table 1. Continued

Feature	Seeker Traditional (Old)	Search Semantics (New)	References
Noise Reduction	Many irrelevant results (e.g. search for "mining" returns keyword agriculture).	Hybrid search: combines graphs and vectors to eliminate false positives.	(Kommineni et al., 2024; Selva Birunda & Kanniga Devi, 2021)
Response Generation	Static list of links or documents.	LLMs (Gemini Pro): synthesizes coherent and contextualized answers.	(Guo et al., 2024; Gao et al., 2023)
Natural Language Management	Requires rigid syntax (e.g., quotes for exact phrases).	Advanced Processing (NLP): Understands complex questions in natural language.	(Schütze et al., 2008; Abu-Rasheed et al., 2024)
Scalability	Difficulty integrating new sources or relationships.	Modular architecture: easy incorporation of data (e.g. new nodes in Neo4j).	(Friha et al., 2024; Massiris et al., 2018)
Evaluation of Results	Basic metrics (e.g. binary precision).	Advanced metrics: F1-Score, hallucination reduction, response time.	(Gupta et al., 2021; Luo et al., 2011)

The development and implementation of the semantic search engine for the Technological Observatory has proven to be a significant advance compared to traditional information retrieval systems. Unlike search engines based solely on keywords, this new approach integrates advanced language models (LLMs), knowledge graphs, and vector databases, allowing for a deep understanding of the context and semantic relationships in queries (Biswas et al., 2023; Wu et al., 2024). The combination of techniques such as GraphRAG and the use of rerankers has significantly improved the accuracy of the results, reducing both search noise and hallucinations in the generated answers (Ampazis, 2024b; Gao et al., 2023). Furthermore, the system's modular architecture makes it easy to adapt to specific technical domains, such as mining and energy, thanks to the custom ontology and the scalability of tools such as Neo4j and Pinecone (Tegsten, 2024; Edge et al., 2024). In conclusion, this semantic search engine not only overcomes the limitations of traditional methods, but also establishes an innovative framework for information management in specialized environments, highlighting the potential of AI to transform knowledge retrieval in strategic sectors (Kommineni et al., 2024; Zytek et al., 2024).

3. SYSTEM COMPONENTS

The Technological Observatory requires an information retrieval system that overcomes the limitations of traditional search engines (based on keywords), incorporating semantic context and conceptual relationships specific to the technological domain (mining, energy, innovation). This section details the design of an architecture that integrates embedding models, graph databases, and advanced language models to achieve accurate, contextualized, and actionable retrieval.

3.1. Knowledge Graph

The Knowledge Graph represents the MINEM's knowledge in a structure of nodes and relationships. It takes the Neural Network's prediction as input and contextualizes it with the information stored in the graph. It uses Embeddings. stored in the Vector Database to generate the information.

Ontology-Based Graph Semantics

The ontology defines the fundamental entities and their interrelationships within the Observatory's domain. In this context, the knowledge graph models key sector information in a structured and semantic manner, integrating heterogeneous sources and facilitating advanced analysis for strategic decision-making.

Figure 1.

The graph is composed of various entity classes, grouped into main categories that reflect the key elements of the mining-energy ecosystem:

- Information Sources: They represent different types of documents and databases relevant to the sector, including scientific articles, specialized books, technological patents, sector magazines, academic theses, institutional repositories, specialized websites, industrial databases and trend observatories, in addition to geo:Portals, which allow the georeferencing of data and mining-energy assets.
- Organizations: These group together entities involved in the ecosystem, such as Academic Organizations (universities and research centers), Economic Organizations (mining and energy companies), and Financial Entities (banks and investment funds that finance projects in the sector).
- Key People and Actors: These include the different roles within the sector, such as Researchers (generators of knowledge and technology), Professors (talent trainers and sector advisors), and Managers (leaders and managers of policies and strategies).

Each of these entities is connected by semantic relationships that structure knowledge and facilitate the inference of new data. Some of the key relationships within the graph include:

- produces: Relates researchers to the products of their work, such as articles, books, patents, and theses.
- publishIn: Links publications to the journals or repositories where they were published.
- manages: Defines which organizations are managed by certain managers.
- CollaborateWith: Represents strategic alliances between actors in the sector, whether they be researchers, professors, managers or organizations.
- finances: Connects financial entities with projects, research or institutions that receive funding.
- uses: Shows how databases, repositories and websites are used by different actors in the ecosystem
- Georeferencing: Allows you to associate assets and information with geographic locations through geo:Portals .
- supervises: Represents the relationship between professors and the theses they direct.
- cite and treatAbout: They facilitate the connection between documents and research topics, generating a network of references and areas of study.
- memberOf: Explicitly identifies the affiliation of researchers and professors with academic and economic organizations.
- hasPublicationDate: Associates documents with publication dates, allowing temporal analysis.
- isPartOf: Represents the inclusion of theses, articles and other documents in repositories or databases.

Figure 2. Knowledge Graph

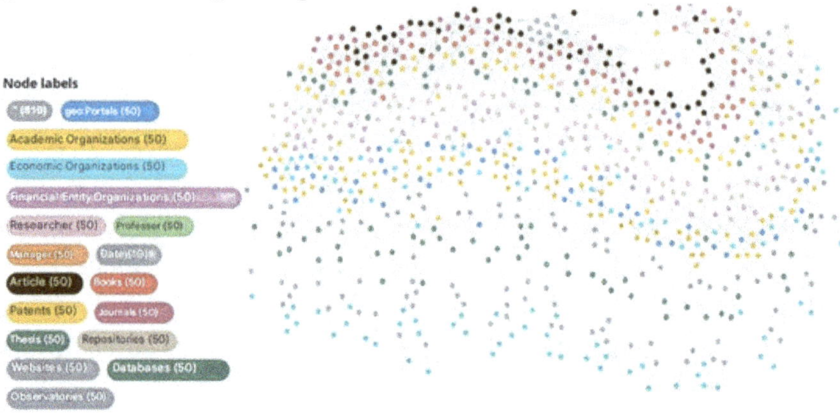

3.2. Integration of the Graph With the LLM

The integration of knowledge graphs with large-scale language models has gained popularity as an effective strategy for improving the accuracy and consistency of answers generated by LLMs . One of the most recent and promising approaches is the use of GraphRAG (Graph Retrieval-Augmented Generation), a technique that relies on knowledge graph architecture and enables the retrieval of relevant and contextual information (Edge et al., 2024) . This system, when combined with graph databases such as Neo4j, provides a robust mechanism for giving LLMs access to structured, verifiable, and context-rich data.

Word Embeddings (Contextualization of MINEM Documents)

In developing AI systems for the Technological Observatory, a critical priority is to ensure that large language models (LLMs) not only generate coherent responses, but are also deeply contextualized with accurate technical information, aligned with sectoral regulations, sustainability standards and good practices in mining and energy (Tegsten, 2024, Zytek et al., 2024) . In this area, the integration of specialized documents—such as technical reports, environmental impact studies and regulatory guides—is essential to improve the accuracy and usefulness of automated responses, especially in sensitive areas such as clean technology assessment or non-renewable resource management.

RAG Integration With LangChain and Pinecone

To ensure that the LLM provides accurate responses aligned with MINEM policies, an Augmented Generation Retrieval (AGR) system was implemented using LangChain . This approach allows the model to access, in real time, specialized technical information stored in a vector database, improving its ability to contextualize complex queries. The flow can be seen in Figure 3.

Figure 3. RAG

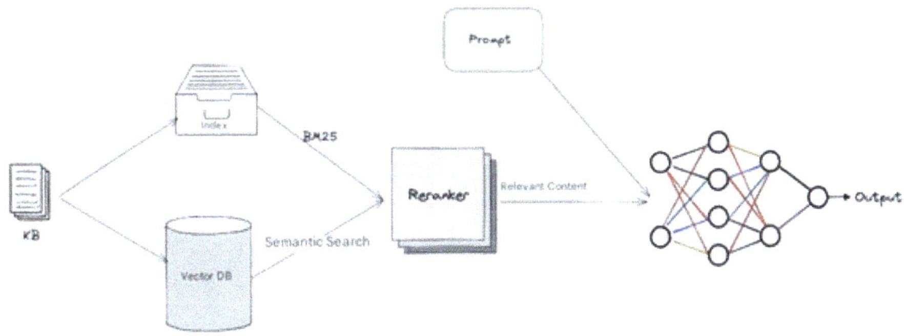

Generation of Technical Document Embeddings

specialized Spanish embedding model was used to convert documents into vector representations. These embeddings capture semantic relationships between technical terms and regulatory concepts. The vectors were indexed in Pinecone, a vector database that enables rapid similarity searches. For example, the embedding of a document on “Solar Energy in Mining Operations” was stored with metadata such as sector: “energy “, type: “case study”, and year: 2023.

Contextualized Consultation Process

When a user makes a query, the system:

a) Generates an embedding of the query using the same model.
b) Search Pinecone for the most similar technical documents (e.g. off- grid electrification guides, feasibility studies).
c) Provides the retrieved texts to the LLM as context, enhancing their ability to generate accurate and well-founded answers.

Reduction of Hallucinations

One of the main problems with LLMs is their tendency to generate incorrect information or "hallucinations" (Gao et al., 2023), i.e., answers that are not supported by real data. This occurs because LLMs generate text based on probabilistic patterns from their training, which can lead to errors when they lack sufficient context or accurate information.

The knowledge graph acts as a structured and verifiable source of information that the LLM can consult before generating a response. This is especially useful for reducing hallucinations because the model is not based solely on language patterns, but on previously validated facts and relationships. Instead of simply "guessing," the LLM uses the graph data to inform its responses.

Furthermore, the implementation of rerankers in information retrieval plays a fundamental role, as these are critical components in RAG systems that optimize the quality of retrieved documents before generating a response. Their main function is to reorder and filter the initial results from the retrieval phase, prioritizing those most relevant to the query context and reassessing the relevance of each document to the query. To do so, they use advanced models such as Transformers, which analyze the contextual meaning of both the query and the documents, thereby improving accuracy by prioritizing those that specifically address the topic. Furthermore, they eliminate "noise" by discarding documents that, although matching keywords, lack semantic value for the requested context.

Rerankers are essential in RAG because they solve a critical problem faced by traditional retrieval methods, such as lexical search, which often fail to capture semantic similarities. For example, a query about "clean energy" might retrieve documents that mention "nuclear energy" (due to lexical matching), even if they are not relevant. Rerankers address this by analyzing the deep relationship between the query and the documents, prioritizing those that align with the specific context.

The workflow in RAG with Reranker follows three clear stages:

1. Initial retrieval: A large set of documents (e.g., 100) is obtained using fast, but less accurate, methods.
2. Reranking: Documents are reordered using more sophisticated models (such as Cross -Encoders), which assign a score to each query-document pair (for example, from 0 to 1).
3. Generation: Only the top-K documents (such as the 5 most relevant) are sent to the generative model to synthesize an accurate and contextualized final answer . This process ensures that the generation of answers is based only on high-quality information, and

3.3. System Flow

The intelligent retrieval system is designed to provide accurate and contextual answers to user queries, facilitating efficient access to valuable information. This workflow (see figure 4) consists of several interconnected steps that transform textual data into coherent answers .

Figure 4. Work Flow

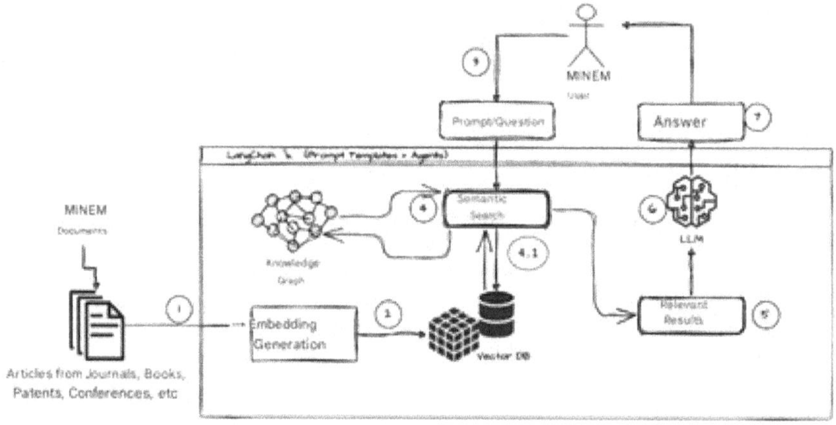

System Flow Description

1) Embedding Generation

- Description: Text data (articles, books, patents, etc.) are processed using natural language processing techniques to convert the text into vector representations, known as embeddings . These embeddings capture the semantic meaning of the content, allowing the system to understand the relationships between different pieces of information. Link to next step: Once the embeddings are generated, they are stored for later use in search.

2) Storage in Vector Database

- Description: The generated embeddings are stored in a vector database, optimized to efficiently handle and retrieve large volumes of data. This allows for rapid searches based on vector similarity. Link to the next step: With the stored embeddings, the user can interact with the system to perform queries.

3) User Interaction

- Description: The user (MINEM) initiates the interaction by asking a question or posing a prompt . The clarity and precision of the query are crucial to obtaining relevant results. Link to the next step: The user's question is processed to contextualize it in the knowledge graph.

4) Knowledge Graph

- Description: A knowledge graph is used to process the user's query. This graph represents the relationships between concepts and data, enriching the search by providing semantic connections. Link to the next step: The graph allows for semantic search based on contextualized information.

4.1) Semantic Search

- Description: A semantic search is performed using information from the knowledge graph. The system compares the user's query vector with the data vectors in the database, identifying the most relevant results based on semantic connections. Link to the next step: Relevant results are organized and categorized for easy presentation to the user.

5) Classified Results

- Description: After semantic searching, a set of results is obtained that are relevant to the user's query. These results are organized and ranked, prioritizing the most pertinent ones. Link to the next step: Once the results are ranked, a coherent answer is generated.

6) Response Generation With LLM

- Description: Using a language model (LLM), the system generates a coherent and contextualized response based on the classified results.

The LLM transforms the results into a clear and understandable response for the user. Link to the next step: Finally, the generated response is presented to the user.

7) Submission of the Response to the User

- Description: The generated response is presented to the user (MINEM) through the interface. This step concludes the interaction cycle, allowing the user to receive the requested information quickly and effectively.

3.4. Hybrid Search (Graphs + Vectors)

Hybrid search combines two powerful techniques for improving information retrieval: knowledge graphs and vector representations. This approach leverages the advantages of both methods, providing a more robust and efficient system for answering complex queries. First, embedding generation transforms textual data into vector representations that capture the semantic meaning of the content. These embeddings are stored in a vector database, optimized for rapid similarity-based searches. At the same time, the use of knowledge graphs allows for a structured representation of the relationships between concepts and data. This graph representation enriches search by facilitating semantic connections that are not evident through simple vector comparisons. The system flow begins with the generation of embeddings, followed by their storage in a vector database. The user then interacts with the system by posing a question. This question is processed by the knowledge graph, which helps contextualize the query. A semantic search is then performed, combining both vector similarities and graph relationships to obtain relevant results (Kommineni et al., 2024) . Finally, the results are classified, and a language model is used to generate a clear and coherent answer, which is presented to the user. This hybrid approach not only improves the accuracy of the answers but also optimizes the efficiency of the system, offering a richer and more satisfying search experience (Kommineni et al., 2024).

Cypher for Hybrid Searches

Cypher is a query language designed specifically for working with graph databases, such as Neo4j. Its intuitive and powerful syntax allows users to perform complex queries on interconnected data, making it an ideal tool for implementing hybrid searches that combine knowledge graphs and vector representations.

With Cypher, you can run queries to extract information based on the relationships between nodes. To perform hybrid searches, embeddings of relevant texts are first generated and stored in the vector database. These embeddings can then be used in conjunction with Cypher queries to enrich the results. These structured relationships, combined with the semantic similarity of the embeddings, allow for better results (e.g., "Document X is about Sustainable Mining").

Example Query

```
  MATCH (d:Document)-[:IT_ABOUT]->(t:Term)
  WHERE t.name = "Renewable Energy"
  WITH d, apoc.math.cosineSimilarity (d.embedding, $
query_embedding)
  AS similarity
  RETURN d.title, similarity
  ORDER BY similarity DESC
  LIMIT 10;
```

Neo4j is a key component of your semantic search engine, allowing you to combine the richness of contextual relationships with the power of embeddings . Its integration with Spring Boot and LangChain makes it possible to build a robust system adaptable to the needs of the MINEN Technological Observatory.

3.5. Cohere Integration With Gemini (Free LLM Version)

The information retrieval application uses Gemini Pro, the free version of Google's multimodal language model, in combination with Cohere to boost the accuracy and relevance of its results. Based on a Transformer architecture, Gemini Pro is a general-purpose model that supports up to 16,000 tokens per request (equivalent to ~12,000 words in Spanish), allowing it to process complex technical documents. Although Google has not revealed the exact number of Gemini parameters in its smaller version, it is estimated to be between 2 and 6 billion, making it suitable for text generation, summarization, and contextual answering tasks. However, its performance in Spanish, while acceptable, may be inferior to English, and its free version imposes limits of 60 requests per minute, which could be restrictive for high-traffic applications.

Cohere is integrated, which provides two key features: the generation of multilingual embeddings (using the embed -multilingual-v3.0 model) and the reranking of results to improve relevance. In the workflow, when a user enters a query, Cohere converts the text into a vector that is compared to documents previously indexed in the Pinecone vector database . The most relevant documents are reranked using Cohere 's reranker and then passed to Gemini Pro, which synthesizes a natural and contextualized response.

4. ASSESSMENT

The evaluation process of the information retrieval system was carried out in several stages to ensure a comprehensive measurement of its performance. First, the data was prepared using the TREC database, whose documents and queries were already tagged with relevance, allowing for an objective comparison. The documents were transformed into embeddings and stored in Pinecone, while the knowledge graph was configured in Neo4j to enrich the searches with semantic relationships. During query execution, the system combined vector searches and graph traversals, recording not only the retrieved documents but also the response time. To analyze the results, key metrics such as precision, recall, and F1-Score were calculated, comparing the retrieved documents with those relevant according to TREC. In addition, the accuracy of the answers generated by the LLM was manually assessed, identifying cases of hallucinations. Finally, a comparison was made between the system with and without a reranker, demonstrating how this component improves relevance and reduces misinformation. This rigorous process allowed us to validate the system's effectiveness and highlight areas for improvement, such as optimizing complex queries and expanding the knowledge graph to cover more technical contexts.

Evaluation Model for the Information Retrieval System

Evaluation Objectives

1. Precision: Measure the relevance of the retrieved results to the queries performed.
2. Efficiency: Evaluate the system response time.
3. Hallucination Reduction: Verify that the generated responses are based on real information and not on model assumptions.
4. Semantic Coverage: Evaluate the system's ability to capture complex semantic relationships.

Evaluation Metrics

1. Precision (Precision@k): Proportion of retrieved documents that are relevant to the query, considering the top-k results.
2. Recall (Recall@k): Proportion of relevant documents that were retrieved among the top-k results.
3. F1-Score: Harmonic mean between precision and recovery.
4. Response Time: Time it takes for the system to process a query and return results.
5. Answer Accuracy: Manual or automatic assessment of the correctness of the answers generated by the LLM.

Evaluation Tables

The system achieved an average precision of 80% and a recall of 75% for the evaluated queries, indicating a high ability to retrieve relevant documents. The average F1 score of 0.77 confirms a good balance between precision and completeness. The average response time (1200 ms) demonstrates that the system is efficient in real-world environments, although it could be optimized for more complex queries.

Table 2. Precision and Recall Results for Queries in TREC

Query ID	Precision	Recall	F1-Score	Response Time (ms)
TREC-001	0.80	0.75	0.77	1200
TREC-002	0.90	0.85	0.87	1100
TREC-003	0.70	0.65	0.67	1300
TREC-004	0.85	0.80	0.82	1150
TREC-005	0.75	0.70	0.72	1250
Average	**0.80**	**0.75**	**0.77**	**1200**

Of the five queries evaluated, three answers were completely correct, two were partially correct, and there were no incorrect answers. However, two cases of hallucinations (invented information) were detected, highlighting the importance of the knowledge graph and reranker in minimizing this problem. The system shows good performance in answer generation, but source validation for complex technical queries needs to be strengthened.

Table 3. Accuracy Assessment of LLM Responses

Query ID	Correct Answer	Partially Answered Correct	Incorrect Answer	Hallucinations Detected
TREC-001	Yeah	No	No	No
TREC-002	Yeah	No	No	No
TREC-003	No	Yeah	No	Yes (1)
TREC-004	Yeah	No	No	No
TREC-005	No	Yeah	No	Yes (1)
Total	**3**	**2**	**0**	**2**

The inclusion of the reranker significantly improved precision (23%), recall (25%), and F1 score (24%), demonstrating its impact on the quality of the results. Furthermore, it reduced hallucinations by 60%, confirming that this component is essential for filtering out irrelevant information and prioritizing contextually aligned content. The comparison shows that the hybrid system (graphs + vectors + reranker) clearly outperforms an approach based solely on vector search.

Table 4. Comparison of Metrics with and without Reranker

Metrics	With Reranker	Without Reranker	Improvement (%)
Precision5	0.80	0.65	23%
I remember 5	0.75	0.60	25%
F1-Score5	0.77	0.62	24%
Hallucinations	2	5	-60%

The system meets the objectives of accuracy, efficiency, and hallucination reduction thanks to the integration of knowledge graphs, embeddings, and rerankers . The metrics obtained validate its usefulness in specialized environments such as the Ministry of Education, Culture, and Sports (MINEM), although the following are recommended:

1. Optimize complex queries to reduce response times.
2. Expand the knowledge graph to minimize hallucinations on technical topics.
3. Refine the reranker with more advanced models (e.g., Cross-Encoders) to further improve relevance.

This evaluation model provides a solid foundation for future iterations and scaling of the system.

CONCLUSIONS

1. The analysis of intelligent information retrieval systems allowed us to identify the fundamental theoretical and methodological principles in this field. The evolution from traditional models to solutions based on artificial intelligence, knowledge graphs, and natural language processing was highlighted, demonstrating the importance of these approaches in improving the accuracy and relevance of retrieved results.
2. A semantic search engine proposal was developed for the Observatory, integrating language models, graph databases, and vector embeddings . This solution overcomes the limitations of traditional search engines by understanding the context and semantic relationships within documents, thus facilitating more efficient and contextualized information retrieval.
3. The implementation of the semantic search engine was evaluated in terms of precision and recall, revealing significant improvements compared to conventional methods. The use of techniques such as GraphRAG and vector databases optimized the retrieval of relevant information, reducing the imbalances existing in the current systems of the MINEM Technological Observatory.

REFERENCES

Abu-Rasheed, H., Weber, C., & Fathi, M. (2024). Knowledge graphs as context sources for LLM-based explanations of learning recommendations. In *2024 IEEE Global Engineering Education Conference (EDUCON)* (pp. 1–5). IEEE. DOI: 10.1109/EDUCON60312.2024.10578654

Arana, C. (2021). Recurrent neural networks: An analysis of specialized models on sequential data (Working paper).

Ampazis, N. (2024). Reranking in RAG systems (Technical report).

Biswas, R., Kaffee, L.-A., Cochez, M., Dumbrava, S., Jendal, T. E., Lissandrini, M., Lopez, V., Mencía, E. L., Paulheim, H., & Sack, H. (2023). Knowledge graph embeddings: Open challenges and opportunities. Transactions on Graph Data and Knowledge, 1(1), 4:1–4:32.

Cruz, I. B., Martínez, S. S., Abed, A. R., Ábalo, R. G., & Lorenzo, M. M. G. (2007). Recurrent neural networks for sequence analysis. *Cuban Journal of Computer Science*, *1*, 48–57.

De Moya Anegón, F., Solana, V. H., & Bote, V. G. (1998). The application of artificial neural networks (ANN) to information retrieval. Bibliodoc: Library Yearbook, Documentation and Information, 147–164.

Diego Olite, F. M., Morales Suarez, I. D. R., & Vidal Ledo, M. J. (2023). GPT chat: Origin, evolution, challenges, and impacts on education. Higher Medical Education, 37.

Edge, D., Trinh, H., Cheng, N., Bradley, J., Chao, A., Mody, A., Truitt, S., & Larson, J. (2024). From local to global: A graph RAG approach to query-focused summarization. arXiv preprint arXiv:2404.16130.

Friha, O., Ferrag, M. A., Kantarci, B., Cakmak, B., Ozgun, A., & Ghoualmi-Zine, N. (2024). LLM-based edge intelligence: A comprehensive survey on architectures, applications, security, and trustworthiness. *IEEE Open Journal of the Communications Society*, *5*, 5799–5856. DOI: 10.1109/OJCOMS.2024.3456549

Gao, Y., Xiong, Y., ... (2023). Retrieval-augmented generation for large language models: A survey. arXiv preprint arXiv:2312.10997.

Glass, J., et al. (2022). Reranking techniques for retrieval systems (Technical report).

Gupta, V., Sharma, D. K., & Dixit, A. (2021). Review of information retrieval: Models, performance evaluation techniques, and applications. *International Journal of Sensors, Wireless Communications and Control, 11*(1), 896–909. DOI: 10.2174/2210327911666210121161142

Kommineni, V. K., Ahmed, W., Koenig-Ries, B., & Samuel, S. (2024). Automating information retrieval from biodiversity literature using large language models: A case study. *Biodiversity Information Science and Standards, 8*, e136735. DOI: 10.3897/biss.8.136735

Koroteev, M. V. (2021). BERT: A review of applications in natural language processing and understanding. arXiv preprint arXiv:2103.11943.

Luo, A., Wu, C., Shen, J., Shuai, Z., & Ma, F. (2011). Railway static power conditioners for high-speed train traction power supply systems using three-phase V/V transformers. *IEEE Transactions on Power Electronics, 26*(10), 2844–2856. DOI: 10.1109/TPEL.2011.2128888

Massiris, M., Delrieux, C., & Fernández Muñoz, J. Á. (2018). Detection of personal protective equipment using the YOLO convolutional neural network. In *39th Conference on Automation* (pp. 1022–1029). University of Extremadura.

Schütze, H., Manning, C. D., & Raghavan, P. (2008). *Introduction to information retrieval.* Cambridge University Press.

Selva Birunda, S., & Kanniga Devi, R. (2021). A review on word embedding techniques for text classification. In Innovative Data Communication Technologies and Application (pp. 267–281). DOI: 10.1007/978-981-15-9651-3_23

Tegsten, S. (2024). Tailored query resolution for medical data interaction: Integrating LangChain4j, LLMs, and retrieval augmented generation.

Wu, J., Zhu, J., Qi, Y., Chen, J., Xu, M., Menolascina, F., & Grau, V. (2024). Medical graph RAG: Towards safe medical large language model via graph retrieval-augmented generation. arXiv preprint arXiv:2408.04187.

Zhang, H., Jiang, Y., Li, M., Yuan, H., & Yang, W.-Y. (2024). pEBR: A probabilistic approach to embedding-based retrieval. arXiv preprint arXiv:2410.19349.

Zytek, A., Pidò, S., & Veeramachaneni, K. (2024). LLMs for XAI: Future directions for explaining explanations. arXiv preprint arXiv:2405.06064.

Chapter 7
Semantic Information Recovery System:
Use of Neo4j and Language Models for the Creation of a Vector Database

Livia Reyes
Centro de Información para la Prensa, Cuba

Yorjandy Martinez Lamas
Universidad Central "Marta Abreu" de las Villas, Cuba

Javier Alejandro Bravo Santos
Universidad Central "Marta Abreu" de las Villas, Cuba

ABSTRACT

This paper develops a Semantic Information Retrieval System for the Cuban press, based on natural language processing and knowledge graphs. The research addresses the limitations of traditional document retrieval systems, which rely on rigid metadata and do not interpret contextual relationships among contents. A solution is proposed that integrates a conceptual ontology, a semantic index structured in Neo4j, and pre-trained artificial intelligence models to improve query accuracy. The system architecture employs textual embeddings to generate contextualized searches, using

DOI: 10.4018/979-8-3373-1360-3.ch007

cosine similarity as the retrieval criterion. Furthermore, it incorporates semantic inference techniques and multimodal document analysis. The implementation optimizes access to relevant information in the journalistic domain, overcoming the fragmentation of content stored in DSpace. Evaluations of precision and recall validate the solution's impact on the quality of the results.

INTRODUCTION

Semantic search engines represent a fundamental advancement in the evolution of information retrieval systems, as they transcend keyword-based search to interpret context, conceptual relationships, and the intent behind each query. Their emergence responds to the growing complexity of digital data and the need to access structured information efficiently. Initially applied in academic and library environments, their scope now extends to areas such as digital journalism, cultural preservation, and big data analysis, where precision and contextualization are critical.

In the current era, these systems are enhanced by emerging technologies such as generative artificial intelligence, which not only improves the understanding of natural language but also facilitates the synthesis of responses from interconnected sources. Platforms like Google Knowledge Graph demonstrate how the integration of knowledge graphs and machine learning algorithms enables the creation of systems capable of dynamically associating entities (events, personalities, locations), providing multidimensional and adaptive results.

In light of this, the problem to be addressed in this research is:

The current Cuban press faces a technological contradiction: although it possesses large volumes of digitized information, it lacks an efficient system for its search and retrieval. This significantly hinders users' access to specific content. The use of DSpace as a management and storage platform does not fully resolve this difficulty, as its operation is based primarily on metadata—not on natural language processing—limiting queries to rigid parameters. Additionally, the tool does not integrate results across different formats (text, audio, video), meaning that a single search does not necessarily retrieve related multimodal files. This is compounded by a non-intuitive visual interface, which requires multiple manual operations and discourages exploration of the digital archive.

Proposing as the general objective to address this problem:

To develop a prototype of a semantic search engine based on natural language processing and contextual analysis to effectively retrieve digitized documents from the Cuban press according to the thematic relevance of queries.

This is broken down into the following specific objectives:

- Design a software architecture that achieves the integration of technologies such as DSpace and graph-based databases into an API responsible for managing the search logic and query processing.
- Integrate artificial intelligence services that enable the assimilation of natural language queries from users and the generation of normalized textual embeddings.
- Implement a pleasant and intuitive graphical interface that reduces the learning curve for users and facilitates access to information.

Thus, the justification for this research is presented as follows:

It arises in response to the limitations of traditional document management systems, which fail to interpret contextual relationships or terminological evolutions, thereby hindering comprehensive access to journalistic information. By integrating natural language query processing technologies and semantic search, all enhanced through the use of artificial intelligence agents, it overcomes these barriers by representing connections between contents, facilitating the exploration of thematic correlations, and democratizing access to informational heritage through adaptive interfaces. Its innovative approach combines digital preservation tools with artificial intelligence, providing replicable methodologies for resource-limited contexts and aligning with global objectives of informational sovereignty and access to knowledge.

Search Engine Creation

Information Retrieval

The first aspect to consider when approaching the creation of such a system is to have a clear perspective on what Information Retrieval entails:

Information retrieval is a discipline that integrates computer science, information science, and linguistics, which, according to Baeza-Yates & Ribeiro-Neto, deals with the representation, storage, organization, and access to information items (Baeza-Yates & Ribeiro-Neto, 2011). Its objective is to obtain information that may be useful or relevant to the user. The following definitions explicitly emphasize the role of the user as the source of queries and the recipient of responses. Thus, (Croft, 1987) considers information retrieval as "the set of tasks through which the user locates and accesses information resources that are relevant to solving the problem at hand. In these tasks, documentary languages, summarization techniques, the description of the documentary object, etc., play a fundamental role." On the other hand, (Korfhage, 1997) states that "the location and presentation to a user of information relevant to an information need is expressed through a query." Information retrieval attempts to solve the problem of finding and organizing relevant documents that satisfy a user's information need, expressed in a specific query language.

As evident from the concepts above, information retrieval emerges as a distinct discipline and field of study and development. Although it shares certain similarities, it differs markedly from what is known as traditional data retrieval:

In data retrieval, the objects under consideration are known data structures. Their representation is based on a predefined, well-defined format with an implicit meaning for each element. For example, a table in a database storing instances of an organization's customers has a set of columns defining the attributes of all customers, and each row corresponds to a specific customer. Each element (attribute) has a known domain, and its semantics are clearly established. On the other hand, in information retrieval, the object of processing is essentially a text document, generally without structure (García, 2020).

In general, the problem of information retrieval must be addressed from two perspectives: computational and human. The computational perspective involves the construction of efficient data structures and algorithms that improve the quality of responses. The human perspective requires the study of user behavior and needs. From a general standpoint, the problem of information retrieval consists of the following elements (García, 2020):

A set of documents containing information of interest (on one or several topics).

Users with information needs that they present to the information retrieval system in the form of a query.

Databases, preferably vector-based or those supporting vector storage and operations. In this context, Neo4j is used as the database system, and queries are specified using the Cypher language, whose semantics are precise.

As a response, an information retrieval system returns references to relevant documents that satisfy the requested information demand, generally in the form of an ordered list.

To fulfill their objectives, these systems must perform some basic tasks, which are formulated as computational procedures:

Logical representation of documents. Some systems only store parts of documents, while others store them in their entirety.

Representation of the user's information need in the form of a query.
Evaluation against a query to establish the relevance of each document.
Ranking of documents considered relevant to form the "Solution" or "Response" set.
Presentation of the response to the user.

Figure 1. General Diagram of an Information Retrieval System Operation

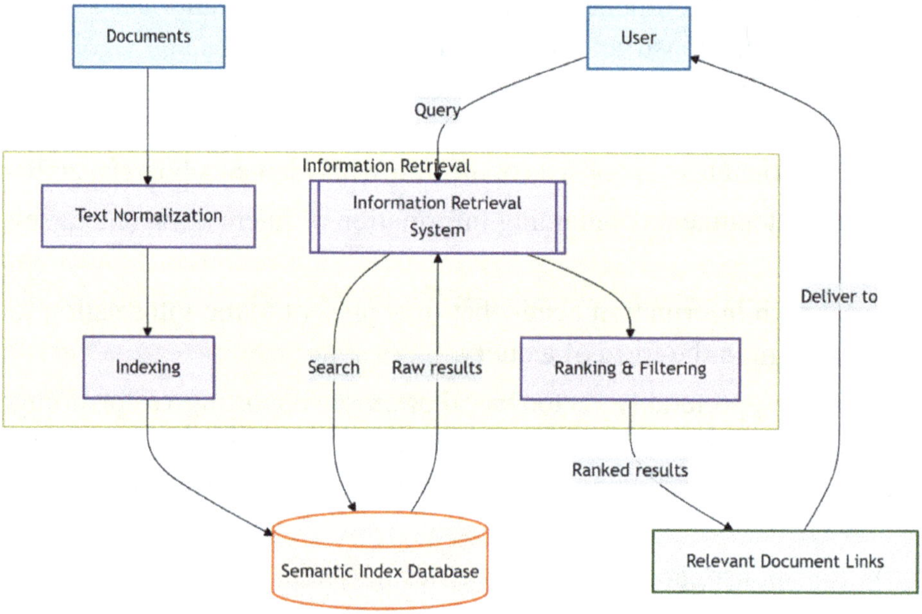

Semantic Index as a Fundamental Component to Ensure Efficiency in the Information Retrieval Process:

It is evident that traversing all documents in a collection each time a query is executed is an impractical solution and generally impossible. To avoid this, documents must be indexed in advance. Indexing is an operation aimed at identifying the terms that represent the content of a document and translating them into a computationally manageable form. When considering a text in natural language, it is easy to observe that not all words are equally representative of the document's semantics. Typically, nouns (or groups of words containing nouns) are the most representative components of a document in terms of content. Therefore, a subset of all words is selected to represent the content of a document. These selected words constitute the document index (García, 2020).

To select keywords, indexing must fulfill two different and potentially opposing objectives:

Be exhaustive, that is, use a sufficiently large number of terms from the document.

Be specific, that is, exclude generic terms that have little semantic value and increase the size of the index.

Once the general concept of a document index in an information retrieval system (IRS) has been reviewed, an implementation approach tailored to the needs of the software to be created must be established. There are many ways to approach the creation and population of this index. In this case, an approach based on the Vector Space Model is used for mapping the documents in the corpus, utilizing text embeddings generated by a Language Model. This easily enables users to query the system in natural language thanks to the calculation of cosine similarity between document vectors and query vectors. To achieve a better understanding of the topic, these concepts must be broken down:

Vector Space Model

The Vector Space Model represents documents and queries as vectors in a vector space where each dimension corresponds to a term in the vocabulary. The foundation of this model is that each term ti from the dictionary V is represented as a vector in a Euclidean vector space of dimension |V|, where each ti has all its components equal to 0 except the one corresponding to the dimension associated with ti in that space, which is equal to 1. Thus, in a 5-dimensional vector space, we would have rock = [1, 0, 0, 0, 0], pop = [0, 1, 0, 0, 0], jazz = [0, 0, 1, 0, 0], heavy = [0, 0, 0, 1, 0], and dance = [0, 0, 0, 0, 1].

In this way, any query q and any document dj∈D can be represented in the vector space as:

$$q = \sum_{i=1}^{|V|} w_{iq} * t_i$$

where wiq and wij are the weights assigned to the term ti for the query q and for each document dj, respectively.

This model assumes that two document vectors that are "close" in the vector space "deal" with the same topic. Therefore, to resolve query vectors, it will search for document vectors that are close in the vector space. Such similarity can be intuitively represented as the projection of one vector onto another, an idea expressed mathematically in terms of the dot product:

$$sim(dj,q)=dj\cdot q$$

Some advantages of the vector space model over the Boolean model lie in its more intuitive geometric interpretation and the ability to weight the representations of queries and documents (García, 2020).

Text Embeddings as an Evolution of the Vector Space Model

Embeddings are numerical representations in the form of vectors that encapsulate the meaning of a word, phrase, or document, enabling them to be processed by machine learning models. They are an essential and widely used tool in many natural language processing (NLP) tasks, such as text classification and generation, search and recommendation systems, and sentiment analysis (Espíndola, 2023).

There are two main types of embeddings: static and dynamic. The key difference lies in the fact that dynamic or contextualized embeddings are those in which the representation of a word varies depending on the context in which it appears, whereas static embeddings have a fixed representation (Huertas, 2019).

The primary techniques and algorithms used for generating static embeddings are Word2Vec and GloVe. Word2Vec involves the use of two key architectures: Continuous Bag of Words (CBoW), which predicts the center word based on the context of surrounding words, and Skip-gram, which works oppositely by predicting the surrounding words based on the center word (Mei, 2020). On the other hand, GloVe (Global Vectors) relies on word co-occurrence statistics in a corpus to learn word representations.

Conversely, some of the most used methods for generating dynamic embeddings include BERT, GPT-2, and Sentence Transformers, all of which are based on the Transformer architecture. This architecture modifies the encoder/decoder pattern of neural networks to implement a self-attention mechanism, which allows the model to process data in any order and focus on the most relevant parts of a sentence.

Language Models and Their Role in Generating Contextualized Text Embeddings

Language Models (LMs) are fundamental computational systems in natural languagc proccssing (NLP) that havc rcvolutionized how machines understand and generate text. Modern LMs, especially those based on Transformer architectures, act as deep representations of linguistic knowledge, capturing not only syntax and grammar but also semantics, context, and certain aspects of real-world knowledge.

The ability to generate rich, contextual representations makes LMs the cornerstone of modern Information Retrieval Systems (IRS). Their application directly impacts the two critical phases of the process:

Processing of the Document Collection (Semantic Indexing): By generating a contextualized embedding for each document or passage, the system moves beyond relying solely on keyword matching. Instead, it constructs a multidimensional semantic space where documents are positioned based on their deep meaning. Documents discussing the same topic but using different terminology (such as synonyms or technical jargon) will have vector representations that are close in this space.

Processing of the User Query: When a user expresses an information need in natural language, the same language model processes the query to generate a contextualized embedding that captures its semantic intent. This enables the system to understand complex, ambiguous, or colloquially expressed queries.

Cosine Similarity Formula in Information Retrieval

Cosine similarity is a mathematical measure that quantifies the degree of similarity between two vectors in a multidimensional space, regardless of their magnitude. This property makes it particularly valuable in information retrieval, where conceptual orientation (meaning) is more important than raw term frequency. Cosine similarity is based on the angle between vectors rather than their magnitude, offering crucial advantages for information retrieval, as it measures orientation rather than vector size, providing a result in the range of 0 (completely dissimilar) to 1 (completely identical). It captures thematic similarity even with different terminologies.

The complete retrieval process using cosine similarity is implemented in the following steps:

Vector Representation

Queries and documents are converted into contextualized embeddings.
Each dimension represents a semantic aspect learned by the model.

Similarity Calculation

$\cos(\theta)$ is calculated between the query vector and each document vector.
This is a computationally intensive operation that requires optimization.

Ranking and Retrieval

Documents are sorted in descending order of similarity value.
A minimum threshold is set to filter out non-relevant results.

Figure 2. Diagram of a semantic information retrieval system using language models and cosine similarity.

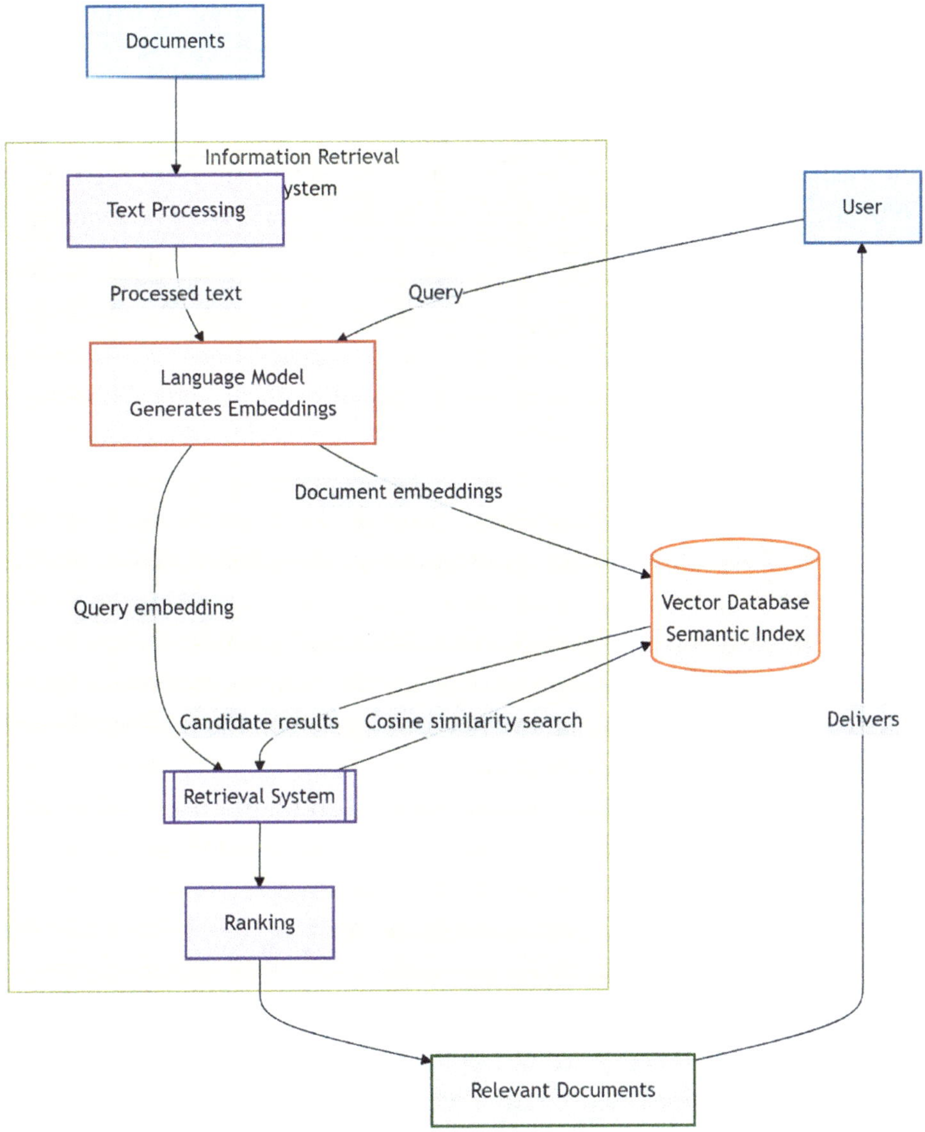

Evaluation of an Information Retrieval System

Information Retrieval Systems (IRS) are susceptible to evaluation, so that their users are in a position to assess their effectiveness and, in this way, gain confidence in them. Blair states that "it is the very nature of IRS that leads to their critical need for evaluation, just like any other field of work that aspires to be classified as a scientific field" (BLAIR, 1990). Baeza-Yates & Ribeiro-Neto states that "an IRS can be evaluated by various criteria, including: execution efficiency, effective data storage, effectiveness in information retrieval, and the range of features the system offers to the user" (YATES, 2002).

Every evaluation process implies an execution program to adequately organize the different tasks related to the main stages (Lara, 2012):

The description of the current state: It is carried out with the objective of searching for and compiling data using appropriate methods and techniques.
The critical analysis of said state: Where a diagnosis is issued about the conditions of what we wish to evaluate, with the purpose of determining whether changes have occurred based on the pre-established design, and in which direction.
The proposition stage: Which allows formulating a set of recommendations based on the results obtained in the previous stage.

Relevance, Precision, and Recall in the Evaluation of Information Retrieval

Information retrieval is defined as the discipline that, for a given query, finds relevant documents rather than simple pattern matches. This reveals a fundamental aspect: the relevance of the results is evaluated in relation to the information need, not the query itself. Broadly speaking, precision (P) is the fraction of retrieved documents that are relevant to a query and provides a measure of the system's "soundness." Precision is not concerned with the total number of documents the system considers relevant. This detail is explained by recall (R), which is defined as the fraction of "truly" relevant documents that are effectively retrieved and thus provides a measure of the system's "completeness." More formally, given the complete set of documents D and a query q, the subset TP $\subseteq$ D is defined as the set of true positives, i.e., retrieved documents that are truly relevant to query q. FP $\subseteq$ D is defined as the set of false positives, i.e., the set of retrieved documents that are not relevant to query q. Additionally, the subset FN $\subseteq$ D is defined as the set of documents that meet the user's needs but are not retrieved by the system. With this notation, precision and recall are defined (García, 2020).

These two measures are highly correlated. Empirically, it has been observed that high recall is accompanied by very low precision and vice versa; that is, an inverse relationship exists between the two measures. Since precision and recall have different advantages and disadvantages, a single evaluation measure that balances both has been defined. It is called the F1-Measure (F1-Score) or the harmonic mean of P and R (García, 2020):

This measure combines precision and recall into a single value ranging between 0 and 1. The interesting aspect of this metric is that a maximum F1 value corresponds to the best compromise between P and R, and its value will only be high when both measures have high values. If F1 = 0, no relevant documents have been retrieved, whereas if F1

= 1, all relevant documents and only these have been retrieved (García, 2020).

Figure 3. Different subsets of the document corpus that emerge after a user query and which must be evaluated to ensure the effectiveness of the system.

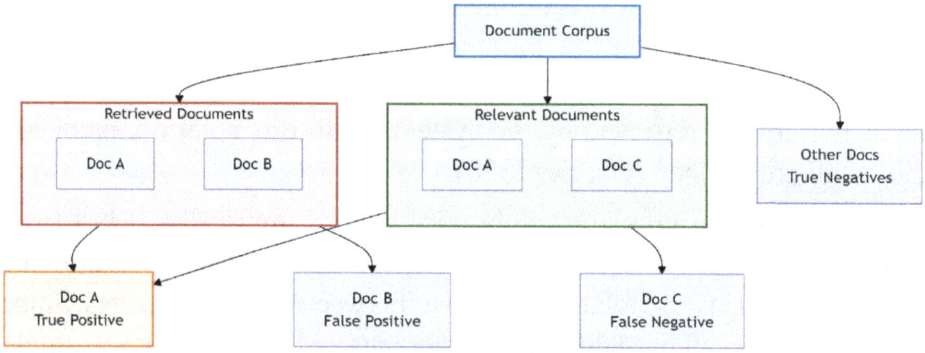

System Implementation Process and Technologies Used in Development

This section details the entire development process of the semantic search engine prototype and describes the technologies used to effectively achieve the stated objectives. The topics to be addressed include the creation of an ontology using Protégé as the foundation for building the semantic index, which will be stored in Neo4j. The characteristics of the language model used for generating embeddings are also outlined, along with how its use was enabled and the advantages it offers in this development.

Design and Construction of the System Ontology

This section details the process of designing and building the ontology that underpins the semantic retrieval system for the Cuban press. This work was based on the contextual description of the business, identifying classes, attributes, and relationships directly from business requirements and the documentary structure of the Cuban press. To ensure rigor in development, principles such as requirement specification, conceptualization, formalization, and iterative implementation were adopted, ensuring coherence between the theoretical model and the practical needs of the system.

The software Protégé was used for the creation of this ontology. Protégé is a free and open-source platform developed by Stanford University, specifically designed for the construction and management of ontologies. Its primary function is to serve as a comprehensive development environment that facilitates the creation, editing, visualization, and validation of ontologies through an intuitive interface and advanced tools. Protégé enables the representation of complex knowledge through standards such as OWL (Web Ontology Language) and RDF (Resource Description Framework), making it an essential tool for modeling knowledge domains with semantic precision.

Its importance in ontology development lies in democratizing access to ontological engineering, allowing both experts and non-technical users to collaborate in the formal structuring of concepts, relationships, and logical rules. This not only optimizes interoperability between intelligent systems and the semantic web but also drives critical applications in areas such as biomedicine, artificial intelligence, and knowledge management, where conceptual clarity and logical consistency are fundamental.

The first step in the development of this ontology was the identification and definition of the ontological classes that constitute the structural core of the system, as they allow capturing the complexity and richness of the Cuban journalistic domain. These classes were identified through a comprehensive business analysis, prioritizing those entities with the highest descriptive and semantic value to represent both key actors and managed documentary resources.

Secondly, the properties that describe and relate these ontological classes were identified. These properties are crucial for adding richness and context to the ecosystem being modeled. They are responsible for interconnecting the classes according to the roles interpreted by each within the system and how they collaborate and interact with one another. They also represent the descriptive and identifying properties held by each of the classes. These properties are divided into Object Properties and Data Properties.

Object Properties: Establish relationships between individuals within the ontology, enabling the linking of entities and representing logical connections between them.

Data Properties: Define the attributes or characteristics of the classes in the ontology. Each of the classes possesses a significant number of descriptive attributes, which have been derived based on business modeling.

Figure 4. Diagram of the system ontology created in Protégé and visualized with the OntoGraf plugin.

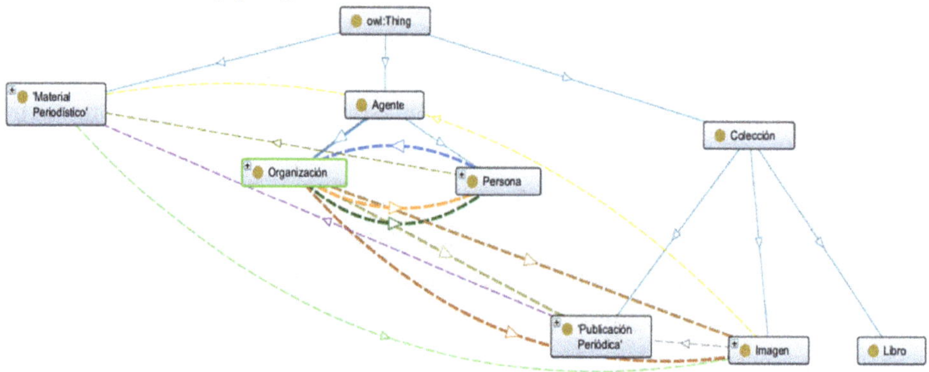

Construction of the System's Semantic Index and Data Loading Process

The semantic index operates as a knowledge graph in Neo4j, designed to integrate exclusively those entities and relationships that possess critical descriptive value in document retrieval. Its architecture replicates the fundamental ontological classes—Periodical Publication, Book, Image, Organization, Person, Collection, and Journalistic Material—derived from the business concept identification processes and ontology modeling described earlier. It is structured into two functional layers: target nodes, which represent the primary documents of the corpus and store both essential metadata (titles, identifiers, URI) and normalized vector representations obtained through an embedding process; and filtering nodes, which act as dynamic facets to constrain search sets through semantic relationships such as:isAuthor or:isPartOf.

In target nodes, embedding processes transform textual contents into numerical vectors. This involves the conversion of linguistic strings (titles, abstracts) into mathematical representations that capture semantic and contextual relationships. Filtering nodes, on the other hand, are limited to storing categorical and relational attributes that enable stratified navigation, without directly intervening in vector comparisons. The result is a dual index capable of executing hybrid searches: combining ontological filters to delimit contexts with vector operations to identify deep similarities.

Example of Cypher Code for Loading Data Into the Semantic Index in Neo4j

The following Cypher query handles the creation of nodes of type Publication, as well as the nodes related to said publication.

Figure 5. Cypher query for the creation of publication-type nodes within the semantic index.

```
MERGE (p:Publication {url:$url, title:$title, thumbnail:$url_thumbnail, identifier: randomUUID()})
ON CREATE SET p.title_embedding = $title_embedding, p.data_embedding = $data_embedding

MERGE (a:Author {name:$author})
MERGE (c:Collection {name:$collection})
MERGE (d:Date {day:$day ,month:$month,year:$year})

MERGE (p)-[:isPartOf]->(c)
MERGE (c)-[:contains]->(p)
MERGE (p)-[:isAuthor]->(a)
MERGE (p)-[:createdAt]->(d)

RETURN p,a,c,d
```

The code segment first describes the creation of a publication using the clause and the passing of its main attributes that distinguish this publication from others in the index. If it was successfully created, it now adds both the embedding attributes of the document's title and the embedding of its content. Following this, the nodes that have a relationship with said publication are created, and finally, the relationships between the publication and the nodes are established. It is worth noting that if the publication already exists in the index, a new publication will not be created; instead, the embedding attributes of the existing one will be updated, with the purpose of allowing the system to change current embeddings to others that provide greater semantic value if needed. The same applies to the nodes related to the publication.

Information Retrieval Process From the Semantic Index

Once the semantic index is populated, queries capable of integrating both metadata-based filters (typical of conventional database management systems) and, primarily, natural language searches are implemented. The core of the process lies in the latter modality, where user queries are transformed into normalized vectors using embedding techniques, replicating the preprocessing applied to documents during loading.

The similarity between the query vector and the stored vectors is calculated using the cosine similarity formula, which quantifies the angular proximity between them in the vector space, yielding values between 0 (total dissimilarity) and 1 (exact equivalence). This approach prioritizes documents whose embeddings reflect contextual alignment with the intent expressed in the query, even in the presence of lexical or syntactic variations.

Although Neo4j does not include native tools for generating embeddings, its Graph Data Science plugin provides optimized functions for cosine similarity calculation, speeding up the identification of matches in graphs with millions of nodes. The results are sorted in descending order by similarity score and can optionally be combined with filters.

Example Cypher Query for Information Retrieval From the Semantic Index

The following query is capable of assimilating both filter parameters and the embedding generated by the user's information request to find the documents with the highest similarity using these arguments.

Figure 6. Cypher query for retrieving information of type [publication] from the system's semantic index.

```
MATCH (p:Publication)-[:isAuthor]->(a:Author)
MATCH (p)-[:isPartOf]->(c:Collection)
MATCH (p)-[:createdAt]->(d:Date)

WHERE ($author_name IS NULL OR a.name = $author_name)
AND ($collection_name IS NULL OR c.name = $collection_name)
AND ($day IS NULL OR d.day = $day)
AND ($month IS NULL OR d.month = $month)
AND ($year IS NULL OR d.year = $year)

 WITH p,a,c,d, gds.similarity.cosine(p.title_embedding, $search_embedding) AS title_similarity, gds.similarity.cosine(p.
 data_embedding, $search_embedding) AS data_similarity

WITH p,a,c,d, CASE WHEN  title_similarity > data_similarity THEN title_similarity ELSE data_similarity END AS final_similarity

WHERE final_similarity > 0.6
RETURN p,a,c,d,final_similarity ORDER BY final_similarity DESC
```

Example of a Cypher Query to Establish the Relationship Between System Documents

It is possible to observe that similarity will not only exist between documents and a user-submitted query, but there is also similarity within the document corpus itself, where one document may share strong thematic similarities with others. Identifying and establishing these similarity relationships is crucial, as they significantly accelerate information search and retrieval. Instead of returning only documents directly related to the user's query in isolation, the system can also retrieve documents interrelated among themselves, enriching the search results. Here, cosine similarity comes into play again, but this time applied iteratively to calculate the relationship between one document and all others in the semantic index.

Figure 7. Cypher query to establish similarity relationships between documents in the corpus that share related themes with each other.

```
MATCH (p:Publication {url: $url_publication})
MATCH (n)
WHERE p <> n AND n.data_embedding IS NOT NULL
WITH p, n, gds.similarity.cosine(p.data_embedding, n.data_embedding) AS similarity
WHERE similarity > 0.7
CREATE (p)-[s:similarTo {score: similarity}]->(n)
RETURN p.title, n.title, s.score
```

All the queries previously presented enable both populating and retrieving data from the semantic index, allowing searches in natural language as well as through metadata filters to achieve the highest possible precision in the results provided to users.

Figure 8. Section of the system's semantic index stored in Neo4j corresponding to periodical publication-type documents and the relationships they share with other nodes.

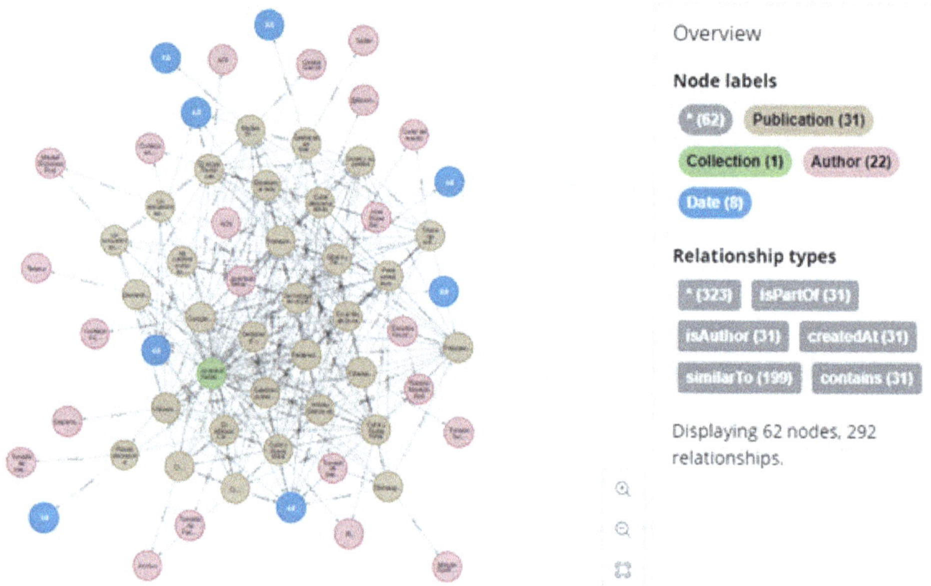

Pre-Trained Models Used as AI Services by the System

This section will address the artificial intelligence agents selected for the system. The platform where they can be obtained will be described, as well as some technical specifications of interest that justify the selection of these specific models.

Hugging Face as a Platform for Obtaining AI Models

This is a collaborative platform and open-source community that has established itself as a fundamental reference in the field of artificial intelligence. Its primary mission is to democratize access to pre-trained AI models, development tools, and datasets, facilitating the implementation of advanced machine learning systems for developers, researchers, and companies. The platform hosts the Model Hub, a centralized repository that offers thousands of pre-trained models, all accessible through libraries such as Transformers.

The practical utility of Hugging Face extends to seamless integrations with ecosystems like PyTorch, TensorFlow, and ONNX. This, coupled with detailed tutorials and active forums, positions the platform as a bridge between academic research and industrial applications, accelerating development cycles and promoting ethical standards through guidelines for the responsible use of AI.

Advantages of the Xenova Model Family on System Performance

The Xenova family on Hugging Face represents a collection of pre-trained models optimized for direct execution in web browsers, eliminating dependency on external servers thanks to their compatibility with ONNX (Open Neural Network Exchange). These models, accessible through the Transformer.js library, enable the integration of advanced AI capabilities—such as natural language processing or text generation—into lightweight and responsive web applications. Their design prioritizes computational efficiency, facilitating rapid inference even on devices with limited resources, and seamlessly integrates with both frontend and backend frameworks, such as Vue.js or Node.js. This approach democratizes the use of AI in decentralized environments, making it ideal for applications requiring data privacy or offline functionality. Xenova thus extends the reach of Hugging Face, bringing powerful models to scenarios where latency or traditional infrastructure costs would be prohibitive.

Transformers.js as an Interface to Access Model Functionalities

This library enables the execution of artificial intelligence models directly in the browser. By loading advanced models such as BERT, Transformers.js reduces latency by eliminating dependency on external servers for text analysis. This library offers full compatibility with models from the Xenova family and reduces complexity in model usage by providing an interface based on pipelines that are easy to program and understand. This ensures that responses are processed locally, enhancing user privacy and reducing the load on server infrastructure (Daniel David Gutierrez Cantillo, 2024).

Main AI Models Used as Agents by the System

Xenova/all-MiniLM-L6-v2

This is a contextual embedding model based on the Transformer architecture, an optimized variant of BERT, designed to convert sentences or paragraphs into 384-dimensional numerical vectors. Its technical core uses Transformer encoders to process text, extracting semantic patterns. This enables it to capture the global meaning of the text, not just individual words. Its primary function within the system is the generation of text embeddings, processing both the textual content of documents and user queries, and generating normalized embeddings to facilitate semantic searches through the calculation of cosine similarity between query and document embeddings.

Evaluation of the Semantic Search Engine for the Press Media Library

The evaluation of the Semantic Information Retrieval System is a fundamental step to determine its effectiveness and accuracy in retrieving documents based on the semantic relevance of queries. Here, a detailed analysis of the current state of the system is presented, describing the main resources stored in the semantic index, which will be one of the primary targets of the evaluations.

As part of the evaluation, quantitative criteria will be defined to measure the system's effectiveness in terms of precision, recall, and F1-score, applying these metrics to a set of representative queries. Specific examples of queries performed and the responses obtained will be included, along with a comparative analysis that demonstrates the quality and relevance of the results provided.

Current State of the System for Evaluation

The semantic retrieval system currently comprises a total corpus of 37 documents, distributed across 31 periodical publications, 5 images, and 1 book. These constitute the target resources for user queries and will be evaluated to measure the system's precision and recall.

Regarding periodical publications, a marked thematic heterogeneity is observed, as the included documents span diverse domains without a defined thematic grouping structure. This implies that, when performing semantic queries on the index, the system may return both highly relevant results and others of lower relevance due to the conceptual dispersion of the resources. However, this situation will not be replicated in the final corpus, which will include a larger number of documents that can be grouped into well-defined thematic sets. For example: economy, health, industry, and politics, enabling more precise and structured retrieval.

On the other hand, image-type resources exhibit considerable thematic homogeneity. This degree of uniformity contributes to the evaluation of the system's precision, as it allows verifying how images are retrieved in response to queries mentioning these historical figures or places. In this case, the system is expected to return images related to these elements with high precision, minimizing noise in the results.

Regarding the single book present in the corpus, its inclusion is key to evaluating the system's ability to discriminate between relevant and irrelevant queries. The fundamental test involves determining whether the system returns the book in response to queries related to its content and, conversely, avoids returning it when the query lacks any semantic connection to it.

Finally, the relevance thresholds used by the system to determine document retrieval are established. Given the small corpus size and the use of normalized embeddings derived from complete titles and descriptions (without token segmentation), a threshold of 0.6 has been defined for document retrieval in queries and a threshold of 0.7 for generating similarity relationships among resources within the semantic index. This approach ensures that the obtained results are effectively representative of the user's search intent, avoiding classification biases and improving the quality of information retrieval.

Results of the Evaluation Metrics on the System

This section will apply evaluation formulas to a set of example queries to quantify the system's effectiveness in information retrieval. The evaluation will primarily focus on periodical publication-type resources, as they are the most abundant and significant within the context of the press. To achieve this, the precision with which the system responds to each search will be analyzed. The results obtained through this evaluation will help identify strengths and areas for improvement in precision, recall, and the generation of similarity relationships within the semantic index, ensuring the system meets the expected quality criteria.

Publication Search

To measure the system's performance in retrieving publications, three user queries were executed, each focused on a distinct domain of information present in the corpus. The objective of this evaluation is to analyze how the system processes and returns relevant results based on the semantics of the stored texts. The selected queries were:

Cuban athletes worldwide
University of Oriente celebrates its day
Participation of Cuban doctors internationally

These queries cover diverse topics, allowing the evaluation of the system's precision across different contexts. The table below details the precision, recall, and F1-score metrics obtained in the evaluation of these queries. The interpretation of these values will help identify strengths and potential adjustments in the relevance threshold configuration to improve document retrieval in broader scenarios.

Table 1.

Query	Relevant Retrieved	Non-Relevant Retrieved	Relevant Not Retrieved	Precision	Recall	F1-Score
1	1	2	2	0.30	0.30	0.30
2	1	0	0	1.00	1.00	1.00
3	1	4	0	0.20	1.00	0.30
Average				0.50	0.76	0.53

After executing the queries, the obtained results show an average precision of 0.5, recall of 0.76, and F1-score of 0.53. Although precision is the lowest metric in this evaluation, this is consistent with the thematic heterogeneity of the publication corpus, which may lead to the retrieval of documents with lower relevance for certain queries.

On the other hand, recall shows a notably high value, as in most cases the system managed to retrieve all existing relevant documents, with only one exception where the entirety of expected responses was not achieved. This demonstrates that, despite the conceptual dispersion of the data, the system is capable of ensuring sufficient coverage of relevant information in the search.

The F1-score, which balances precision and recall, shows acceptable performance within the context of the current corpus. In conclusion, the results reflect that the system maintains adequate performance in the retrieval of publications, ensuring that users access pertinent resources within a document set of varied themes. The high recall suggests that the search engine is capable of correctly identifying documents related to the user's query, reinforcing the feasibility of its application in real-world scenarios.

Figure 9.

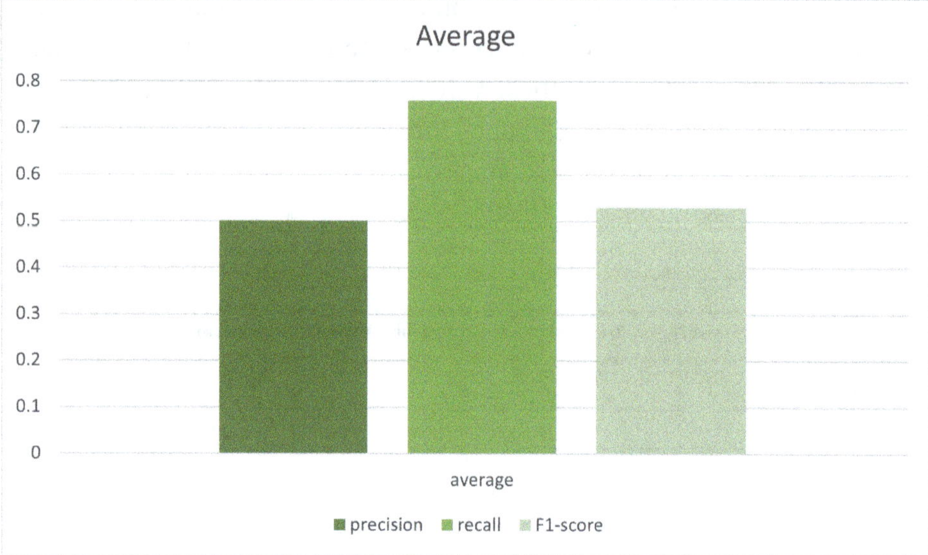

CONCLUSION

This work has materialized a concrete proposal to enhance information retrieval in the journalistic domain. Based on the identification of a real-world problem and the definition of clear objectives, a solution was developed that combines semantic approaches, emerging technologies, and sound design practices. The results and insights are summarized in the following conclusions.

Regarding the design of a software architecture capable of integrating DSpace with graph-based databases, partial but significant fulfillment was achieved. Although a direct connection to the press DSpace services was not possible due to its ongoing development phase, a modular and scalable architecture was successfully built, fully compatible with the Cypher language for interaction with Neo4j. The necessary structural models were developed to manage each type of resource instantiated in the semantic index, preparing the technical environment for future seamless integration. Consequently, once access to the definitive DSpace data is enabled, migration to the semantic index can be performed without system restructuring, requiring only the channeling of data through the pre-existing interfaces for processing and storage. This proactive preparation demonstrates strategic architectural foresight, oriented toward sustainability and system growth.

The integration of artificial intelligence services capable of processing natural language queries and generating normalized textual embeddings was fully achieved. This was made possible through the incorporation of Hugging Face's Transformers.js library, which enabled the local execution of models from the Xenova family, specifically designed for semantic representation tasks. This integration allowed the system to interpret user queries with significant contextual understanding, and through the use of cosine similarity calculations, it successfully identified the most semantically aligned documents. Furthermore, the same embedding model facilitated the establishment of internal relationships among resources within the semantic index, applying the same vector comparison logic, thereby adding an additional layer of precision in thematic identification and content grouping. This advancement not only improves retrieval quality but also demonstrates the practical utility of AI models in building truly intelligent search systems.

Finally, the implementation of a user-friendly graphical interface that minimizes the learning curve for users was also fully accomplished. Leveraging Vue.js as the primary frontend framework enabled the creation of a reactive, organized, and visually clear interface with short response times and an intuitive structure. By applying robust user-centered design principles and drawing inspiration from established search systems, a comfortable navigation experience was achieved. The interface not only displays results organized by resource type but also provides access to detailed metadata, exploration of similar resources, and an easy-to-use advanced filtering system. This set of features creates a versatile and accessible search environment, designed for users with varying levels of technological familiarity, and reinforces the system's role as an effective tool for document retrieval in real-world contexts.

The implementation of this prototype has demonstrated that it is possible to build semantic solutions tailored to local contexts without relying on complex infrastructures or proprietary platforms. The adopted approach—based on artificial intelligence, knowledge graph representation, and similarity search mechanisms—reflects a level of technical maturity that establishes a solid foundation for future evolution. Beyond the functional achievements, the development process has yielded significant insights into the modular integration of technologies, the semantic organization of content, and the importance of designing accessible user experiences. Collectively, this work contributes to the modernization of document retrieval systems in cultural and academic environments, paving the way for further research and applications that strengthen technological sovereignty in knowledge management.

REFERENCES

Baeza-Yates, R., & Ribeiro-Neto, B. (2011). *Modern information retrieval: The concepts and technology behind search* (2nd ed.). Addison-Wesley.

Blair, D. C. (1990). *Language and representation in information retrieval.* Elsevier Science Publishers.

Croft, W. B. (1987). Approaches to intelligent information retrieval. *Information Processing & Management, 23*(4), 249–254.

Espíndola, G. (2023, March 3). ¿Qué son los embeddings y cómo se utilizan en la inteligencia artificial con python? Medium. https://gustavo-espindola.medium.com/qu%C3%A9-son-los-embeddings-y-c%C3%B3mo-se-utilizan-en-la-inteligencia-artificial-con-python-45b751ed86a5

García, B. T. (2020). *Introducción a la recuperación de información.* Universitat Oberta de Catalunya.

Huertas, A. (2019, October 14). Clasificación de textos state-of-the-art con embeddings contextuales. Medium. https://afhuertas.medium.com/clasificaci%C3%B3n-de-textos-state-of-art-con-embeddings-contextuales-58cb29767669

Korfhage, R. R. (1997). *Information storage and retrieval.* Wiley Computer Publishing.

Lara, A. V. (2012). Evaluación del sistema de recuperación de información de la herramienta de gestión bibliotecaria ABCD versión 1.0.6 [Undergraduate thesis, Universidad Central "Marta Abreu" de Las Villas]. https://dspace.uclv.edu.cu/items/e9a5aae6-17f6-45f1-b510-179a9f41029c

Mei, T. (2020, September 8). From static embedding to contextualized embedding. Medium. https://ted-mei.medium.com/from-static-embedding-to-contextualized-embedding-fe604886b2bc

Mercado, S. A., Gutiérrez, D. D., & Henríquez, D. D. (2024). SafeRecords, una solución de software para la anonimización de registros médicos usando modelos de reconocimiento de entidades [Undergraduate project, Universidad del Norte].

Yates, B. (2002). *Modelos de recuperación de información.* Addison-Wesley.

Chapter 8
Image Classification-Based Detection System of the Mite (Phyllocoptruta oleivora) Using Machine Learning Models

Everardo L. Huerta-Lopez
Autonomous University of Tamaulipas, Mexico

Ana B. Rios-Alvarado
Autonomous University of Tamaulipas, Mexico

Tania Y. Guerrero-Meléndez
http://orcid.org/0000-0003-1834-2431
Autonomous University of Tamaulipas, Mexico

Jose L. Martinez-Rodriguez
http://orcid.org/0000-0002-1276-6957
Autonomous University of Tamaulipas, Mexico

DOI: 10.4018/979-8-3373-1360-3.ch008

ABSTRACT

This work presents an automatic detection system for the mite Phyllocoptruta oleivora using deep learning image classification. Three convolutional archi- tectures (a base CNN, MobileNetV2, and ResNet50) are compared under a homogeneous preprocessing, transfer learning, and data augmentation protocol. From a set of images captured in the field and validated by experts, the results show that a lightweight model such as MobileNetV2 offers the best balance between performance, robustness, and computational efficiency for deployment in agricultural environments. On the other hand, ResNet50 is presented as a competitive alternative when greater computing power is available. Design con- siderations, limitations, and future directions oriented toward mobile applications and monitoring platforms in precision agriculture are discussed.

1 INTRODUCTION

Agriculture is an essential activity for societal development and has existed for generations. Citrus farming in Mexico is particularly important for both domestic con- sumption and export, generating employment and development in various regions and involving approximately 67,000 Mexican families (Valencia Sandoval & Duana Avila, 2019). This activity provides multiple social and economic benefits. However, it constantly faces threats, with pests being a major concern. One example is the citrus mite (Phyllocoptruta oleivora), which signifi- cantly affects fruit productivity and quality. Due to its tiny size and rapid reproduction rate, this pest represents a constant challenge for producers (Landeros et al., 2003).

Traditionally, farmers have relied on expert visual inspections to detect pests, a process that is slow, costly, and often subjective. In response, technological advances—particularly in computer vision, digital image processing, and machine learning—provide new opportunities for automating crop phytosanitary monitoring. These tools help develop models that identify visual patterns associated with dis- eases and pests, enabling more accurate, rapid, and data-driven decision-making (Mittal et al., 2024). Within the framework of Agriculture 4.0, the integration of technologies like smart sensors, data analytics, robotics, and artificial intelligence aims to optimize produc- tion processes. The use of machine learning for automatic pest detection, in particular, contributes to more sustainable, efficient, and profitable crop management (Wang et al., 2025).

This chapter presents the development of an automatic detection system for the citrus mite (Phyllocoptruta oleivora). The system utilizes machine learning to identify the presence of the mite from digital images of crop leaves, serving as a potential tool to enhance traditional pest management practices. A key feature of this study is its specific agricultural context, employing a novel dataset of images captured directly from citrus fields in Tamaulipas, Mexico.

The core of our investigation involves a comparative analysis of three distinct convolutional neural network (CNN) architectures: a custom-built CNN, along with the pre-trained models ResNet50 and MobileNetV2. The objective is to identify the model best suited for this application. To ensure a fair and meaningful comparison, all models were trained, validated, and tested on the same dataset and under consistent conditions. This structured evaluation offers clear insights into the practical trade-offs and advantages of each architecture for real-world agricultural monitoring (Lara-Rodríguez et al., 2023; García-Palomera et al., 2024).

2 RELATED WORK

The use of machine learning models has gained prominence over the last decade, having a significant impact on agriculture, particularly in image classification tasks and in the detection of pests and diseases (Waqas et al., 2025). These activities are part of Agriculture 4.0, a trend that promotes the digitalization and automation of agricultural processes through technologies such as computer vision, sensors, and neural networks (García Palomera et al., 2024; Addanki et al., 2025).

Among the various machine learning techniques proposed for the agricultural domain, those based on deep neural networks—especially pre-trained models and foun- dational architectures like Convolutional

Neural Networks (CNNs), MobileNetV2, and ResNet50—are particularly prominent (Rai & Bansal, 2025; El Sakka et al., 2025).

CNNs have proven effective in identifying complex visual patterns in agricultural field images. Architectures such as CNNs extract relevant features at different levels of depth, making them useful for tasks such as binary or multiclass classification of leaf, stem, or fruit images (Lu et al., 2021; Lin et al., 2025).

Models such as MobileNetV2 are widely used for efficient real-time image classifi- cation. This model is capable of recognizing and classifying multiple categories within an image, making it an attractive option for farmers through mobile applications in the field, where fast and reliable processing is required (Paz Garcia & Pachay Ruiz, 2024; Balasooriya et al., 2025).

ResNet50 employs a deep residual network architecture that has been shown to be effective in agricultural studies for managing complex scenarios and improving accuracy (Mulay et al., 2025).

In citrus, the detection of *Huanglongbing* (HLB) has been demonstrated using deep networks with transfer learning, highlighting field feasibility and the importance of data curation, standardized preprocessing, and augmentation; furthermore, the use of macro and per-class metrics is recommended (Gómez-Flores et al., 2022). In stone fruit, CNNs have been val- idated under rigorous experimental protocols (stratified splits, cross-validation, and overfitting control), and in avocado a robust and portable neural-network-based pro- totype has been documented for on-device inference (Lara-Rodríguez et al., 2023; García-Palomera et al., 2024).Taken together, these studies support the use of convolutional architectures with transfer learning and data augmentation for agricultural pests and set the stage for the analysis presented below. Several studies have applied these techniques for the identification of both pests and diseases. However, the detection of the citrus mite *Phyllocoptruta oleivora* has received little attention, mainly due to its small size and the difficulty of capturing its presence in field images.

Due to the limited research on the citrus mite, a comparison of machine learn- ing models is required, particularly for regions like Tamaulipas which exhibit unique climatic features.

3 MATERIALS AND METHODS

This research contributes to the field of computer vision applied to precision agri- culture, specifically in the automatic detection of the mite *Phyllocoptruta oleivora*. This study follows a methodology that encompasses image acquisition, labeling, and subsequent analysis. The proposed methodology is illustrated in Figure 1, and its constituent stages are described in detail below.

3.1 Image Acquisition and Labeling

The initial phase consisted of dataset collection, a critical step since the quality and diversity of the images directly influence the models' generalization capacity. For this work, the image dataset was acquired directly by the authors using devices specifically suited for field capture. The dataset considers the following conditions:

- **Resolution and quality:** The images were captured using the camera of an iPhone 13 smartphone at a resolution of 12 MP (3024 × 4032), providing sufficient sharpness to highlight important features of the pest or agricultural condition.

Figure 1. Proposed methodology for image classification

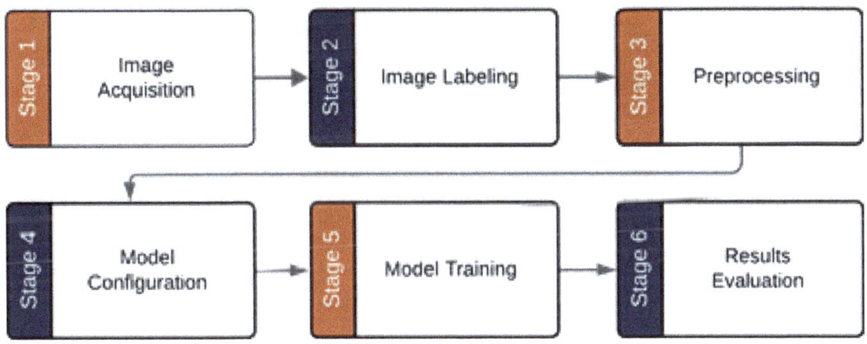

• **Labeling:** The images were manually classified by an expert into their respective categories: *healthy fruit* and *mites*.
• **Data augmentation:** In experiment version v1, additional transformations were applied, including rotations, translations, zoom, blurring, Gaussian noise, and contrast variations. These were carried out through three parallel augmentation branches, according to the function make v1 augmented ds defined in the code (Kusrini et al., 2020).

An original image bank was developed, consisting of 3,154 images collected and labeled in the field, later reviewed and validated by plant health experts to ensure labeling reliability. The images were classified into two main categories:

• **Healthy fruit:** 1,610 images (51%) Figure 2

Figure 2. Healthy fruit image

• **Mites:** 1,544 images (49%) Figure 3

Figure 3. Mite image

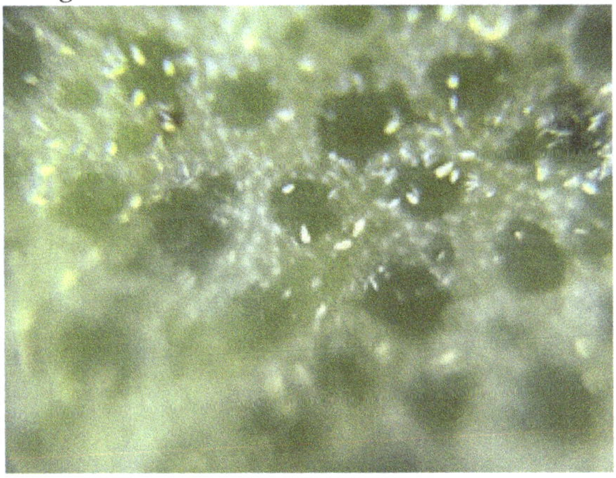

The balance between the two classes is appropriate, providing robust train- ing and evaluation of machine learning models. A balanced dataset prevents bias toward a dominant class, enabling accurate assessment of the performance of different architectures.

Regarding, the dataset split and experimental conditions, to standardize the training, validation, and testing processes, the following conditions were applied:

- 70% Training: 2,207 images
- 20% Validation: 631 images
- 10% Testing: 316 images
- Same data source and split proportions across all versions
- Each experiment version (v0, v1, and v2) was trained for 60 epochs, totaling three configurations per model
- Equivalent image size (224×224 pixels) and preprocessing parameters were main- tained
- Uniform batch size, binary cross-entropy loss function, and Adam optimizer were used as the standard configuration

3.2 Image Preprocessing

Preprocessing ensured that the input data were compatible with the network architectures (Sánchez Martínez, 2018).

- **Normalization:** Pixel values were scaled to the range [0,1]. For ResNet50 and MobileNetV2, architecture-specific preprocessing functions were applied, first scal- ing to [0,255].
- **Resizing:** Images were resized to 224×224 pixels, the size required by ResNet50 and MobileNetV2.
- **Color conversion:** The RGB color space was used.
- **Noise reduction:** Gaussian and median filters were applied during augmentation.

3.3 Model Design and Configuration

Three main architectures were implemented using specific functions in the code (build cnn, build resnet50, build mobilenetv2):

- **Custom CNN:** A baseline convolutional network with Conv2D, MaxPooling2D, and Dense layers, used as a reference for comparison.
- **ResNet50:** A model pretrained on ImageNet, initially configured in *frozen* mode (feature extraction) and subsequently fine-tuned in version v2.
- **MobileNetV2:** A model optimized for mobile devices, also with pretrained weights on ImageNet. In v2, fine-tuning of the last 40 layers was enabled, and an alpha=1.0 factor was applied to control the network width.

Across all architectures, hyperparameters such as learning rate, batch size, and dropout probability were configured, varying according to the experimental version.

3.4 Model Training

Training consisted of optimizing the neural network weights to minimize the loss function.

- **Loss function:** Binary cross-entropy was used, with the option of *label smoothing*.
- **Optimizers:** Adam was the main optimizer, with learning rates tailored to each version (from 10^{-3} to 10^{-5} in MobileNetV2 fine-tuning).
- **Regularization:** Techniques such as dropout and L2 penalty were applied to the custom CNN.
- **Monitoring:** EarlyStopping was implemented on validation loss to stop training if no improvement was observed over several epochs.

Three experimental configurations were carried out:

- **Version v0:** Baseline training without augmentation.
- **Version v1:** With data augmentation (*blur*, *noise*, *contrast*).
- **Version v2:** Hyperparameter tuning, with stronger regularization in the CNN, *dropout* in ResNet50, and fine-tuning in MobileNetV2.

3.5 Evaluation and Validation

Evaluation was performed on an independent test set using standard classification metrics.

- **Metrics:** Accuracy, precision, recall, and F1-score, reported both macro-averaged and per class.
- **Confusion matrix:** Used to analyze the most frequently misclassified categories.
- **ROC curve and AUC:** Applied for binary classification (*healthy fruit* vs. *mites*).
- **Threshold calibration:** The decision threshold was adjusted on the validation set to maximize the F1-score, instead of using the fixed threshold of 0.5.
- **Automated reporting:** Each model exported a .txt file with detailed metrics and a metrics summary.csv file with the global comparison.

4 RESULTS AND DISCUSSION

Three architectures (CNN, MobileNetV2, and ResNet50) were evaluated under three experimental configurations (v0, v1, v2), each trained for 60 epochs, keeping the data split, image size, and preprocessing constant. The global and per-class metrics obtained are presented below.

Table 1. Summary by model and version (60 epochs): Accuracy, F1 macro, Precision and Recall per class

Model	Ver.	Accuracy	F1 macro	Prec. Mites	Prec. Healthy	Rec. Mites	Rec. Healthy
	v0	0.9652	0.9652	0.95	0.9808	0.9806	0.9503
CNN	v1	0.962	0.962	0.9554	0.9686	0.9677	0.9565
	v2	0.9114	0.9113	0.915	0.908	0.9032	0.9193
	v0	0.9367	0.9365	0.9655	0.9123	0.9032	0.9689
ResNet50	v1	0.9747	0.9747	0.9804	0.9693	0.9677	0.9814
	v2	0.5063	0.3418	0.3333	0.508	0.0065	0.9876
	v0	0.9304	0.9304	0.9236	0.9371	0.9355	0.9255
MobileNetV2	v1	0.9335	0.9332	0.9786	0.8977	0.8839	0.9814
	v2	0.9873	0.9873	0.9935	0.9816	0.9806	0.9938

Global performance (Accuracy and *F1 macro*). The best configuration was MobileNetV2 v2, with *accuracy* = 0.9873 and *F1 macro* = 0.9873, followed by ResNet50 v1 (0.9747 for both metrics) and CNN v0/v1 (0.9652 and 0.9620). On average (v0–v2), MobileNetV2 achieved the highest mean *accuracy* (≈ 0.950), followed by CNN (≈ 0.946), and further behind, ResNet50 (≈ 0.806), evidencing the greater stability of MobileNetV2 across versions.

Per-class analysis. With 60 epochs, MobileNetV2 v2 achieved the best simulta- neous per-class maxima: *precision* on "Mites" = 0.9935 and *recall* on "Healthy fruit" = 0.9938, in addition to *precision* on "Healthy fruit" = 0.9816 and *recall* on "Mites" = 0.9806 (tied with CNN v0). ResNet50 v1 remained highly competitive at the per- class level (e.g., *precision* on "Mites" = 0.9804; *recall* on "Healthy fruit" = 0.9814), but ResNet50 v2 showed a severe collapse in the "Mites" class (*recall* = 0.0065), suggesting decision imbalance or extreme overfitting in that configuration.

Implications. The results indicate that deeper fine-tuning of MobileNetV2 in v2 was decisive for achieving the best overall performance, while ResNet50 requires more careful control of *early stopping* and learning rate to avoid instabilities in prolonged training. From an operational perspective, MobileNetV2 v2 emerges as the preferred option for deployment due to its combination of maximum *accuracy/F1* and robust per-class performance.

5 LIMITATIONS

Although there have been technological advances in the fields of machine learning and computer vision, certain limitations remain when applying these techniques in real agricultural environments.

First, the main difficulty lies in the quality and diversity of the images. Factors such as uncontrolled lighting, variations in focus, the presence of unwanted particles, stains, or overlapping with other pests make it difficult to determine the presence of the mite *(Phyllocoptruta oleivora).*

Second, another challenge in data acquisition is the scarcity of public databases and class imbalance within existing datasets, as well as variations in image resolution, which restrict the training capacity of models and their ability to generalize.

Third, each machine learning model has its own limitations. CNNs can be fast but restricted; MobileNetV2 is ideal for real-time classification and mobile applica- tions, although it can be sensitive to low-contrast or very low-resolution images; while ResNet50 requires longer training times and greater computational resources.

Model performance shows significant variation depending on the selection of hyperparameters, highlighting the need to compare results under homogeneous and controlled conditions.

Automated pest detection presents multiple challenges. The most significant diffi- culties in automatic pest detection systems are attributed to a variety of factors that affect both training quality and model prediction. In the case of the mite *(Phyllo- coptruta oleivora)*, these challenges arise from its microscopic size and limited visual features.

The main problems encountered in automatic image classification are related to:

- Insufficient resolution or blurring, which prevents distinguishing the mite's main characteristics, especially in uncontrolled environments or images collected in the field.
- The presence of similar elements such as impurities, stains, or leaf textures, leading to false positives mistakenly identified as pests.
- Variations in characteristics such as lighting, capture angle and camera type, which reduce the generalization capacity of the models.
- Incorrect labeling and class imbalance, affecting training quality by introducing noise into the classes or by producing unbalanced data in the classes.

The creation of a dataset or image bank requires a rigorous selection of models and parameters, along with comparisons across architectures capable of adequately addressing the conditions described in this work.

6 CONCLUSIONS

This work presented the development of an automatic detection system for the mite *Phyllocoptruta oleivora* through image classification with machine learning models. The main contributions include: (i) the creation of a balanced dataset with field- collected images validated by plant health experts, and (ii) the systematic comparison of three architectures (CNN, MobileNetV2, and ResNet50) trained under the same data partition and preprocessing scheme, across three versions (v0, v1, v2), each with 60 epochs.

In global terms, the best configuration was achieved with MobileNetV2 v2, reaching the highest values of *accuracy* and *F1 macro* (both = 0.9873), demonstrat- ing excellent generalization capacity when applying deeper fine-tuning. As runner-up, ResNet50 v1 showed competitive performance (*accuracy* = 0.9747, *F1 macro* = 0.9747). The CNN proved solid in v0–v1 (0.9652 and 0.9620), although it declined in v2 (0.9113), suggesting great- er sensitivity to hyperparameter configuration during extended training.

At the class level, MobileNetV2 v2 simultaneously achieved outstanding metrics: *precision* on "Mites" = 0.9935 and *recall* on "Healthy fruit" = 0.9938, as well as *precision* on "Healthy fruit" = 0.9816 and *recall* on "Mites" = 0.9806 (the latter tied with CNN v0). ResNet50 v1 also performed strongly per class (*precision* on "Mites" = 0.9804; *recall* on "Healthy fruit" = 0.9814). In contrast, ResNet50 v2 collapsed in the "Mites" class (*recall* = 0.0065), highlighting the need to control *early stopping*, learning rate, and fine-tuning depth.

Overall, the findings suggest that MobileNetV2 v2 is the preferred option for deployment due to its combination of high global performance and computational efficiency, while ResNet50 v1 remains a robust alternative when prioritizing a deeper network with strong per-class performance. Future work will focus on expanding the dataset, exploring adaptive augmentation schemes, and strengthening regularization and learning rate control to stabilize fine-tuning in deep architectures.

REFERENCES

Addanki, U. K., Devareddi, R. B., Kamarajugadda, K. K., Pavani, M., & Gera, P. (2025). Machine learning-powered intrusion detection system for agriculture 4.0: Securing the next generation of farming. *International Journal of Innovative Research and Scientific Studies*, *8*(1), 1964–1978. DOI: 10.53894/ijirss.v8i1.4840

Balasooriya, R., Adithya, E., Gunarathne, M., Silva, T., & Lokuliyana, S. Wije- siri, P.: An explainable deep learning framework for coconut disease detection using mobilenetv2, super-resolution, and grad-cam++. In: *2025 International Conference on Data Science and Its Applications (ICoDSA)*, pp. 985–990 (2025). IEEE DOI: 10.1109/ICoDSA67155.2025.11157166

El Sakka, M., Ivanovici, M., Chaari, L., & Mothe, J. (2025). A review of cnn applications in smart agriculture using multimodal data. *Sensors (Basel)*, *25*(2), 472. DOI: 10.3390/s25020472 PMID: 39860841

G'omez-Flores, W., Garza-Saldan˜a, J. J., & Varela-Fuentes, S. E. (2022). A huanglongbing detection method for orange trees based on deep neural networks and transfer learning. *IEEE Access : Practical Innovations, Open Solutions*, *10*, 116686–116696. DOI: 10.1109/ACCESS.2022.3219481

García-Palomera, J., Verduzco-Ram'ırez, J., & Barrios-Hern'andez, C. (2024). Garc'ıa- Virgen, J., Mor'an-L'opez, L.: Prototipo para la detecci'on de aran˜a cristalina en cultivos de aguacate aplicando redes neuronales. *Revista ELECTRO*, *46*(1), 49–54.

Kusrini, K., Suputa, S., Setyanto, A., Agastya, I. M. A., Priantoro, H., Chandramouli, K., & Izquierdo, E. (2020). Chan- dramouli, K., Izquierdo, E.: Data augmentation for automated pest classification in mango farms. *Computers and Electronics in Agriculture*, *179*, 105842. DOI: 10.1016/j.compag.2020.105842

Landeros, J., Balderas, J., Badii, M.H., S´anchez, V.M., Guerrero, E., Flores, A.E.: Distribuci´on espacial y fluctuaci´on poblacional de phyllocoptruta oleivora (ashmead)(acari: Eriophyidae) en c´ıtricos de gu¨emez, tamaulipas. Acta zool´ogica mexicana (89), 129–138 (2003)

Lara-Rodríguez, L. D., L'opez-Mel'endez, E., & Castellanos-Corzo, A. L. (2023). Com- paraci'on de redes neuronales convolucionales (rnc) para la detecci'on de plagas en el cultivo del durazno en departamento norte de santander, colombia. *Informador T'ecnico*, *87*(2), 150–164. DOI: 10.23850/22565035.5805

Lin, L. H.-M., Lien, W.-C., Cheng, C. Y.-T., Lee, Y.-C., Lin, Y.-T., Kuo, C.-C., Lai, Y.-T., & Peng, Y.-T. (2025). A rapid household mite detection and classification technology based on artificial intelligence-enhanced scanned images. *Internet of Things : Engineering Cyber Physical Human Systems*, *29*, 101484. DOI: 10.1016/j.iot.2024.101484

Lu, J., Tan, L., & Jiang, H. (2021). Review on convolutional neural network (cnn) applied to plant leaf disease classification. *Agriculture*, *11*(8), 707. DOI: 10.3390/agriculture11080707

Mittal, M., Gupta, V., Aamash, M., & Upadhyay, T. (2024). Machine learning for pest detection and infestation prediction: A comprehensive review. *Wiley Interdisciplinary Reviews. Data Mining and Knowledge Discovery*, *14*(5), 1551. DOI: 10.1002/widm.1551

Mulay, V.M., Rao, M., Kumar, K.V.: Ensemble based deep learning models for crop and weed differentiation. Measurement: Digitalization, 100009 (2025)

Paz Garcia, R. C., & Pachay Ruiz, S. A. Sistema web y m'ovil para la detecci'on de nivel de incidencia y severidad de la plaga coptoborus ochromactonus en planta- ciones de balsa en la finca digna elizabeth. PhD thesis, Universidad Agraria del Ecuador (2024)

Rai, R., & Bansal, P. Smart agriculture 4.0: Precision crop disease identification and classification using advanced ai techniques. In: *International Conference on Recent Advancements and Modernisations in Sustainable Intelligent Technologies and Applications (RAMSITA 2025)*, pp. 583 598 (2025). Atlantis Press DOI: 10.2991/978-94-6463-716-8_45

Sánchez Martínez, M.: Detecci´on de personas mediante t´ecnicas de aprendizaje autom´atico: Svm y cnn (2018)

Valencia Sandoval, K., Duana Avila, D.: Los c´ıtricos en m´exico: an´alisis de eficiencia t´ecnica. An´alisis econ´omico 34(87), 269–283 (2019)

Wang, S., Xu, D., Liang, H., Bai, Y., Li, X., Zhou, J., Su, C., & Wei, W. (2025). Advances in deep learning applications for plant disease and pest detection: A review. *Remote Sensing (Basel), 17*(4), 698. DOI: 10.3390/rs17040698

Waqas, M., Naseem, A., Humphries, U.W., Hlaing, P.T., Dechpichai, P., Wang- wongchai, A.: Applications of machine learning and deep learning in agriculture: A comprehensive review. Green Technologies and Sustainability, 100199 (2025)

Chapter 9
Integration of Large Language Models and Knowledge Graphs in Semantic Web:
A Bibliometric Analysis of Scientific Production

Francisco Isaí Morales-Sáenz
http://orcid.org/0000-0001-9740-149X
Autonomous University of Tamaulipas, Mexico

ABSTRACT

The convergence between Large Language Models (LLMs) and Knowledge Graphs (KGs) represents an emerging paradigm in artificial intelligence that combines natural language processing capabilities with structured reasoning. This study presents a comprehensive bibliometric analysis of 230 documents indexed in Web of Science, characterizing the intellectual structure, scientific production trends, and thematic evolution of the field. Results reveal exponential growth with an annual rate of 48.12%, leadership of Chinese institutions, and thematic structuring into six main clusters: reasoning on graphs with LLMs, semantic data mining, entity linking, decision-making systems, domain knowledge extraction, and rec-

DOI: 10.4018/979-8-3373-1360-3.ch009

ommender systems. Theoretical implications reveal the synthesis between connectionist and symbolic approaches, materializing the Semantic Web vision through natural language interfaces.

INTRODUCTION

The convergence between natural language models (LLM) and knowledge graphs (KG), documented in multiple studies (Villazón-Terrazas et al., 2021, 2022, 2023, 2025), represents one of the most significant advances in contemporary artificial intelligence. This synergistic integration combines the natural language understanding and generation capabilities of LLMs with the structured representation and logical reasoning of KGs, creating more robust, explainable, and efficient AI systems (Cai et al., 2025; Dehal et al., 2025). The Semantic Web, originally conceived as an extension of the World Wide Web that enables machines to understand and interpret data meaningfully, finds in this technological fusion a catalyst to materialize its original vision (Silva & Terra, 2023). LLMs, particularly generative models such as GPT-4 and its variants, have demonstrated exceptional capabilities in natural language processing tasks, while KGs provide the ontological and semantic structure necessary to represent knowledge in a formal and queryable manner (Li & Xu, 2024; Yang et al., 2025).

Analysis of specialized literature reveals that various authors have addressed this integration from multiple methodological and applied perspectives. Cai et al. (2025) identified three main fusion strategies that have emerged in recent literature: KG-enhanced LLMs (KEL), where knowledge graphs enrich the capabilities of language models; LLM-enhanced KGs (LEK), where LLMs improve the construction and completeness of graphs; and collaborative LLMs and KGs (LKC), which represents a bidirectional collaboration approach. This taxonomy provides a conceptual framework for understanding the different approaches that researchers are adopting to integrate these technologies. Complementarily, Liu et al. (2025) conducted a review on the use of LLMs for knowledge graph embedding, demonstrating how pre-trained models with parameters in the order of hundreds of millions substantially improve knowledge representation tasks. For their part, Dehal et al. (2025) highlighted the reciprocal relationship between both technologies, where LLMs automate KG construction through entity recognition, relation extraction, and schema generation, while KGs provide LLMs with factual contextualization and structured reasoning capabilities.

Moreover, authors such as Yang et al. (2025) proposed a systematic four-layer framework encompassing data, model, technology, and application dimensions to analyze this integration, addressing both the capabilities and limitations of LLMs in natural language processing and the strengths and challenges of KGs in knowledge representation (Tiwari et al., 2024; Ortiz-Rodríguez et al., 2023). This proposal represents a significant advance toward the systematization of knowledge in this emerging field, providing a conceptual structure that facilitates comparison between different approaches and the identification of research opportunities.

Existing literature reviews have documented specific applications in various domains that demonstrate the transformative potential of this technological integration. In the construction sector, Zheng et al. (2025) explored the automation of contract review through LLM-enhanced KGs, demonstrating that this integration overcomes the limitations of methods based solely on traditional natural language processing, which typically were limited to text classification or segmented label prediction. Meanwhile, Liang et al. (2025) highlighted how LLMs can enhance KGs in the era of Human-AI collaboration, facilitating the extraction and reuse of domain knowledge, a crucial aspect for success in the design of complex knowledge-intensive products.

In the healthcare field, applications have demonstrated particular relevance due to the complex and multidimensional nature of medical data. Al Khatib et al. (2024) conducted a review on patient-centered knowledge graphs (PCKGs), which integrate various types of health data to provide holistic and multidimensional understanding, enabling more personalized and effective care. This approach represents a paradigm shift toward healthcare systems where the integration of information from multiple sources facilitates more accurate diagnoses and personalized treatments. Similarly, Serra et al. (2025) updated knowledge on KGs and their applications in drug discovery, comparing existing graph types and their relevance in the pharmaceutical field, evidencing how these technologies are accelerating the development process of new drugs through the identification of non-obvious relationships between chemical compounds, biological targets, and mechanisms of action.

Data processing constitutes a central axis in this technological convergence, representing one of the most significant challenges in the Big Data era. Dey (2024) reviewed how KGs drive data processing for business intelligence, enabling the linking of disparate application data and processing large volumes of unstructured data such as emails, call logs, social networks, and news to derive essential elements for complex organizational decision-making. This capability for integrating heterogeneous data represents a significant competitive advantage for organizations seeking to extract value from their information assets.

While the analyzed literature reviews demonstrate considerable progress achieved in the integration of LLMs and KGs across multiple application domains, fusion methodologies, and technical architectures, critical analysis reveals a significant limitation shared by these studies: the absence of bibliometric methodologies that reveal the social and intellectual structure of research in this domain. Existing reviews have provided valuable conceptual taxonomies, identified specific technical challenges, and documented success cases through predominantly qualitative and narrative approaches; however, none have employed bibliographic coupling or co-word analysis techniques to map the field's intellectual structure or analyze international collaboration patterns. This gap represents a significant opportunity for those seeking to understand not only what is being researched, but also who is leading these efforts, how they are collaborating, which institutions are driving the field, and where trends are heading in terms of scientific productivity, emerging fronts, and thematic evolution.

Therefore, the research objective is to conduct a bibliometric analysis on the integration of Large Language Models, Knowledge Graphs, and Semantic Web, focusing on data processing, knowledge extraction, and AI capabilities, characterizing scientific production, identifying key actors, mapping the intellectual structure, and analyzing collaboration networks to identify gaps and future research opportunities that contribute to providing a comprehensive overview of how this technological integration is developing and its implications for the scientific community.

METHODOLOGY

For the development of this research, a bibliometric approach was adopted to analyze scientific production on the integration of Large Language Models (LLMs) and Knowledge Graphs (KGs) in the context of the Semantic Web. This type of approach enables mapping the intellectual development of a field, identifying research patterns, emerging fronts, and collaboration networks through systematic analysis of scientific publications and their metadata (Donthu et al., 2021; Zupic & Čater, 2015). This methodological design is particularly appropriate for emerging research fields where understanding the social and intellectual structure of produced knowledge is required (Aria & Cuccurullo, 2017).

Web of Science (WoS) was selected as the primary data source due to its recognition as the most prestigious bibliographic database in international scientific evaluation, its rigorous selection process for indexed journals, and its extensive coverage of high-impact publications across multiple disciplines (Birkle et al., 2020). This platform provides complete and structured bibliometric information on citations, institutional affiliations, international collaborations, and cited references—essential characteristics for comprehensive bibliometric analyses (Pranckutė, 2021).

The search strategy was designed by combining key terms related to three fundamental conceptual dimensions: (1) large language models, (2) knowledge graphs and semantic web, and (3) processing capabilities and knowledge extraction. The search string employed was: *(("large language model*" OR "LLM*" OR "generative AI") AND ("knowledge graph*" OR "semantic web") AND ("knowledge extraction" OR "data processing" OR "reasoning" OR "AI capabilit*")).* This search strategy was applied to title, abstract, and keyword fields, following the recommendations of Gusenbauer and Haddaway (2020) to maximize sensitivity and precision in systematic literature reviews.

The search executed in Web of Science retrieved a total of 230 documents that met the established selection criteria. Bibliographic data were exported in BibTeX format from the platform, including the complete record with cited references. Data were processed using the bibliometrix package (Aria & Cuccurullo, 2017) in the R programming environment.

This bibliometric analysis software has been widely validated in scientific literature and enables comprehensive analyses of scientific production, citation structure, collaborations, and thematic evolution (Moral-Muñoz et al., 2020).

For the visualization of collaboration networks and thematic maps, VOSviewer was used, specialized software for the construction and visualization of bibliometric maps. This tool employs clustering algorithms that identify clusters of related elements and visualization techniques based on multidimensional scaling that position elements in two-dimensional maps where proximity reflects the intensity of relationships (Van Eck & Waltman, 2010).

RESULTS

The bibliometric analysis retrieved a total of 230 scientific documents indexed in Web of Science that met the established selection criteria. The temporal distribution of publications reveals exponential growth in research on the integration of Large Language Models and Knowledge Graphs, with an annual growth rate of 48.12%.

Annual production shows notable progression: in 2023, only 4 articles were published, a figure that increased to 43 documents in 2024, finally experiencing considerable growth in 2025 with 183 publications. This reflects over such a short period evidences a research domain of very recent interest, whose development has accelerated coinciding with the massification of advanced generative models such as GPT-4 and its successors. This temporal trend suggests that the field is in an initial development phase characterized by intensive methodological exploration and establishment of conceptual foundations.

MOST RELEVANT JOURNALS

Analysis of publication sources identifies the journals that are leading knowledge dissemination in this emerging field. Electronics positions itself as the most productive journal with 14 publications, followed by Applied

Sciences Basel and IEEE Access with 10 publications each, and Advanced Engineering Informatics with 9 publications. Other relevant journals include Expert Systems with Applications and Knowledge-Based Systems with 7 publications each, Information Processing & Management with 5 publications, and IEEE Transactions on Knowledge and Data Engineering, Information Fusion, and Mathematics with 4 publications each (Figure 1).

The predominance of multidisciplinary open-access journals reflects the emerging and rapidly evolving nature of the field, where accelerated knowledge dissemination is a priority. The significant presence of journals specialized in knowledge engineering, intelligent systems, and applied informatics evidences the interdisciplinary nature of the field, where artificial intelligence, software engineering, knowledge representation, and domain-specific applications converge.

Figure 1. Most Relevant Journals

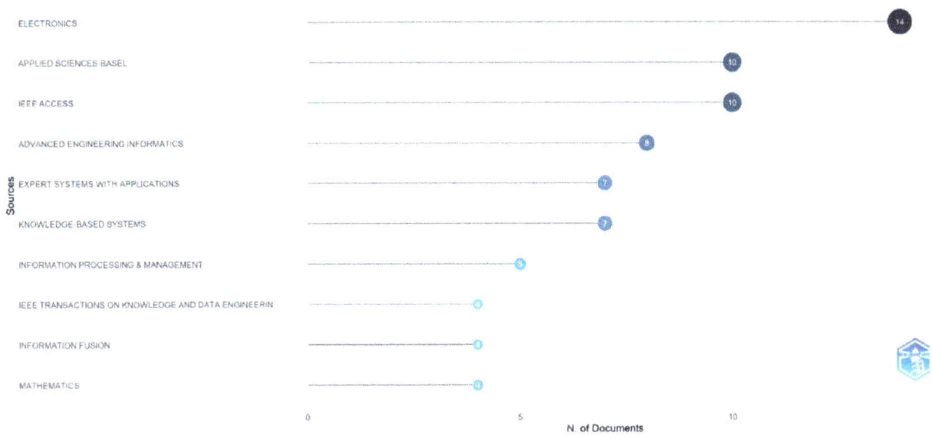

Source: Own elaboration based on Web of Science data using bibliometrix.

The prominent presence of journals with high impact factors in Q1 and Q2 quartiles of the Journal Citation Reports indicates that research in this domain is being published in high-quality academic sources, which is an indicator of the maturity and scientific rigor of the research developed. The diversity of publication sources reflects the thematic transversality of the field and its relevance for multiple scientific communities.

LEADING RESEARCH INSTITUTIONS

Institutional productivity analysis (Table 1) reveals a significant concentration of research in Chinese academic institutions, which dominate the ranking of the ten most productive universities. The Chinese Academy of Sciences leads with 25 publications, followed by Tsinghua University (13 articles), Nanjing University (11 articles), and Wuhan University (9 articles). This institutional distribution suggests a coordinated national strategy by China to position itself as a leader in research on artificial intelligence and emerging technologies, consistent with explicit government policies of investment in AI and technological development.Among non-Chinese institutions, the University of California System stands out with 7 publications, evidencing the competitiveness of American research centers in this field. The presence of specialized institutions such as the National University of Defense Technology and the Beijing Institute of Technology also signals strategic interest in defense and security applications of these integrated technologies.

Table 1. Institutions with the Highest Scientific Production on the Topic

Institution	N° of articles
Chinese Academy of Sciences	25
Tsinghua University	13
Nanjing University	11
Wuhan University	9
National University of Defense Technology - China	8
Beijing Institute Of Technology	7
University of California System	7
University of Chinese Academy of Sciences, Cas	7
Zhejiang University	7
China Agricultural University	6

Source: Own elaboration based on Web of Science data.

CORRESPONDING AUTHOR'S COUNTRY

Analysis by country of corresponding author affiliation (Figure 2) confirms China's leadership in the field's scientific production, with participation representing more than 60% of the total documents analyzed. The United States positions itself in second place with significantly lower participation, followed by countries such as India, the United Kingdom, Germany, and Australia, which show growing but still incipient research activity. This geographic distribution reflects not only research and development capabilities but also strategic investments in high-performance computational infrastructure, access to large datasets, and science and technology policies that prioritize artificial intelligence as an area of national development.

Figure 2. Distribution of Scientific Production by Corresponding Author's Country

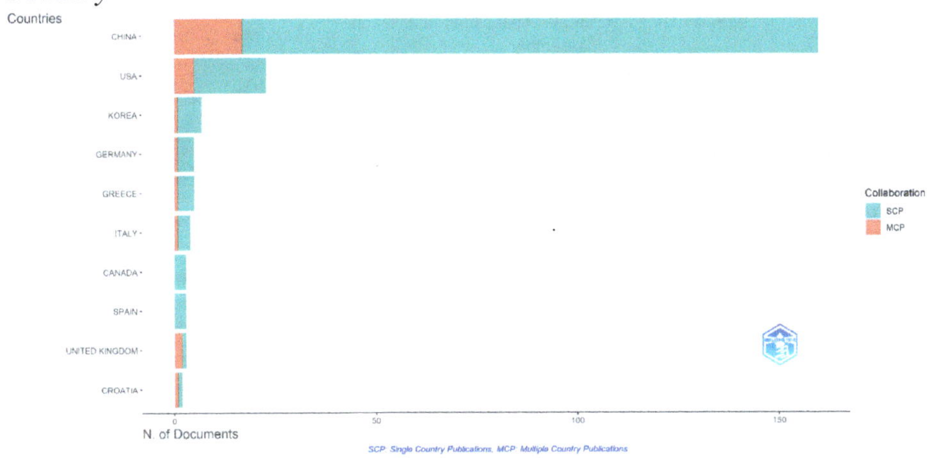

Source: Own elaboration based on Web of Science data.

Note: SCP = Single Country Publications; MCP = Multiple Country Publications (international collaboration publications).

MOST CITED DOCUMENTS

Citation analysis identifies the works that have exerted the greatest influence on the field's development (Table 2).

Table 2. Most Cited Documents

Author	Title	Journal	Citations
Pan et al. (2024)	Unifying Large Language Models and Knowledge Graphs: A Roadmap	*IEEE Transactions on Knowledge and Data Engineering*	*381*
Xiao et al. (2023)	Knowledge graph-based manufacturing process planning: A state-of-the-art review	*Journal of Manufacturing Systems*	*83*
Zhou et al. (2024)	CausalKGPT: Industrial structure causal knowledge-enhanced large language model for cause analysis of quality problems in aerospace product manufacturing	*Advanced Engineering Informatics*	*70*
Yang et al. (2024)	Give us the Facts: Enhancing Large Language Models With Knowledge Graphs for Fact-Aware Language Modeling	*IEEE Transactions on Knowledge and Data Engineering*	*61*
Liu (2024)	Joint Knowledge Graph and Large Language Model for Fault Diagnosis and Its Application in Aviation Assembly	*IEEE Transactions on Industrial Informatics*	*57*
Zhu et al. (2024)	LLMs for knowledge graph construction and reasoning: recent capabilities and future opportunities	*World Wide Web*	*56*
Chen et al. (2024)	Enhancing emergency decision-making with knowledge graphs and large language models	*International Journal of Disaster Risk Reduction*	*24*
Ghafarollahi y Buehler (2025)	SciAgents: Automating Scientific Discovery Through Bioinspired Multi-Agent Intelligent Graph Reasoning	*Advanced Materials*	*18*
Guo et al. (2024)	KnowledgeNavigator: leveraging large language models for enhanced reasoning over knowledge graph	*Complex & Intelligent Systems*	*16*
Liu y Cheng (2024)	MAKG: A maritime accident knowledge graph for intelligent accident analysis and management	*Ocean Engineering*	*15*

Source: Own elaboration based on Web of Science data.

The most cited document is the article by Pan et al. (2024) published in IEEE Transactions on Knowledge and Data Engineering, which has received 381 citations with a normalized citation rate of 19.86 citations per year. This work represents a fundamental contribution to the systematization of methods for integrating LLMs and KGs, proposing conceptual taxonomies and reference frameworks that have been widely adopted by the scientific community.

The second document is the work by Xiao et al. (2023) in Journal of Manufacturing Systems with 83 citations, which addresses specific applications in intelligent manufacturing systems. This article is particularly relevant as one of the first contributions published (2023) that demonstrated the feasibility of integrating LLMs with domain-specific industrial knowledge graphs, establishing a methodological paradigm subsequently replicated across multiple sectors.

Other cited works include contributions by Zhou et al. (2024) in Advanced Engineering Informatics (70 citations), Yang et al. (2024) in IEEE Transactions on Knowledge and Data Engineering (61 citations), and Liu et al. (2024) in IEEE Transactions on Industrial Informatics (57 citations). The high normalized citation rate of these works, considering their recent publication, suggests they are configuring the theoretical and methodological foundations of the field. The most recent article among those highly cited is by Ghafarollahi et al. (2025) in Advanced Materials, which with 18 citations and a normalized rate of 13.72 represents an emerging research front in the application of these technologies to advanced materials discovery.

KEYWORD CLOUD

The word cloud (Figure 3), generated from the frequency of terms in titles, abstracts, and keywords of the 230 analyzed documents, provides a visual representation of the central concepts that structure the scientific discourse in the field of study. The size of each term is proportional to its frequency of occurrence, allowing identification of conceptual hierarchies and thematic emphases.

Figure 3. Keyword Cloud

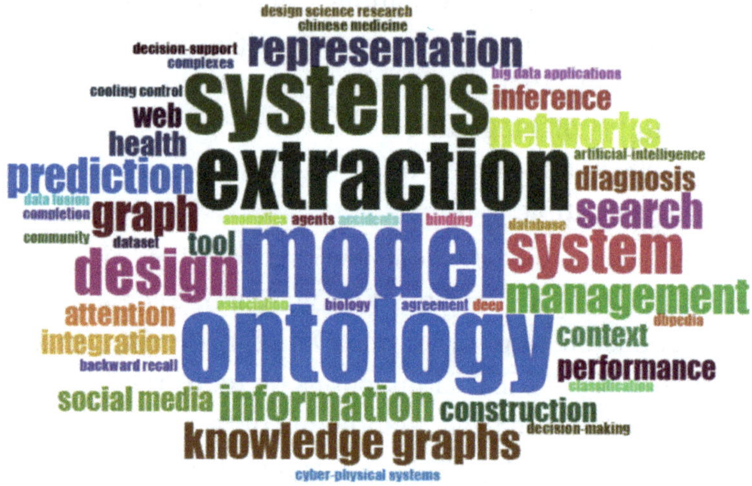

Source: Own elaboration based on Web of Science data using bibliometrix.

The keyword cloud reveals a field structured around four main axes: (1) foundations of knowledge representation (ontology, graphs, information, semantics); (2) automated construction methodologies (extraction, design, construction, generation); (3) intelligent processing capabilities (systems, models, inference, prediction, reasoning); and (4) domain-specific applications (health, diagnosis, management, decision support, manufacturing). This thematic structure confirms that the field integrates theoretical concerns about formal knowledge representation with methodological developments in knowledge engineering automation and practical applications in diverse sectors where the combination of natural language understanding and structured reasoning generates differential value.

KEY TERMS NETWORK

Co-occurrence analysis of keywords using VOSviewer (Figure 4) enabled identification of six main thematic clusters that structure the research field, in addition to a set of peripheral terms representing emerging areas.

Figure 4. Network of Conceptual Relationships

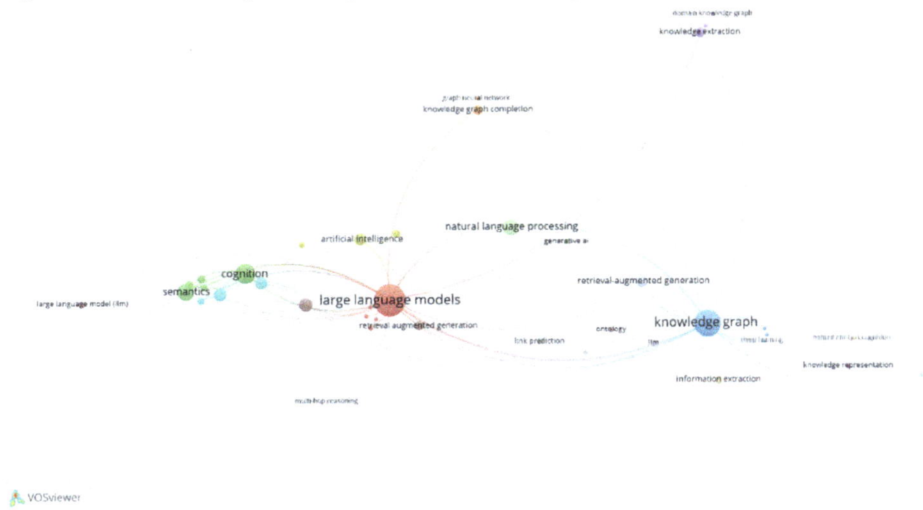

Source: Own elaboration based on Web of Science data using VOSviewer.

The first cluster addresses elements related to reasoning on knowledge graphs with LLMs. It groups elements focused on the use of graph neural networks, knowledge bases, knowledge graph reasoning, and large language models. Works in this cluster focus on how LLMs can improve logical and deductive reasoning capabilities on graph structures, as well as on hybrid architectures that combine dense vector representations with structured symbolic reasoning.

The second cluster contains elements related to data mining and semantic extraction. This thematic grouping includes adaptation models, cognition, data mining, feature extraction, and semantics. Research in this cluster is oriented toward methods that allow LLMs to learn more diverse semantic representations through the incorporation of structured knowledge, as well as transfer learning techniques that adapt pretrained generative models to specific domains using knowledge graphs as structured background knowledge.

The third cluster is characterized by terms such as chain of thought, deep learning, entity linking, and knowledge graphs. This cluster represents research on advanced prompting techniques that guide LLMs through step-by-step structured reasoning processes, linking textual mentions with entities in knowledge graphs to improve factual accuracy and traceability of generated responses.

Regarding cluster 4, it addresses elements related to artificial intelligence systems for decision-making. It groups terms associated with artificial intelligence, decision-making, and machine learning. Works in this category explore applications of LLM-KG integration in decision support systems, where structured knowledge provides factual context and logical constraints that guide the generation of recommendations and predictive analyses in complex domains.

Cluster 5, composed of terms such as domain knowledge graphs, knowledge extraction, and large language models, represents research on automated construction of specialized knowledge graphs using LLMs for tasks of named entity recognition, relation extraction, and ontology population from unstructured textual corpora.

The sixth grouping includes elements such as data models, recommender systems, and training. Research in this cluster addresses how knowledge graphs can improve recommender systems by providing explicit semantic representations of users, items, and contexts, as well as methods for training hybrid models that combine neural embeddings with explicit relational structure.

CONCLUSIONS

The present study reveals that the convergence between Large Language Models (LLMs) and Knowledge Graphs (KGs) does not merely constitute an incremental technical innovation, but rather the emergence of an epistemological paradigm that redefines the possibilities of artificial intelligence and materializes, after two decades, the original vision of the Semantic Web. The systematic analysis of 230 documents reveals that this integration responds to a structural need: to overcome the fundamental limitations of both pure statistical learning and isolated symbolic representation through architectures that combine the flexibility of neural processing with the logical guarantees of structured reasoning.

The neuro-symbolic synthesis documented in this study transcends historical dichotomies in artificial intelligence between connectionist and symbolic approaches. The findings suggest that advanced AI systems will require hybrid architectures where rapid and intuitive processing modules (LLMs) coexist with deliberate and verifiable reasoning capabilities (KGs). This convergence has profound epistemological consequences: it redefines what "knowledge" means in artificial systems, shifting focus from purely statistical representations toward explicit semantic structures (Tiwari et al., 2022) that enable traceability, explainability, and controlled knowledge updating.

China's dominant leadership, concentrating more than 60% of scientific production and seven of the ten most productive institutions, signals a fundamental reconfiguration of global equilibria in advanced technological knowledge generation. This pattern reflects sustained strategic investments, coherent government policies that prioritize AI as an area of national development, and high-performance computational infrastructures that enable large-scale experimentation. The significantly lower participation of Western institutions suggests that historical competitive advantages in technological research can erode rapidly in emerging fields where adoption speed and resource mobilization capacity are determinants.

For countries and regions with currently limited participation, this geographic concentration poses urgent strategic dilemmas. LLM-KG integration technologies incorporate ontologies, conceptual structures, and cultural biases of those who develop them. A global infrastructure of structured knowledge dominated by actors from a specific geographic region could perpetuate epistemic asymmetries, subordinate local knowledge, and generate technological dependencies with lasting economic and political consequences. Global epistemic justice requires democratization of research and development capabilities, plural representation in ontology construction, and policies that prevent monopolies in knowledge infrastructures that will configure globally deployed AI systems.

The identified emerging fronts—prompt engineering, factual precision evaluation, adaptation to specialized domains—represent the surface of a much broader space of potentially transformative research. Currently, peripheral domains such as education, law, digital humanities, and environmental sustainability offer exceptional opportunities to explore (Jabbar M.A. et al., 2022) method transferability toward contexts with distinctive epistemic characteristics: tacit knowledge difficult to formalize, inherent conceptual ambiguity, legitimate interpretive pluralism, and complex ethical dimensions that resist simplistic algorithmic codification.

Interdisciplinary integration with cognitive sciences, philosophy of language, computational linguistics, and epistemology could fundamentally enrich theoretical understanding of how neuro-symbolic architectures relate to human cognition, conceptual representation, and logical reasoning. Fundamental questions remain open: What aspects of human knowledge can be captured through structured symbolic representations versus distributed sub-symbolic processing? How do formal ontologies relate to natural conceptual categories in human cognition? What does "understanding" mean in hybrid systems that combine statistical processing with symbolic reasoning? These questions require rigorous research that transcends traditional disciplinary boundaries.

The integration of Large Language Models and Knowledge Graphs represents more than a technological development; it constitutes an epistemological inflection point in artificial intelligence. This study documents the accelerated emergence of a field that promises to overcome fundamental limitations of previous paradigms, but also evidences concentrations of epistemic power, unresolved ethical challenges, and geographic asymmetries in research capabilities that raise questions about equity, governance, and justice in the configuration of global knowledge infrastructures.

The bibliometric analysis provides a systematic mapping of the field's intellectual and social structure, but its most significant contribution lies in evidencing what we still do not fully comprehend: how to ensure that increasingly powerful systems of automated processing and reasoning over structured knowledge serve equitable human flourishing, respect epistemic pluralism, and are governed democratically. The speed of technological development has far exceeded collective capacity for ethical reflection, policy formulation, and establishment of governance frameworks. Closing this gap is not merely a technical challenge but a civilizational imperative that requires urgent mobilization of interdisciplinary research, dialogue among diverse actors, and political will to prioritize the common good over short-term competitive advantages.

REFERENCES

Al Khatib, H. S., Neupan, S., Manchukonda, H. K., Golilarz, N. A., Mittal, S., Amirlatifi, A., & Rahimi, S. (2024). Patient-centric knowledge graphs: a survey of current methods, challenges, and applications. *Frontiers in Artificiall Intelligence, 7*(1388479.). DOI: 10.3389/frai.2024.1388479

Aria, M., & Cuccurullo, C. (2017). Bibliometrix: An R-tool for comprehensive science mapping analysis. *Journal of Informetrics, 11*(4), 959–975. https://doi.org/https://doi.org/10.1016/j.joi.2017.08.007. DOI: 10.1016/j.joi.2017.08.007

Birkle, C., Pendlebury, D. A., Schnell, J., & Adams, J. (2020). Web of Science as a Data Source for Research on Scientific and Scholarly Activity. *Quantitative Science Studies, 1*(1), 363–376. https://doi.org/https://doi.org/10.1162/qss_a_00018. DOI: 10.1162/qss_a_00018

Cai, L., Yu, C., Kang, Y., Fu, Y., Zhang, H., & Zhao, Y. (2025). Practices, opportunities and challenges in the fusion of knowledge graphs and large language models. *Frontiers of Computer Science, 7*, 1590632. DOI: 10.3389/fcomp.2025.1590632

Chen, M., Tao, Z., Tang, W., Qin, T., Yang, R., & Zhu, C. (2024). Enhancing emergency decision-making with knowledge graphs and large language models☆. *International Journal of Disaster Risk Reduction, 113*, 104804. DOI: 10.1016/j.ijdrr.2024.104804

Dehal, R. S., Sharma, M., & Rajabi, E. (2025). Knowledge Graphs and Their Reciprocal Relationship with Large Language Models. *Machine Learning and Knowledge Extraction, 7*(38), 38. Advance online publication. DOI: 10.3390/make7020038

Dey, L. (2024). Knowledge graph-driven data processing for business intelligence. *Wiley Interdisciplinary Reviews. Data Mining and Knowledge Discovery, 14*(3), e1529. DOI: 10.1002/widm.1529

Donthu, N., Kumar, S., Mukherjee, D., Pandey, N., & Marc, W. (2021). How to conduct a bibliometric analysis: An overview and guidelines. *Journal of Business Research*, *133*, 285–296. https://doi.org/https://doi.org/10.1016/j.jbusres.2021.04.070. DOI: 10.1016/j.jbusres.2021.04.070

Ghafarollahi, A., & Buehler, M. J. (2024). SciAgents: Automating Scientific Discovery Through Bioinspired Multi-Agent Intelligent Graph Reasoning. *Advanced Materials*, *37*(22), 2413523. Advance online publication. DOI: 10.1002/adma.202413523 PMID: 39696898

Guo, T., Yang, Q., Wang, C., Liu, Y., Pan, L., Tang, J., & Wen, Y. (2024). KnowledgeNavigator: Leveraging large language models for enhanced reasoning over knowledge graph. *Complex & Intelligent Systems*, *10*(5), 7063–7076. DOI: 10.1007/s40747-024-01527-8

Gusenbauer, M., & Haddaway, N. R. (2020). Which academic search systems are suitable for systematic reviews or meta-analyses? Evaluating retrieval qualities of Google Scholar, PubMed, and 26 other resources. *Research Synthesis Methods*, *11*(2), 181–217. DOI: 10.1002/jrsm.1378 PMID: 31614060

Jabbar, M. A., Tiwari, S., & Ortiz-Rodriguez, F. (2022). *Smart Urban Computing Applications*. River Publishers. DOI: 10.1201/9781003373247

Li, D., & Xu, F. (2024). Synergizing Knowledge Graphs with Large Language Models: A Comprehensive Review and Future Prospects. *Computer Science*. https://doi.org//arXiv.2407.18470DOI: 10.48550

Liang, X., Wang, Z., & Liu, J. (2025). A survey of large language model-augmented knowledge graphs for advanced complex product design. *Journal of Manufacturing Systems*, *80*, 883–901. DOI: 10.1016/j.jmsy.2025.04.016

Liu, B., Fan, Y., Xu, N., Hou, S., Li, X., & Li, Q. (2025). Large Language Models for Knowledge Graph Embedding: A Survey. *Mathematics*, *13*(14), 2244. Advance online publication. DOI: 10.3390/math13142244

Liu, D., & Cheng, L. (2024). MAKG: A maritime accident knowledge graph for intelligent accident analysis and management. *Ocean Engineering*, *312*, 119280. DOI: 10.1016/j.oceaneng.2024.119280

Liu, P., Qian, L., Zhao, X., & Tao, B. (2024). Joint Knowledge Graph and Large Language Model for Fault Diagnosis and Its Application in Aviation Assembly. *IEEE Transactions on Industrial Informatics*, *20*(6), 8160–8169. DOI: 10.1109/TII.2024.3366977

Moral-Muñoz, J. A., Herrera-Viedma, E., Santisteban-Espejo, A., & Cobo, M. J. (2020). Software tools for conducting bibliometric analysis in science: An up-to-date review. *El Profesional de la Información*, *29*(1). Advance online publication. DOI: 10.3145/epi.2020.ene.03

Ortiz-Rodríguez, F., Villazón-Terrazas, B., Tiwari, S., & Bobed, C. (Eds.). (2023). Knowledge Graphs and Semantic Web: 5th Iberoamerican Conference, KGSWC 2023, Zaragoza, Spain, November 13–15, 2023, Proceedings. Springer Nature.

Pan, S., Luo, L., Wang, Y., Chen, C., Wang, J., & Wu, X. (2024). Unifying large language models and knowledge graphs: A roadmap. *IEEE Transactions on Knowledge and Data Engineering*, *36*(7), 3580–3599. DOI: 10.1109/TKDE.2024.3352100

Pan, S., Luo, L., Wang, Y., Chen, C., Wang, J., & Wu, X. (2024). Unifying Large Language Models and Knowledge Graphs: A Roadmap. *IEEE Transactions on Knowledge and Data Engineering*, *36*(7), 3580–3599. DOI: 10.1109/TKDE.2024.3352100

Pranckuté, R. (2021). Web of Science (WoS) and Scopus: The Titans of Bibliographic Information in Today's Academic World. *Publications / MDPI*, *9*(1), 12. Advance online publication. DOI: 10.3390/publications9010012

Serra, A., Fratello, M., Federico, A., & Greco, D. (2025). An update on knowledge graphs and their current and potential applications in drug discovery. *Expert Opinion on Drug Discovery*, *20*(5), 599–619. DOI: 10.1080/17460441.2025.2490253 PMID: 40223439

Silva, A. L., & Terra, A. L. (2023). Cultural heritage on the Semantic Web: The Europeana Data Model. *IFLA Journal*, *50*(1), 93–107. DOI: 10.1177/03400352231202506

Tiwari, S., Ortiz-Rodríguez, F., & Jabbar, M. A. (2022). Semantic modeling for healthcare applications: An introduction. In *Semantic Models in IoT and eHealth Applications* (pp. 1–17). Academic Press., DOI: 10.1016/B978-0-32-391773-5.00007-8

Tiwari, S., Villazón-Terrazas, B., Ortiz-Rodríguez, F., & Sahri, S. (Eds.). (2024). Knowledge Graphs and Semantic Web: 6th International Conference, KGSWC 2024, Paris, France, December 11–13, 2024, Proceedings. Springer Nature.

Van Eck, N. J., & Waltman, L. (2010). Software survey: VOSviewer, a computer program for bibliometric mapping. *Scientometrics, 84*(2), 523–538. DOI: 10.1007/s11192-009-0146-3 PMID: 20585380

Villazón-Terrazas, B., Ortiz-Rodríguez, F., Tiwari, S., Goyal, A., & Jabbar, M. A. (Eds.). (2021). *Knowledge Graphs and Semantic Web: Third Iberoamerican Conference, KGSWC 2021, Kingsville, TX, USA, November 22–24, 2021, Proceedings*. Springer Nature.

Villazón-Terrazas, B., Ortiz-Rodríguez, F., Tiwari, S., Riechert, T., & Marx, E. (Eds.). (2025). *Knowledge Graphs and Semantic Web: 7th International Conference, KGSWC 2025, Leipzig, Germany, November 26–28, 2025, Proceedings*. Springer Nature.

Villazón-Terrazas, B., Ortiz-Rodríguez, F., Tiwari, S., Sicilia, M. A., & Martín-Moncunill, D. (Eds.). (2022). *Knowledge Graphs and Semantic Web: 4th Iberoamerican Conference, KGSWC 2022, Madrid, Spain, November 21–23, 2022, Proceedings*. Springer Nature.

Xiao, Y., Zheng, S., Shi, J., Du, X., & Hong, J. (2023). Knowledge graph-based manufacturing process planning: A state-of-the-art review. *Journal of Manufacturing Systems, 70*, 417–435. DOI: 10.1016/j.jmsy.2023.08.006

Yang, L., Chen, H., Li, Z., Ding, X., & Wu, X. (2024). Give us the Facts: Enhancing Large Language Models With Knowledge Graphs for Fact-Aware Language Modeling. *IEEE Transactions on Knowledge and Data Engineering, 36*(7), 3091–3110. Advance online publication. DOI: 10.1109/TKDE.2024.3360454

Yang, Z., Yuan, S., Shao, Z., Li, W., & Liu, R. (2025). A review on synergizing knowledge graphs and large language models. *Computing*, *107*(143), 143. Advance online publication. DOI: 10.1007/s00607-025-01499-8

Zheng, C., Wong, S., Su, X., Tang, Y., Nawaz, A., & Kassem, M. (2025). Automating construction contract review using knowledge graph-enhanced large language models. *Automation in Construction*, *175*, 106179. DOI: 10.1016/j.autcon.2025.106179

Zhou, B., Li, X., Liu, T., Xu, K., Liu, W., & Bao, J. (2024). CausalKGPT: Industrial structure causal knowledge-enhanced large language model for cause analysis of quality problems in aerospace product manufacturing. *Advanced Engineering Informatics*, *59*, 102333. DOI: 10.1016/j.aei.2023.102333

Zhu, Y., Wang, X., Chen, J., Qiao, S., Ou, Y., Yao, Y., Deng, S., Chen, H., & Zhang, N. (2024). LLMs for knowledge graph construction and reasoning: Recent capabilities and future opportunities. *World Wide Web (Bussum)*, *27*(58), 58. Advance online publication. DOI: 10.1007/s11280-024-01297-w

Zupic, I., & Čater, T. (2015). Bibliometric methods in management and organization. *Organizational Research Methods*, *18*(3), 429–472. https://doi.org/https://doi.org/10.1177/109442811456262. DOI: 10.1177/1094428114562629

Chapter 10

AI-Integrated Learning Environment in Higher Education: Challenges and Opportunities

Vivek Gupta
Sharda University, India

Fernando Ortiz-Rodriguez
http://orcid.org/0000-0003-2084-3462
Tamaulipas Autonomous University, Mexico

ABSTRACT

E-learning platforms are rapidly increasing in demand to transform the landscape of education as they are strengthened by machine learning and artificial intelligence (AI). The integration of AI in higher education improves Massive Open Online Courses (MOOCs) and Virtual Learning Environments (VLEs) in intelligent tutoring and personalized learning, making e-learning and other academic tasks more efficient. This paper explores the potential of AI in online education systems along with proposed solutions. The primary aim of this paper is to highlight the current opportunities and challenges.

DOI: 10.4018/979-8-3373-1360-3.ch010

1 INTRODUCTION

Artificial intelligence (AI) is a key component in different fields such as education, healthcare, industries, and finance. AI is gaining attention. increasingly more and more and resulting successful achievements in recent years. Education is one of the prominent areas where AI plays an important role in transforming the academia with various AI techniques. AI powered tools has potential for facing promising challenges and improving the teaching and learning tasks in higher education. AI technologies are empowering to automate administrative tasks, personalize learning experiences, reduc- ing workloads, improving student progress and cumulating instant feedback along with decision making (Al-Zahrani, 2024; Chu et al., 2022; Dai & Ke, 2022; Zheng et al., 2023). AI integrated tools such as intelligent tutoring systems (ITS), (adaptive) educational apps and learning management systems (LMS) are providing better access to data and improved engagement by resource availability and strong accessibility (Harley et al., 2015; Nesbit et al., 2014). AI tools are significant to make decisions in educational system by identifying trends, correlations and patterns and analyzing huge data sets. This can enhance the resource allocation, strategic planning, and policy development to make strong data driven decisions for student and institutions (Debo, 2024).

AI in higher education is an evolving and dynamic area of research and become effective to explore the significance of AI in educational, social and ethical areas. It is required to explore the current developments in this field and summarize the find- ings. This paper has conducted a review to highlight the research in the area of AI in e-learning and virtual education. Rest of the sections are organized as follows: Section 2 has conducted a review of various survey papers related with AI in education and summarize their findings. Section 3 highlighted how the education system was trans- formed with artificial intelligence. Section 4 has discussed the promising challenges to be taken care and finally concluded in section 5.

2 LITERATURE REVIEW

Online learning (Pappano, 2012) is not a new process, it focuses on acquiring knowledge within an electronic environment that includes network infrastructure, artificial intelligence, communication technologies and multimedia tools. The traditional model of the edu- cation system was limited with limited physical classrooms and localized instruction with limited resources. Internet has made a revolutionary change and introduces an online education system for teaching and learning where knowledge can be accessed in a tangible form. Generally, the Massive Open Online Course (MOOC) platform played a vital role in creating an online education system that included educational innovation and technological advancement. This section will analyze existing research to explore current opportunities and challenges. Table 1 has discussed several survey articles to explore the role of Artificial Intelligence in education.

Dogan et al. (2023) analyzed 276 research articles to propose a systematic review of related studies using data mining and analytics approaches, and highlighted three dominant clusters such as: AI techniques in teaching and learning tasks, Behavioral Prediction Using AI and AI empowered adaptive and personalized learning.

Fauvel et al. (2018) has proposed a survey to examine the role of Ai in Massive Open Online Courses (MOOCs) and prepared a taxonomy in three categories: Learner Modeling; Improving Learning Experience;and Learner Assessment to Integrate AI for MOOCs.

Gligorea et al. (2023) has proposed an analysis of integration of AI / ML (cluster algo- rithms, recommendation systems, and deep learning models) into adaptive learning systems to improve educational results. They also identified key challenges of AI/Ml in explainable AI (XAI), real-time learning adaptation, and human-AI collaboration.

Ifenthaler et al. (2024) have contributed to a comprehensive review to analyze chal- lenges, key trends, and policy recommendations for AI in education. They used a

Table 1. Exploring Artificial Intelligence in Education: Surveyr

Ref	Scope	Type of Article	Methodology	Technical Contribution	Future Direction
(Dogan et al., 2023)	AI in e-learning and online education	Survey	a multi-method approach with text and data mining, and social network analysis (SNA)	bibliometric analysis of 276 publications	development of human-centered AI models
(Fauvel et al., 2018)	AI in MOOCs	Survey	organized and structured review of AI Applications	a taxonomy with learner modeling and assessment and learning experience.	identify the key areas to enhance the MOOCs
(Gligorea et al., 2023)	AI/ML in adaptive e-learning	Survey	a systematic literature review of 63 research articles	highlighting role of AI/ML approaches in e-learning	identifying key challenges of AI/Ml
(Ifenthaler et al., 2024)	AI in education (privacy, trust, ethics)	Survey	Delphi study to analyze AI's impact on education by involving 33 international experts	explores role of AI in adaptive learning, augmenting teaching, and decision-making support	filling the gaps in AI's role in education, policymaking, and learning analytics.
(Wang et al., 2024)	AI in education	Survey	systematic literature review (SLR)	identify AI trends in education including quantitative bibliometric analysis and qualitative content analysis	to evolve more studies on human-AI, emotional AI, and ethical AI frameworks.
(Kuleto et al., 2021)	AI/ML in higher education	Survey	mixed-method approach combining statistical modeling, and document analysis	implements correlation analysis, composite reliability testing, and regression modeling using SmartPLS3 software	proposing concrete AI and ML platforms
(Ilić et al., 2023)	AI-based tech- niques in e-learning	Survey	bibliometric and content analysis	categorization of intelligent techniques for e-learning	focus on AI-driven learning models

Delphi study to analyze the impact of AI on education by involving 33 international experts.

Wang et al. (2024) have proposed a systematic review to explore artificial intelligence in education by performing a bibliometric analysis of 2,223 research articles and selected 125 articles to analyze the main findings. This paper has highlighted the primary domains of AI applications, principal research themes, and their key findings along with the status of primary research design elements.

Kuleto et al. (2021) has highlighted the role of AI/ML in higher education and proposed a mixed-method approach that combines review of the literature, survey research, sta- tistical modeling and document analysis. The major contribution to conducts a survey of 103 students in Serbia to assess AI/ML knowledge and perceptions in higher edu- cation.

Ilic et al. (2023) proposed a comprehensive study on innovations in the area of e- learning and conducted a survey to analyze the effectiveness of intelligent techniques in e-learning environments. The findings of this research conclude that AI-supported systems can provide fully personalized learning experience.

3 TRANSFORMING EDUCATION THROUGH ARTIFICIAL INTELLIGENCE

Artificial Intelligence (AI) emerged in every field of daily life and education is one of the most important areas. It is a technology to integrate machine learning, cog- nition, emotion recognition, data storage, human-computer interaction, and decision making (Yang et al., 2024). Zhai et al. (2021) has explored five key AI elements, widely applied in education: visualization, complex algorithms, XR (virtual / augmented / mixed real- ity), neuroscience and wearable technology. The course content can be personalized and customized according to student needs by adapting machine learning algorithms and can also improve the quality and experience of student learning (Chen et al., 2020). Figure **1** presents the areas where AI is widely applied.

Figure 1. AI in Education

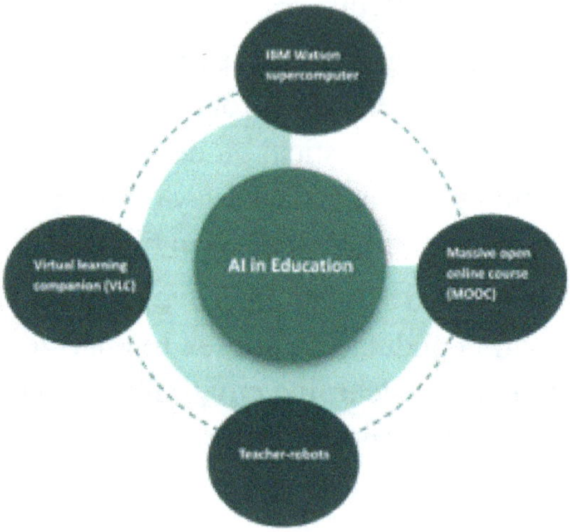

(Al Braiki et al., 2020)

IBM Watson supercomputer is used in higher education as one of the examples of artificial intelligence. Another feature of AI, the brain-computer interface (BCI) (Contributors, 2022) is introduced to automate the education system. BCI is an association between a brain and a device to conduct external activity. Artificial intelligence is supporting teacher robots called teacher bots as a complex algorithm to make an environment for person- alized learning. They can be presented as a machine-based hardware or software to play the role of a teaching assistant to conduct the exams (Popenici & Kerr, 2017). A virtual learning companion (VLC) is considered as an AI-driven teaching assistant, capable to mimic human-like behavior to support personalized learning. Massive open online courses (MOOC) also have become a prominent tool in higher education today. Although it is not presented as an AI technique, it is considered as a plateform where AI can be applied. It fol- lows a classroom-based approach, covering all phases from content delivery to making exercises, scheduling exams, and assessing the performance of students.

Currently, Generative AI, as an AI system, is widely used in education to develop AI algorithms to produce novel content such as text, music, graphics, or any other type of content. Deep learning models: Generative Adversarial Networks (GANs) or Variational Autoencoders (VAEs), generally applied in AI systems for images while for language, usually depends on the Transformer architecture used in Natural Language Processing (NLP) (Zhao et al., 2024).

Figure 2. Impacts of AI in Education

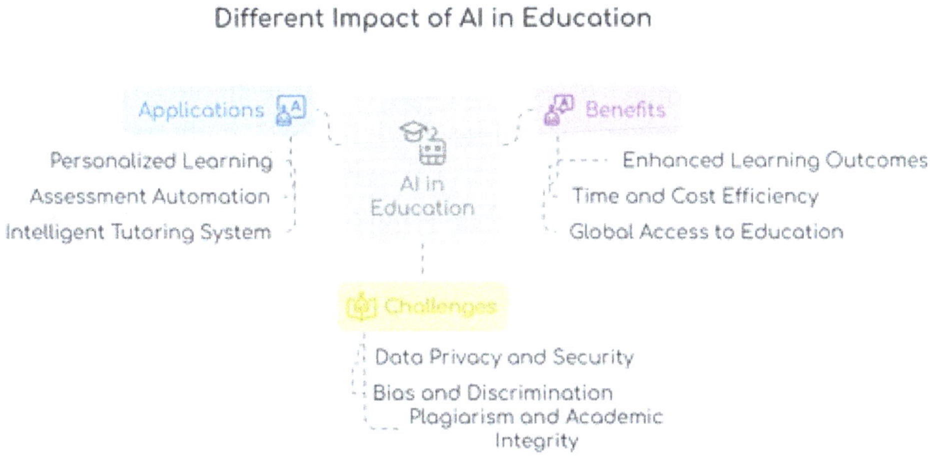

(Kamalov et al., 2023)

AI algorithms are deployed in various academic tasks, such as automatic generation of learning content (Madhavi et al., 2023), language learning tools] (Winaitham, 2022), creative writing (Javaid et al., 2023), artistic creation (Vartiainen et al., 2023), and virtual experiments and simulations (Lee & Kim, 2023). To improve educational tasks, there is a transformative approach combining the capability of symbolic and neural AI to develop intelligent and adaptable personalized teaching tools (Jaldi et al., 2025). Firuz et al. (2023) explored the effectivenmess of AI in education by conducting a survey to analyze existing studies focusing on advantages, applications and challenges. Figure **2** has highlighted various impacts of AI in education. They have summarized the key advantages in different categories: (1) improved learning outcomes, (2) global access to quality education, (3) time and cost efficiency.

3.1 AI-Driven Approaches in E-Learning

Recently, e-learning has been widely applied for various educational tasks and mak- ing education available to the community. Various options are available in e-learning with advanced technologies (Monahan et al., 2008). E-learning widely encompasses all types of educa- tional technology used in teaching and learning. It is synonymous with internet-based training (IBT), computer-based training (CBT), technology-enhanced learning (TEL), computer-assisted instruction (CAI), multimedia learning, virtual learning environ- ments (VLE), virtual education, web-based training (WBT) (Current Trends in E Learning, 2025). Various techniques involved in e-learning such as mobile learning (m-learning), Social media, HTML5, Cloud-based learning, Gamification, MOOCs etc.

3.2 AI in Assessment

Artificial intelligence (AI) holds a significant role in evaluating student progress effi- ciently and effectively (Kakungulu Samuel, 2024). Assessment tasks are the backbone of the education system in improving teaching and learning processes effectively day by day. Various assessment practices are involved, from light-weight evaluations to massive high-stakes evaluations. Currently, integration of AI in education transforms the learning and teaching processes. Different AI technologies are involved in assessment tasks such as ML/DL techniques. Support vector machine and decision tree classifiers are applied for Learning Outcome evaluation in teaching courses. Na¨ıve Bayes classifiers, k-nearest neighbor, and natural language processing-based assessment are applied for qualitative evaluation of written work.

4 CHALLENGES

Although AI has transformed the education system, there are several rapidly grow- ing issues such as privacy and data security, plagiarism, bias and discrimination, and academic integrity and student-teacher relationship (Kamalov et al., 2023). The factor of data security and privacy is a crucial factor in every technology. User data, location and communi- cation details are prominently required monitoring in the AI applications with in the education system. AI techniques go through educational systems and acquiring and processing a huge amount of sensitive data such as academic records, students' per- sonal data, and behavioral patterns. In this scenario, there are high chances of risks for misusing or unauthorized access of the sensitive data (Timan & Mann, 2021). Several efforts, measures and awareness generation have been taken at various educational system levels. It is challenging to preserving academic integrity and skilled personnel development for incorporating AI techniques (Rane, 2024).

5 CONCLUSION

The integration of AI in higher education has provided new opportunities for intel- ligent assessment, personalized learning, and efficient educational administration. This paper has reviewed current literature and presented key insights into the use of AI technologies in MOOCs, VLEs, and other digital learning environments. While the adoption of AI brings significant benefits—such as improved learning outcomes, scalability, and accessibility—it also poses complex challenges including data privacy, ethical concerns, and the evolving role of educators. To harness AI's full potential in education, stakeholders must balance innovation with responsible governance, ensuring that AI-enhanced learning systems are transparent, inclusive, and aligned with pedagogical goals. Ongoing research, cross-disciplinary collaboration, and policy frameworks will be essential in shaping a future where AI serves as a transformative and equitable force in higher education.

REFERENCES

Al Braiki, B., Harous, S., Zaki, N., & Alnajjar, F. (2020). Artificial intelligence in education and assessment methods. *Bulletin of Electrical Engineering and Informatics*, *9*(5), 1998–2007. DOI: 10.11591/eei.v9i5.1984

Al-Zahrani, A. M. (2024). From traditionalism to algorithms: Embracing artificial intel- ligence for effective university teaching and learning. *TECHNOLOGY*, *2*(2), 103.

Chen, L., Chen, P., & Lin, Z. (2020). Artificial intelligence in education: A review. *IEEE Access : Practical Innovations, Open Solutions*, *8*, 75264–75278. DOI: 10.1109/ACCESS.2020.2988510

Chu, H.-C., Hwang, G.-H., Tu, Y.-F., & Yang, K.-H. (2022). Roles and research trends of artificial intelligence in higher education: A systematic review of the top 50 most-cited articles. *Australasian Journal of Educational Technology*, *38*(3), 22–42.

Contributors, T.: What is brain-computer interface (bci)?-definition from whatis. com. WhatIs. com (2022)

Current Trends in E Learning & (2025); Communication technologies—ebooks.inflibnet.ac.in. https://ebooks.inflibnet.ac.in/ae01/chapter/current-trends-in-e-learning/. [Accessed 29-04-2025]

Dai, C.-P., & Ke, F. (2022). Educational applications of artificial intelligence in simulation- based learning: A systematic mapping review. *Computers and Education: Artificial Intelligence*, *3*, 100087. DOI: 10.1016/j.caeai.2022.100087

Debo, D.: Ai in higher education: Opportunities and challenges. Researchgate. net (2024)

Dogan, M. E., Goru Dogan, T., & Bozkurt, A. (2023). The use of artificial intelligence (ai) in online learning and distance education processes: A systematic review of empirical studies. *Applied Sciences (Basel, Switzerland)*, *13*(5), 3056. DOI: 10.3390/app13053056

Fauvel, S., Yu, H., Miao, C., Cui, L., Song, H., Zhang, L., Li, X., & Leung, C. Artificial intelligence powered moocs: a brief survey. In: *2018 IEEE International Conference on Agents (ICA)*, pp. 56–61 (2018). IEEE DOI: 10.1109/AGENTS.2018.8460059

Gligorea, I., Cioca, M., Oancea, R., Gorski, A.-T., Gorski, H., & Tudorache, P. (2023). Adaptive learning using artificial intelligence in e-learning: A literature review. *Education Sciences*, *13*(12), 1216. DOI: 10.3390/educsci13121216

Harley, J. M., Bouchet, F., Hussain, M. S., Azevedo, R., & Calvo, R. (2015). A multi- componential analysis of emotions during complex learning with an intelligent multi-agent system. *Computers in Human Behavior*, *48*, 615–625. DOI: 10.1016/j.chb.2015.02.013

Ifenthaler, D., Majumdar, R., Gorissen, P., Judge, M., Mishra, S., Raffaghelli, J., Shimada, A.: Artificial intelligence in education: Implications for policymakers, researchers, and practitioners. Technology, Knowledge and Learning, 1–18 (2024)

Ili'c, M., Miki'c, V., Kopanja, L., & Vesin, B. (2023). Intelligent techniques in e-learning: A literature review. *Artificial Intelligence Review*, *56*(12), 14907–14953. DOI: 10.1007/s10462-023-10508-1

Jaldi, C. D., Ilkou, E., Schroeder, N., & Shimizu, C. (2025). Education in the era of neurosymbolic ai. *Journal of Web Semantics*, *85*, 100857. DOI: 10.1016/j.websem.2024.100857

Javaid, M., Haleem, A., Singh, R. P., Khan, S., & Khan, I. H. (2023). Unlocking the opportunities through chatgpt tool towards ameliorating the education system. BenchCouncil Transactions on Benchmarks. *Standards and Evaluations*, *3*(2), 100115.

Kakungulu Samuel, J.: The role of artificial intelligence in educational assessment (2024)

Kamalov, F., Santandreu Calonge, D., & Gurrib, I. (2023). New era of artificial intelli- gence in education: Towards a sustainable multifaceted revolution. *Sustainability (Basel)*, *15*(16), 12451. DOI: 10.3390/su151612451

Kuleto, V., Ili'c, M., Dumangiu, M., Rankovi'c, M., Martins, O. M., P˘aun, D., & Mihoreanu, L. (2021). Exploring opportunities and challenges of artificial intelligence and machine learning in higher education institutions. *Sustainability (Basel), 13*(18), 10424. DOI: 10.3390/su131810424

Lee, J., & Kim, Y. (2023). Sustainable educational metaverse content and system based on deep learning for enhancing learner immersion. *Sustainability (Basel), 15*(16), 12663. DOI: 10.3390/su151612663

Madhavi, E., Sivapurapu, L., Koppula, V., Rani, P., & Sreehari, V. (2023). Develop- ing learners' english-speaking skills using ict and ai tools. *Journal of Advanced Research in Applied Sciences and Engineering Technology, 32*(2), 142–153. DOI: 10.37934/araset.32.2.142153

Monahan, T., McArdle, G., & Bertolotto, M. (2008). Virtual reality for collaborative e- learning. *Computers & Education, 50*(4), 1339–1353. DOI: 10.1016/j.compedu.2006.12.008

Nesbit, J. C., Adesope, O. O., Liu, Q., & Ma, W. How effective are intelligent tutor- ing systems in computer science education? In: 2014 IEEE 14th International Conference on Advanced Learning Technologies, pp. 99–103 (2014). IEEE

Pappano, L. The year of the mooc. The New York Times **2**(12), 2012 (2012)

Popenici, S. A., & Kerr, S. (2017). Exploring the impact of artificial intelligence on teaching and learning in higher education. *Research and Practice in Technology Enhanced Learning, 12*(1), 22. DOI: 10.1186/s41039-017-0062-8 PMID: 30595727

Rane, N. (2024). Enhancing the quality of teaching and learning through gemini, chatgpt, and similar generative artificial intelligence: Challenges, future prospects, and ethical considerations in education. *TESOL and Technology Studies*, *5*(1), 1–6. DOI: 10.48185/tts.v5i1.1000

Timan, T., & Mann, Z. (2021). Data protection in the era of artificial intelligence: trends, existing solutions and recommendations for privacy-preserving technologies. In *The Elements of Big Data Value: Foundations of the Research and Innovation Ecosystem* (pp. 153–175). Springer. DOI: 10.1007/978-3-030-68176-0_7

Vartiainen, H., Tedre, M., Jormanainen, I.: Co-creating digital art with generative ai in k-9 education: Socio-material insights. International Journal of education through art **19**(3), 405–423 (2023)

Wang, S., Wang, F., Zhu, Z., Wang, J., Tran, T., & Du, Z. (2024). Artificial intelligence in education: A systematic literature review. *Expert Systems with Applications*, *252*, 124167. DOI: 10.1016/j.eswa.2024.124167

Winaitham, W. The scientific review of ai functions of enhancement english learning and teaching. In: 2022 13th International Conference on Information and Communication Technology Convergence (ICTC), pp. 148–152 (2022). IEEE DOI: 10.1109/ICTC55196.2022.9952632

Yang, Y., Sun, W., Sun, D., & Salas-Pilco, S. Z. (2024). Navigating the ai-enhanced stem education landscape: A decade of insights, trends, and opportunities. *Research in Science & Technological Education*, 1–25.

Zhai, X., Chu, X., Chai, C. S., Jong, M. S. Y., Istenic, A., Spector, M., Liu, J.-B., Yuan, J., & Li, Y. (2021). A review of artificial intelligence (ai) in education from 2010 to 2020. *Complexity*, *2021*(1), 8812542. DOI: 10.1155/2021/8812542

Zhao, H.-G., Li, X.-Z., & Kang, X. (2024). Development of an artificial intelligence curricu- lum design for children in taiwan and its impact on learning outcomes. *Humanities & Social Sciences Communications*, *11*(1), 1–17. DOI: 10.1057/s41599-024-03839-z

Zheng, W., Lu, S., Cai, Z., Wang, R., Wang, L., & Yin, L. (2023). Palbert: An improved question answering model. *Computer Modeling in Engineering & Sciences*, *10*, •••.

Compilation of References

Abu-Rasheed, H., Weber, C., & Fathi, M. (2024). Knowledge graphs as context sources for LLM-based explanations of learning recommendations. In *2024 IEEE Global Engineering Education Conference (EDUCON)* (pp. 1–5). IEEE. DOI: 10.1109/EDUCON60312.2024.10578654

Addanki, U. K., Devareddi, R. B., Kamarajugadda, K. K., Pavani, M., & Gera, P. (2025). Machine learning-powered intrusion detection system for agriculture 4.0: Securing the next generation of farming. *International Journal of Innovative Research and Scientific Studies*, *8*(1), 1964–1978. DOI: 10.53894/ijirss.v8i1.4840

Al Braiki, B., Harous, S., Zaki, N., & Alnajjar, F. (2020). Artificial intelligence in education and assessment methods. *Bulletin of Electrical Engineering and Informatics*, *9*(5), 1998–2007. DOI: 10.11591/eei.v9i5.1984

Al Khatib, H. S., Neupan, S., Manchukonda, H. K., Golilarz, N. A., Mittal, S., Amirlatifi, A., & Rahimi, S. (2024). Patient-centric knowledge graphs: a survey of current methods, challenges, and applications. *Frontiers in Artificiall Intelligence, 7*(1388479.). DOI: 10.3389/frai.2024.1388479

Almahmood, R. J. K., & Tekerek, A. (2022). Issues and solutions in deep learning-enabled recommendation systems within the e-commerce field. *Applied Sciences (Basel, Switzerland)*, *12*(21), 11256. DOI: 10.3390/app122111256

Alshwaheen, T. I., Hau, Y. W., Ass'Ad, N., & Abualsamen, M. M. (2020). A novel and reliable framework of patient deterioration prediction in intensive care unit based on long short-term memory-recurrent neural network. *IEEE Access : Practical Innovations, Open Solutions*, *9*, 3894–3918. DOI: 10.1109/ACCESS.2020.3047186

Al-Zahrani, A. M. (2024). From traditionalism to algorithms: Embracing artificial intel- ligence for effective university teaching and learning. *TECHNOLOGY*, *2*(2), 103.

Ampazis, N. (2024). Reranking in RAG systems (Technical report).

Anand, A., Lyu, L., Idahl, M., Wang, Y., Wallat, J., & Zhang, Z. (2022). "Explainable information retrieval: A survey." *arXiv preprint arXiv:2211.02405.*

Arana, C. (2021). Recurrent neural networks: An analysis of specialized models on sequential data (Working paper).

Aria, M., & Cuccurullo, C. (2017). Bibliometrix: An R-tool for comprehensive science mapping analysis. *Journal of Informetrics*, *11*(4), 959–975. https://doi.org/https://doi.org/10.1016/j.joi.2017.08.007. DOI: 10.1016/j.joi.2017.08.007

Asteris, P. G., Gavriilaki, E., Touloumenidou, T., Koravou, E.-E., Koutra, M., Papayanni, P. G., Pouleres, A., Karali, V., Lemonis, M. E., Mamou, A., Skentou, A. D., Papalexandri, A., Varelas, C., Chatzopoulou, F., Chatzidimitriou, M., Chatzidimitriou, D., Veleni, A., Rapti, E., Kioumis, I., & Anagnostopoulos, A. (2022). Genetic prediction of ICU hospitalization and mortality in COVID-19 patients using artificial neural networks. *Journal of Cellular and Molecular Medicine*, *26*(5), 1445–1455. DOI: 10.1111/jcmm.17098 PMID: 35064759

Badii, C., Bellini, P., Cenni, D., Difino, A., Nesi, P., & Paolucci, M. (2017). Analysis and assessment of a knowledge based smart city architecture providing service APIs. *Future Generation Computer Systems*, *75*, 14–29. DOI: 10.1016/j.future.2017.05.001

Bae, K., Ryu, H., & Shin, H. (2019). "Does Adam optimizer keep close to the optimal point?" *arXiv preprint arXiv:1911.00289.*

Baeza-Yates, R., & Ribeiro-Neto, B. (2011). *Modern information retrieval: The concepts and technology behind search* (2nd ed.). Addison-Wesley.

Bai, J., Luo, C., Li, Z., Yin, Q., Yin, B., & Song, Y. (2023, August). Knowledge graph reasoning over entities and numerical values. In *Proceedings of the 29th ACM SIGKDD Conference on Knowledge Discovery and Data Mining* (pp. 57-68). DOI: 10.1145/3580305.3599399

Balasooriya, R., Adithya, E., Gunarathne, M., Silva, T., & Lokuliyana, S. Wije- siri, P.: An explainable deep learning framework for coconut disease detection using mobilenetv2, super-resolution, and grad-cam++. In: *2025 International Conference on Data Science and Its Applications (ICoDSA)*, pp. 985–990 (2025). IEEE DOI: 10.1109/ICoDSA67155.2025.11157166

Barrasa, J., & Webber, J. (2023). *Building Knowledge Graphs.* O'Reilly Media, Inc.

Berka, P. (2020). Sentiment analysis using rule-based and case-based reasoning. *Journal of Intelligent Information Systems*, *55*(1), 51–66. DOI: 10.1007/s10844-019-00591-8

Berners-Lee, T., Hendler, J., & Lassila, O. (2001). The Semantic Web. *Scientific American*, *284*(5), 34–43. DOI: 10.1038/scientificamerican0501-34 PMID: 11681174

Biewald, L. (2020). *Experiment tracking with weights and biases* [Software]. wandb.com. https://www.wandb.com/

Birkle, C., Pendlebury, D. A., Schnell, J., & Adams, J. (2020). Web of Science as a Data Source for Research on Scientific and Scholarly Activity. *Quantitative Science Studies*, *1*(1), 363–376. https://doi.org/https://doi.org/10.1162/qss_a_00018. DOI: 10.1162/qss_a_00018

Biswas, R., Kaffee, L.-A., Cochez, M., Dumbrava, S., Jendal, T. E., Lissandrini, M., Lopez, V., Mencía, E. L., Paulheim, H., & Sack, H. (2023). Knowledge graph embeddings: Open challenges and opportunities. Transactions on Graph Data and Knowledge, 1(1), 4:1–4:32.

Blair, D. C. (1990). *Language and representation in information retrieval.* Elsevier Science Publishers.

Brasse, J., Broder, H. R., Förster, M., Klier, M., & Sigler, I. (2023). Explainable artificial intelligence in information systems: A review of the status quo and future research directions. *Electronic Markets*, *33*(1), 26. DOI: 10.1007/s12525-023-00644-5

Bratanic, T. (2024). *Graph Algorithms for Data Science: With Examples in Neo4j.* Simon and Schuster.

Bronstein, M. M., Bruna, J., Cohen, T., & Veličković, P. (2021). Geometric deep learning: Grids, groups, graphs, geodesics, and gauges. *arXiv preprint arXiv:2104.13478.*

Burkart, N., & Huber, M. F. (2021). A survey on the explainability of supervised machine learning. *Journal of Artificial Intelligence Research, 70*, 245–317. DOI: 10.1613/jair.1.12228

Cai, L., Yu, C., Kang, Y., Fu, Y., Zhang, H., & Zhao, Y. (2025). Practices, opportunities and challenges in the fusion of knowledge graphs and large language models. *Frontiers of Computer Science*, *7*, 1590632. DOI: 10.3389/fcomp.2025.1590632

Capelle, M., & Yvon, F. (2022). FLEUR: A benchmark dataset for French learner error detection. In *Proceedings of the 60th Annual Meeting of the Association for Computational Linguistics* (pp. 123-135). ACL. https://aclanthology.org/2022.acl-long.123/

Chang, Y., Wang, X., Wang, J., Wu, Y., Yang, L., Zhu, K., Chen, H., Yi, X., Wang, C., Wang, Y., Ye, W., Zhang, Y., Chang, Y., Yu, P. S., Yang, Q., & Xie, X. (2024). A survey on evaluation of large language models. *ACM Transactions on Intelligent Systems and Technology, 15*(3), 1–45. DOI: 10.1145/3641289

Chen, Z., Mao, H., Liu, J., Song, Y., Li, B., Jin, W., . . . Tang, J. (2024). Text-space Graph Foundation Models: Comprehensive Benchmarks and New Insights. *arXiv preprint arXiv:2406.10727*. DOI: 10.52202/079017-0239

Chen, Z., Zhang, Y., Fang, Y., Geng, Y., Guo, L., Chen, X., . . . Chen, H. (2024). Knowledge Graphs Meet Multi-Modal Learning: A Comprehensive Survey. *arXiv preprint arXiv:2402.05391*.

Chen, J., Yang, Y., Peng, L., Chen, L., & Ge, X. (2022). Knowledge graph representation learning-based forest fire prediction. *Remote Sensing (Basel)*, *14*(17), 4391. DOI: 10.3390/rs14174391

Chen, J., Zhang, R., Guo, J., Fan, Y., & Cheng, X. (2022). "GERE: Generative evidence retrieval for fact verification." In *Proceedings of the 45th International ACM SIGIR Conference*, 2184-2189. DOI: 10.1145/3477495.3531827

Chen, L., Chen, P., & Lin, Z. (2020). Artificial intelligence in education: A review. *IEEE Access : Practical Innovations, Open Solutions*, *8*, 75264–75278. DOI: 10.1109/ACCESS.2020.2988510

Chen, M., Tao, Z., Tang, W., Qin, T., Yang, R., & Zhu, C. (2024). Enhancing emergency decision-making with knowledge graphs and large language models☆. *International Journal of Disaster Risk Reduction*, *113*, 104804. DOI: 10.1016/j.ijdrr.2024.104804

Chen, X., Jia, S., & Xiang, Y. (2020). A review: Knowledge reasoning over knowledge graph. *Expert Systems with Applications*, *141*, 112948. DOI: 10.1016/j.eswa.2019.112948

Chen, Z., Chen, L., Villar, S., & Bruna, J. (2020). Can graph neural networks count substructures? *Advances in Neural Information Processing Systems*, *33*, 10383 10395.

Chu, H.-C., Hwang, G.-H., Tu, Y.-F., & Yang, K.-H. (2022). Roles and research trends of artificial intelligence in higher education: A systematic review of the top 50 most-cited articles. *Australasian Journal of Educational Technology*, *38*(3), 22–42.

Contributors, T.: What is brain-computer interface (bci)?-definition from whatis. com. WhatIs. com (2022)

Council of Europe. (2020). *Common European Framework of Reference for languages: Learning, teaching, assessment*. Edinumen.

Croft, W. B. (1987). Approaches to intelligent information retrieval. *Information Processing & Management, 23*(4), 249–254.

Cruz, I. B., Martínez, S. S., Abed, A. R., Ábalo, R. G., & Lorenzo, M. M. G. (2007). Recurrent neural networks for sequence analysis. *Cuban Journal of Computer Science, 1*, 48–57.

Cui, Z., Chen, H., Cui, L., Liu, S., Liu, X., Xu, G., & Yin, H. (2022). Reinforced KGs reasoning for explainable sequential recommendation. *World Wide Web (Bussum), 25*(2), 631–654. DOI: 10.1007/s11280-021-00902-6

Current Trends in E Learning & (2025); Communication technologies—ebooks.inflibnet.ac.in. https://ebooks.inflibnet.ac.in/ae01/chapter/ current-trends-in-e-learning/. [Accessed 29-04-2025]

Dai, C.-P., & Ke, F. (2022). Educational applications of artificial intelligence in simulation- based learning: A systematic mapping review. *Computers and Education: Artificial Intelligence, 3*, 100087. DOI: 10.1016/j.caeai.2022.100087

De Moya Anegón, F., Solana, V. H., & Bote, V. G. (1998). The application of artificial neural networks (ANN) to information retrieval. Bibliodoc: Library Yearbook, Documentation and Information, 147–164.

Debo, D.: Ai in higher education: Opportunities and challenges. Researchgate. net (2024)

Dehal, R. S., Sharma, M., & Rajabi, E. (2025). Knowledge Graphs and Their Reciprocal Relationship with Large Language Models. *Machine Learning and Knowledge Extraction, 7*(38), 38. Advance online publication. DOI: 10.3390/make7020038

Dessì, D., Osborne, F., Reforgiato Recupero, D., Buscaldi, D., Motta, E., & Sack, H. (2020). AI-KG: an automatically generated knowledge graph of artificial intelligence. In *The Semantic Web–ISWC 2020: 19th International Semantic Web Conference, Athens, Greece, November 2–6, 2020* [Springer International Publishing.]. *Proceedings, 19*(Part II), 127–143.

Dey, L. (2024). Knowledge graph-driven data processing for business intelligence. *Wiley Interdisciplinary Reviews. Data Mining and Knowledge Discovery, 14*(3), e1529. DOI: 10.1002/widm.1529

Dieber, J., & Kirrane, S. (2020). "Why model why? Assessing the strengths and limitations of LIME." *arXiv preprint arXiv:2012.00093*.

Diego Olite, F. M., Morales Suarez, I. D. R., & Vidal Ledo, M. J. (2023). GPT chat: Origin, evolution, challenges, and impacts on education. Higher Medical Education, 37.

Dogan, M. E., Goru Dogan, T., & Bozkurt, A. (2023). The use of artificial intelligence (ai) in online learning and distance education processes: A systematic review of empirical studies. *Applied Sciences (Basel, Switzerland), 13*(5), 3056. DOI: 10.3390/app13053056

Dong, X. L., & Rekatsinas, T. (2018, May). Data integration and machine learning: A natural synergy. In *Proceedings of the 2018 international conference on management of data* (pp. 1645-1650). DOI: 10.1145/3183713.3197387

Donthu, N., Kumar, S., Mukherjee, D., Pandey, N., & Marc, W. (2021). How to conduct a bibliometric analysis: An overview and guidelines. *Journal of Business Research, 133*, 285–296. https://doi.org/https://doi.org/10.1016/j.jbusres.2021.04.070. DOI: 10.1016/j.jbusres.2021.04.070

Dwivedi, R., Dave, D., Naik, H., Singhal, S., Omer, R., Patel, P., Qian, B., Wen, Z., Shah, T., Morgan, G., & Ranjan, R. (2023). Explainable AI (XAI): Core ideas, techniques, and solutions. *ACM Computing Surveys, 55*(9), 1–33. DOI: 10.1145/3561048

Edge, D., Trinh, H., Cheng, N., Bradley, J., Chao, A., Mody, A., Truitt, S., & Larson, J. (2024). From local to global: A graph RAG approach to query-focused summarization. arXiv preprint arXiv:2404.16130.

El Sakka, M., Ivanovici, M., Chaari, L., & Mothe, J. (2025). A review of cnn applications in smart agriculture using multimodal data. *Sensors (Basel)*, *25*(2), 472. DOI: 10.3390/s25020472 PMID: 39860841

EnterpriseDB. (2024). Transforming Real-Time Analytics and AI Workloads with PostgreSQL.

Espíndola, G. (2023, March 3). ¿Qué son los embeddings y cómo se utilizan en la inteligencia artificial con python? Medium. https://gustavo-espindola.medium.com/qu%C3%A9-son-los-embeddings-y-c%C3%B3mo-se-utilizan-en-la-inteligencia-artificial-con-python-45b751ed86a5

Fabre, R., Azeroual, O., Schöpfel, J., Bellot, P., & Egret, D. (2023). A Multiverse Graph to Help Scientific Reasoning from Web Usage: Interpretable Patterns of Assessor Shifts in GRAPHYP. *Future Internet*, *15*(4), 147. DOI: 10.3390/fi15040147

Fauvel, S., Yu, H., Miao, C., Cui, L., Song, H., Zhang, L., Li, X., & Leung, C. Artificial intelligence powered moocs: a brief survey. In: *2018 IEEE International Conference on Agents (ICA)*, pp. 56–61 (2018). IEEE DOI: 10.1109/AGENTS.2018.8460059

Fei, H., Ren, Y., Zhang, Y., Ji, D., & Liang, X. (2021). Enriching contextualized language model from knowledge graph for biomedical information extraction. *Briefings in Bioinformatics*, *22*(3), bbaa110. DOI: 10.1093/bib/bbaa110 PMID: 32591802

Fivetran (2023). 12 Best Open Source Database Software in 2023.

Friha, O., Ferrag, M. A., Kantarci, B., Cakmak, B., Ozgun, A., & Ghoulami-Zine, N. (2024). LLM-based edge intelligence: A comprehensive survey on architectures, applications, security and trustworthiness. *IEEE Open Journal of the Communications Society*, *5*, 5799–5856. DOI: 10.1109/OJCOMS.2024.3456549

G'omez-Flores, W., Garza-Saldan˜a, J. J., & Varela-Fuentes, S. E. (2022). A huanglongbing detection method for orange trees based on deep neural networks and transfer learning. *IEEE Access : Practical Innovations, Open Solutions*, *10*, 116686–116696. DOI: 10.1109/ACCESS.2022.3219481

Gao, Y., Xiong, Y., ... (2023). Retrieval-augmented generation for large language models: A survey. arXiv preprint arXiv:2312.10997.

García, B. T. (2020). *Introducción a la recuperación de información.* Universitat Oberta de Catalunya.

García-Palomera, J., Verduzco-Ram'ırez, J., & Barrios-Hern'andez, C. (2024). Garc'ıa- Virgen, J., Mor'an-L'opez, L.: Prototipo para la detecci'on de aran˜a cristalina en cultivos de aguacate aplicando redes neuronales. *Revista ELECTRO*, *46*(1), 49–54.

Gavranović, B., Lessard, P., Dudzik, A. J., von Glehn, T., Araújo, J. G. M., & Veličković, P. Position: Categorical Deep Learning is an Algebraic Theory of All Architectures. In *Forty-first International Conference on Machine Learning*.

GeeksforGeeks. (2024). *Comparing MySQL.* PostgreSQL, and MongoDB.

Ghafarollahi, A., & Buehler, M. J. (2024). SciAgents: Automating Scientific Discovery Through Bioinspired Multi-Agent Intelligent Graph Reasoning. *Advanced Materials*, *37*(22), 2413523. Advance online publication. DOI: 10.1002/adma.202413523 PMID: 39696898

Glass, J., et al. (2022). Reranking techniques for retrieval systems (Technical report).

Gligorea, I., Cioca, M., Oancea, R., Gorski, A.-T., Gorski, H., & Tudorache, P. (2023). Adaptive learning using artificial intelligence in e-learning: A literature review. *Education Sciences*, *13*(12), 1216. DOI: 10.3390/educsci13121216

Google Research. (2023). *Colaboratory: Frequently asked questions.* https://research.google.com/colaboratory/faq.html

Goyal, P., & Ferrara, E. (2018). Graph embedding techniques, applications, and performance: A survey. *Knowledge-Based Systems, 151*, 78–94. DOI: 10.1016/j.knosys.2018.03.022

Grimm, S. (2009). Knowledge representation and ontologies. In *Scientific data mining and knowledge discovery: Principles and foundations* (pp. 111–137). Springer Berlin Heidelberg. DOI: 10.1007/978-3-642-02788-8_6

Guo, T., Yang, Q., Wang, C., Liu, Y., Pan, L., Tang, J., & Wen, Y. (2024). KnowledgeNavigator: Leveraging large language models for enhanced reasoning over knowledge graph. *Complex & Intelligent Systems, 10*(5), 7063–7076. DOI: 10.1007/s40747-024-01527-8

Gupta, V., Sharma, D. K., & Dixit, A. (2021). Review of information retrieval: Models, performance evaluation techniques, and applications. *International Journal of Sensors, Wireless Communications and Control, 11*(1), 896–909. DOI: 10.2174/2210327911666210121161142

Gusenbauer, M., & Haddaway, N. R. (2020). Which academic search systems are suitable for systematic reviews or meta-analyses? Evaluating retrieval qualities of Google Scholar, PubMed, and 26 other resources. *Research Synthesis Methods, 11*(2), 181–217. DOI: 10.1002/jrsm.1378 PMID: 31614060

Harley, J. M., Bouchet, F., Hussain, M. S., Azevedo, R., & Calvo, R. (2015). A multi- componential analysis of emotions during complex learning with an intelligent multi-agent system. *Computers in Human Behavior, 48*, 615–625. DOI: 10.1016/j.chb.2015.02.013

Hogan, A., Luna Dong, X., Vrandečić, D., & Weikum, G. (2025). Large Language Models, Knowledge Graphs and Search Engines: A Crossroads for Answering Users' Questions. arXiv e-prints, arXiv-2501.

Huang, X., Zhang, J., Li, D., & Li, P. (2019, January). Knowledge graph embedding based question answering. In *Proceedings of the twelfth ACM international conference on web search and data mining* (pp. 105-113). DOI: 10.1145/3289600.3290956

Huertas, A. (2019, October 14). Clasificación de textos state-of-the-art con embeddings contextuales. Medium. https://afhuertas.medium.com/clasificaci%C3%B3n-de-textos-state-of-art-con-embeddings-contextuales-58cb29767669

Hu, W., Fey, M., Zitnik, M., Dong, Y., Ren, H., Liu, B., & Leskovec, J. (2020). Open graph benchmark: Datasets for machine learning on graphs. *Advances in Neural Information Processing Systems*, *33*, 22118–22133.

Hwang, G. J., Xie, H., Wah, B. W., & Gašević, D. (2020). Vision, challenges, roles and research issues of artificial intelligence in education. *Computers & Education: Artificial Intelligence*, *1*, 100001.

Ifenthaler, D., Majumdar, R., Gorissen, P., Judge, M., Mishra, S., Raffaghelli, J., Shimada, A.: Artificial intelligence in education: Implications for policymakers, researchers, and practitioners. Technology, Knowledge and Learning, 1–18 (2024)

Ili'c, M., Miki'c, V., Kopanja, L., & Vesin, B. (2023). Intelligent techniques in e-learning: A literature review. *Artificial Intelligence Review*, *56*(12), 14907–14953. DOI: 10.1007/s10462-023-10508-1

Institut Français. (n.d.). *Studies on AI-assisted language learning*. Retrieved from https://www.institutfrancais.com

Jabbar, M. A., Tiwari, S., & Ortiz-Rodriguez, F. (2022). *Smart Urban Computing Applications*. River Publishers. DOI: 10.1201/9781003373247

Jaldi, C. D., Ilkou, E., Schroeder, N., & Shimizu, C. (2025). Education in the era of neurosymbolic ai. *Journal of Web Semantics*, *85*, 100857. DOI: 10.1016/j.websem.2024.100857

Javaid, M., Haleem, A., Singh, R. P., Khan, S., & Khan, I. H. (2023). Unlocking the opportunities through chatgpt tool towards ameliorating the education system. BenchCouncil Transactions on Benchmarks. *Standards and Evaluations*, *3*(2), 100115.

Ji, S., Pan, S., Cambria, E., Marttinen, P., & Philip, S. Y. (2021). A survey on knowledge graphs: Representation, acquisition, and applications. *IEEE Transactions on Neural Networks and Learning Systems, 33*(2), 494–514. DOI: 10.1109/TNNLS.2021.3070843 PMID: 33900922

Kakungulu Samuel, J.: The role of artificial intelligence in educational assessment (2024)

Kamalov, F., Santandreu Calonge, D., & Gurrib, I. (2023). New era of artificial intelli- gence in education: Towards a sustainable multifaceted revolution. *Sustainability (Basel), 15*(16), 12451. DOI: 10.3390/su151612451

Kass, R., & Finin, T. (1988). The need for user models in generating expert system explanations. *International Journal of Expert Systems, 1*(4).

Kasula, B. Y. (2024). Advancements in AI-driven healthcare: A comprehensive review of diagnostics, treatment, and patient care integration. *International Journal of Machine Learning for Sustainable Development, 6*(1), 1–5.

Kau, A., He, X., Nambissan, A., Astudillo, A., Yin, H., & Aryani, A. (2024). Combining Knowledge Graphs and Large Language Models. *arXiv preprint arXiv:2407.06564.*

Kessler, S., Schroeder, D., Korlakov, S., Hettlich, V., Kalkhoff, S., Moazemi, S., Lichtenberg, A., Schmid, F., & Aubin, H. (2023). Predicting readmission to the cardiovascular intensive care unit using recurrent neural networks. *Digital Health, 9*, 20552076221149529. DOI: 10.1177/20552076221149529 PMID: 36644663

Kinsta (2024). The Best in Open Source Database Software: Top 10 Picks.

Kommineni, V. K., Ahmed, W., Koenig-Ries, B., & Samuel, S. (2024). Automating information retrieval from biodiversity literature using large language models: A case study. *Biodiversity Information Science and Standards, 8*, e136735. DOI: 10.3897/biss.8.136735

Korfhage, R. R. (1997). *Information storage and retrieval.* Wiley Computer Publishing.

Koroteev, M. V. (2021). BERT: A review of applications in natural language processing and understanding. arXiv preprint arXiv:2103.11943.

Kuleto, V., Ili'c, M., Dumangiu, M., Rankovi'c, M., Martins, O. M., P˘aun, D., & Mihoreanu, L. (2021). Exploring opportunities and challenges of artificial intelligence and machine learning in higher education institutions. *Sustainability (Basel)*, *13*(18), 10424. DOI: 10.3390/su131810424

Kumar, H., Singh, M. K., Gupta, M. P., & Madaan, J. (2020). Moving towards smart cities: Solutions that lead to the Smart City Transformation Framework. *Technological Forecasting and Social Change*, *153*, 119281. DOI: 10.1016/j.techfore.2018.04.024

Kusrini, K., Suputa, S., Setyanto, A., Agastya, I. M. A., Priantoro, H., Chandramouli, K., & Izquierdo, E. (2020). Chan- dramouli, K., Izquierdo, E.: Data augmentation for automated pest classification in mango farms. *Computers and Electronics in Agriculture*, *179*, 105842. DOI: 10.1016/j.compag.2020.105842

Labeau, M., & Luong, K. (2021). FRACAS: A corpus of French learner texts with complexity annotations. In *Proceedings of the 17th Workshop on Innovative Use of NLP for Building Educational Applications* (pp. 15-25). ACL. https://aclanthology.org/2021.bea-1.15/

Landeros, J., Balderas, J., Badii, M.H., S´anchez, V.M., Guerrero, E., Flores, A.E.: Distribuci´on espacial y fluctuaci´on poblacional de phyllocoptruta oleivora (ashmead)(acari: Eriophyidae) en c´ıtricos de gu¨emez, tamaulipas. Acta zool´ogica mexicana (89), 129–138 (2003)

Lara, A. V. (2012). Evaluación del sistema de recuperación de información de la herramienta de gestión bibliotecaria ABCD versión 1.0.6 [Undergraduate thesis, Universidad Central "Marta Abreu" de Las Villas]. https://dspace.uclv.edu.cu/items/e9a5aae6-17f6-45f1-b510-179a9f41029c

Lara-Rodríguez, L. D., L'opez-Mel'endez, E., & Castellanos-Corzo, A. L. (2023). Com- paraci'on de redes neuronales convolucionales (rnc) para la detecci'on de plagas en el cultivo del durazno en departamento norte de santander, colombia. *Informador T'ecnico*, *87*(2), 150–164. DOI: 10.23850/22565035.5805

Lee, J., & Kim, Y. (2023). Sustainable educational metaverse content and system based on deep learning for enhancing learner immersion. *Sustainability (Basel), 15*(16), 12663. DOI: 10.3390/su151612663

Lelong, J., Errazine, A., & Blangero, A. (2025). Agentic rag with knowledge graphs for complex multi-hop reasoning in real-world applications. arXiv preprint arXiv:2507.16507. DOI: 10.3233/FAIA251445

Lewis, P., Perez, E., Piktus, A., Petroni, F., Karpukhin, V., Goyal, N., & Kiela, D. (2020). Retrieval-augmented generation for knowledge-intensive nlp tasks. *Advances in Neural Information Processing Systems, 33*, 9459–9474.

Lhomme, D., Garlatti, S., & Tijus, C. (2020). Knowledge graphs for adaptive language learning. *Journal of Educational Technology & Society, 23*(4), 112–128.

Li, D., & Xu, F. (2024). Synergizing Knowledge Graphs with Large Language Models: A Comprehensive Review and Future Prospects. *Computer Science*. https://doi.org//arXiv.2407.18470DOI: 10.48550

Liang, X., Wang, Z., & Liu, J. (2025). A survey of large language model-augmented knowledge graphs for advanced complex product design. *Journal of Manufacturing Systems, 80*, 883–901. DOI: 10.1016/j.jmsy.2025.04.016

Lin, L. H.-M., Lien, W.-C., Cheng, C. Y.-T., Lee, Y.-C., Lin, Y.-T., Kuo, C.-C., Lai, Y.-T., & Peng, Y.-T. (2025). A rapid household mite detection and classification technology based on artificial intelligence-enhanced scanned images. *Internet of Things : Engineering Cyber Physical Human Systems, 29*, 101484. DOI: 10.1016/j.iot.2024.101484

Liu, B., Fan, Y., Xu, N., Hou, S., Li, X., & Li, Q. (2025). Large Language Models for Knowledge Graph Embedding: A Survey. *Mathematics, 13*(14), 2244. Advance online publication. DOI: 10.3390/math13142244

Liu, D., & Cheng, L. (2024). MAKG: A maritime accident knowledge graph for intelligent accident analysis and management. *Ocean Engineering, 312*, 119280. DOI: 10.1016/j.oceaneng.2024.119280

Liu, P., Qian, L., Zhao, X., & Tao, B. (2024). Joint Knowledge Graph and Large Language Model for Fault Diagnosis and Its Application in Aviation Assembly. *IEEE Transactions on Industrial Informatics*, *20*(6), 8160–8169. DOI: 10.1109/TII.2024.3366977

Li, Z., Liu, H., Zhang, Z., Liu, T., & Xiong, N. N. (2021). Learning knowledge graph embedding with heterogeneous relation attention networks. *IEEE Transactions on Neural Networks and Learning Systems*, *33*(8), 3961–3973. DOI: 10.1109/TNNLS.2021.3055147 PMID: 33606639

Luckin, R., Holmes, W., Griffiths, M., & Forcier, L. B. (2016). *Intelligence unleashed: An argument for AI in education*. Pearson.

Lu, J., Tan, L., & Jiang, H. (2021). Review on convolutional neural network (cnn) applied to plant leaf disease classification. *Agriculture*, *11*(8), 707. DOI: 10.3390/agriculture11080707

Luo, A., Wu, C., Shen, J., Shuai, Z., & Ma, F. (2011). Railway static power conditioners for high-speed train traction power supply systems using three-phase V/V transformers. *IEEE Transactions on Power Electronics*, *26*(10), 2844–2856. DOI: 10.1109/TPEL.2011.2128888

Madhavi, E., Sivapurapu, L., Koppula, V., Rani, P., & Sreehari, V. (2023). Develop- ing learners' english-speaking skills using ict and ai tools. *Journal of Advanced Research in Applied Sciences and Engineering Technology*, *32*(2), 142–153. DOI: 10.37934/araset.32.2.142153

Malec, S. A., Taneja, S. B., Albert, S. M., Shaaban, C. E., Karim, H. T., Levine, A. S., & Boyce, R. D. (2023). Causal feature selection using a knowledge graph combining structured knowledge from the biomedical literature and ontologies: A use case studying depression as a risk factor for Alzheimer's disease. *Journal of Biomedical Informatics*, *142*, 104368. DOI: 10.1016/j.jbi.2023.104368 PMID: 37086959

Manning, C. D. (2022). Human language understanding & reasoning. *Daedalus*, *151*(2), 127–138. DOI: 10.1162/daed_a_01905

Massiris, M., Delrieux, C., & Fernández Muñoz, J. Á. (2018). Detection of personal protective equipment using the YOLO convolutional neural network. In *39th Conference on Automation* (pp. 1022–1029). University of Extremadura.

McCaffrey, P.. (2024). Evaluating use of generative artificial intelligence in clinical pathology practice: Opportunities and the way forward. *Archives of Pathology & Laboratory Medicine*. PMID: 39384182

McDermott, R. (2025). *From Unstructured Text to Interactive Knowledge Graphs Using LLMs*. Retrieved from Medium.

Mei, T. (2020, September 8). From static embedding to contextualized embedding. Medium. https://ted-mei.medium.com/from-static-embedding-to-contextualized-embedding-fe604886b2bc

Mercado, S. A., Gutiérrez, D. D., & Henríquez, D. D. (2024). SafeRecords, una solución de software para la anonimización de registros médicos usando modelos de reconocimiento de entidades [Undergraduate project, Universidad del Norte].

Mittal, M., Gupta, V., Aamash, M., & Upadhyay, T. (2024). Machine learning for pest detection and infestation prediction: A comprehensive review. *Wiley Interdisciplinary Reviews. Data Mining and Knowledge Discovery, 14*(5), 1551. DOI: 10.1002/widm.1551

Monahan, T., McArdle, G., & Bertolotto, M. (2008). Virtual reality for collaborative e- learning. *Computers & Education, 50*(4), 1339–1353. DOI: 10.1016/j.compedu.2006.12.008

Moral-Muñoz, J. A., Herrera-Viedma, E., Santisteban-Espejo, A., & Cobo, M. J. (2020). Software tools for conducting bibliometric analysis in science: An up-to-date review. *El Profesional de la Información, 29*(1). Advance online publication. DOI: 10.3145/epi.2020.ene.03

Morris, C., Frasca, F., Dym, N., Maron, H., Ceylan, I. I., & Levie, R.. & Jegelka, S. Position: Future Directions in the Theory of Graph Machine Learning. In *Forty-first International Conference on Machine Learning*.

Mosca, E., Szigeti, F., Tragianni, S., Gallagher, D., & Groh, G. (2022). "SHAP-based explanation methods: A review for NLP interpretability." In *Proceedings of the 29th International Conference on Computational Linguistics*, 4593-4603.

Mulay, V.M., Rao, M., Kumar, K.V.: Ensemble based deep learning models for crop and weed differentiation. Measurement: Digitalization, 100009 (2025)

Munn, M., & Pitman, D. (2022). *Explainable AI for practitioners*. O'Reilly Media, Inc.

Navigli, R., & Ponzetto, S. P. (2012). BabelNet: The automatic construction of a multilingual semantic network. *Artificial Intelligence*, *193*, 217–250. DOI: 10.1016/j.artint.2012.07.001

Nesbit, J. C., Adesope, O. O., Liu, Q., & Ma, W. How effective are intelligent tutor- ing systems in computer science education? In: 2014 IEEE 14th International Conference on Advanced Learning Technologies, pp. 99–103 (2014). IEEE

Open, A. I. (2023). *GPT-4 technical report* (arXiv:2303.08774). arXiv. https://arxiv.org/abs/2303.08774

Ortiz-Rodriguez, F., Villazón-Terrazas, B., Tiwari, S., & Bobed, C. (Eds.). (2023). *Knowledge Graphs and Semantic Web: 5th Iberoamerican Conference and 4th Indo-American Conference, KGSWC 2023, Proceedings*. Springer Nature. Jabbar, M. A., Tiwari, S., & Ortiz-Rodriguez, F. (Eds.). (2023). *Smart Urban Computing Applications*. CRC Press.

Ortiz-Rodríguez, F., Villazón-Terrazas, B., Tiwari, S., & Bobed, C. (Eds.). (2023). Knowledge Graphs and Semantic Web: 5th Iberoamerican Conference, KGSWC 2023, Zaragoza, Spain, November 13–15, 2023, Proceedings. Springer Nature.

Ortiz-Rodriguez, F., Leyva-Mederos, A., Tiwari, S., Hernandez-Quintana, A. R., & Martinez-Rodriguez, J. L. (Eds.). (2024). *Semantic Web Technologies and Applications in Artificial Intelligence of Things*. IGI Global. DOI: 10.4018/979-8-3693-1487-6

Ortiz-Rodriguez, F., Medina-Quintero, J. M., Tiwari, S., & Villanueva, V. (2022). EGODO Ontology: Sharing, Retrieving, and Exchanging Legal Documentation Across E-Government. In *Futuristic Trends for Sustainable Development and Sustainable Ecosystems*. IGI Global. DOI: 10.4018/978-1-6684-4225-8.ch016

Paleyes, A., Urma, R. G., & Lawrence, N. D. (2022). Challenges in deploying machine learning: A survey of case studies. *ACM Computing Surveys*, *55*(6), 1–29. DOI: 10.1145/3533378

Pan, S., Luo, L., Wang, Y., Chen, C., Wang, J., & Wu, X. (2024, July). Unifying Large Language Models and Knowledge Graphs: A Roadmap. *IEEE Transactions on Knowledge and Data Engineering*, *36*(7), 3580–3599. DOI: 10.1109/TKDE.2024.3352100

Papamarkou, T., Birdal, T., Bronstein, M. M., Carlsson, G. E., Curry, J., Gao, Y., & Zamzmi, G. (2024). Position: Topological Deep Learning is the New Frontier for Relational Learning. In *Forty-first International Conference on Machine Learning*.

Pappano, L. The year of the mooc. The New York Times **2**(12), 2012 (2012)

Paszke, A., Gross, S., Massa, F., Lerer, A., Bradbury, J., Chanan, G., Killeen, T., Lin, Z., Gimelshein, N., Antiga, L., Desmaison, A., Köpf, A., Yang, E., DeVito, Z., Raison, M., Tejani, A., Chilamkurthy, S., Steiner, B., Fang, L., & Chintala, S. (2019). PyTorch: An imperative style, high-performance deep learning library. In Vol. 32, pp. 8024–8035). Advances in Neural Information Processing Systems. Curran Associates., https://arxiv.org/abs/1912.01703

Patil, R., Boit, S., Gudivada, V., & Nandigam, J. (2023). A survey of text representation and embedding techniques in NLP. *IEEE Access : Practical Innovations, Open Solutions*, *11*, 36120–36146. DOI: 10.1109/ACCESS.2023.3266377

Paz Garcia, R. C., & Pachay Ruiz, S. A. Sistema web y m'ovil para la detecci'on de nivel de incidencia y severidad de la plaga coptoborus ochromactonus en planta- ciones de balsa en la finca digna elizabeth. PhD thesis, Universidad Agraria del Ecuador (2024)

Percona (2023). The Ultimate Guide to Open Source Databases.

Popenici, S. A., & Kerr, S. (2017). Exploring the impact of artificial intelligence on teaching and learning in higher education. *Research and Practice in Technology Enhanced Learning*, *12*(1), 22. DOI: 10.1186/s41039-017-0062-8 PMID: 30595727

PostgreSQL Global Development Group (2025).PostgreSQL Documentation.

Pranckuté, R. (2021). Web of Science (WoS) and Scopus: The Titans of Bibliographic Information in Today's Academic World. *Publications / MDPI*, *9*(1), 12. Advance online publication. DOI: 10.3390/publications9010012

Pratt, M. K. (2021). *5 challenges IT faces using open source data management*. TechTarget.

Quan, Y., Xiong, Z. K., Zhang, K. X., Zhang, Q. Y., Zhang, W., & Zhang, H. Y. (2023). Evolution-strengthened knowledge graph enables predicting the targetability and druggability of genes. *PNAS Nexus*, *2*(5), pgad147. DOI: 10.1093/pnasnexus/pgad147 PMID: 37188275

Rai, R., & Bansal, P. Smart agriculture 4.0: Precision crop disease identification and classification using advanced ai techniques. In: *International Conference on Recent Advancements and Modernisations in Sustainable Intelligent Technologies and Applications (RAMSITA 2025)*, pp. 583–598 (2025). Atlantis Press DOI: 10.2991/978-94-6463-716-8_45

Rane, N. (2024). Enhancing the quality of teaching and learning through gemini, chatgpt, and similar generative artificial intelligence: Challenges, future prospects, and ethical considerations in education. *TESOL and Technology Studies*, *5*(1), 1–6. DOI: 10.48185/tts.v5i1.1000

Redgate Software (2025). DB-Engines Ranking.

Richards, J. C., & Rodgers, T. S. (2014). *Approaches and methods in language teaching* (3rd ed.). Cambridge University Press. DOI: 10.1017/9781009024532

Rizzo, G., Pereira, B., Varga, A., Van Erp, M., & Cano Basave, A. E. (2017). Lessons learnt from the Named Entity rEcognition and Linking (NEEL) challenge series. *Semantic Web*, *8*(5), 667–700. DOI: 10.3233/SW-170276

Rossi, A., Barbosa, D., Firmani, D., Matinata, A., & Merialdo, P. (2021). Knowledge graph embedding for link prediction: A comparative analysis. [TKDD]. *ACM Transactions on Knowledge Discovery from Data*, *15*(2), 1–49. DOI: 10.1145/3424672

RTInsights. (2024). 7 Reasons PostgreSQL is a Great Choice for AI Projects.

Sánchez Martínez, M.: Detecci´on de personas mediante t´ecnicas de aprendizaje autom´atico: Svm y cnn (2018)

Santos, A., Colaço, A. R., Nielsen, A. B., Niu, L., Strauss, M., Geyer, P. E., Coscia, F., Albrechtsen, N. J. W., Mundt, F., Jensen, L. J., & Mann, M. (2022). A knowledge graph to interpret clinical proteomics data. *Nature Biotechnology*, *40*(5), 692–702. DOI: 10.1038/s41587-021-01145-6 PMID: 35102292

Scholz, R. W., & Tietje, O. (2002). Embedded case study methods: Integrating quantitative and qualitative knowledge. *Sage (Atlanta, Ga.).*

Schütze, H., Manning, C. D., & Raghavan, P. (2008). *Introduction to information retrieval.* Cambridge University Press.

Selva Birunda, S., & Kanniga Devi, R. (2021). A review on word embedding techniques for text classification. In Innovative Data Communication Technologies and Application (pp. 267–281). DOI: 10.1007/978-981-15-9651-3_23

Serra, A., Fratello, M., Federico, A., & Greco, D. (2025). An update on knowledge graphs and their current and potential applications in drug discovery. *Expert Opinion on Drug Discovery*, *20*(5), 599–619. DOI: 10.1080/17460441.2025.2490253 PMID: 40223439

Shimizu, R., Matsutani, M., & Goto, M. (2022). An explainable recommendation framework based on an improved knowledge graph attention network with massive volumes of side information. *Knowledge-Based Systems, 239*, 107970. DOI: 10.1016/j.knosys.2021.107970

Silva, A. L., & Terra, A. L. (2023). Cultural heritage on the Semantic Web: The Europeana Data Model. *IFLA Journal, 50*(1), 93–107. DOI: 10.1177/03400352231202506

Su, C., Tong, J., Zhu, Y., Cui, P., & Wang, F. (2020). Network embedding in biomedical data science. *Briefings in Bioinformatics, 21*(1), 182–197. DOI: 10.1093/bib/bby117 PMID: 30535359

Sun, X., Zhang, J., Wu, X., Cheng, H., Xiong, Y., & Li, J. (2023). Graph prompt learning: A comprehensive survey and beyond. *arXiv preprint arXiv:2311.16534.*

Sun, Z., Yang, J., Zhang, J., Bozzon, A., Huang, L. K., & Xu, C. (2018, September). Recurrent knowledge graph embedding for effective recommendation. In *Proceedings of the 12th ACM conference on recommender systems* (pp. 297-305). DOI: 10.1145/3240323.3240361

Tamine, L., & Goeuriot, L. (2021). Semantic information retrieval on medical texts: Research challenges, survey, and open issues. *ACM Computing Surveys, 54*(7), 1–38. DOI: 10.1145/3462476

TechTarget (2024). 12 Top Open Source Databases to Consider.

TecTarget (2023). 7 Top Technologies for Metaverse Development.

Tegsten, S. (2024). Tailored query resolution for medical data interaction: Integrating LangChain4j, LLMs, and retrieval augmented generation.

Tiddi, I., & Schlobach, S. (2022). Knowledge graphs as tools for explainable machine learning: A survey. *Artificial Intelligence, 302*, 103627. DOI: 10.1016/j.artint.2021.103627

Timan, T., & Mann, Z. (2021). Data protection in the era of artificial intelligence: trends, existing solutions and recommendations for privacy-preserving technologies. In *The Elements of Big Data Value: Foundations of the Research and Innovation Ecosystem* (pp. 153–175). Springer. DOI: 10.1007/978-3-030-68176-0_7

Timescale. (2024). State of PostgreSQL 2024: PostgreSQL and AI.

Tiwari, S., Villazón-Terrazas, B., Ortiz-Rodríguez, F., & Sahri, S. (Eds.). (2024). Knowledge Graphs and Semantic Web: 6th International Conference, KGSWC 2024, Paris, France, December 11–13, 2024, Proceedings. Springer Nature.

Tiwari, S., Ortiz-Rodriguez, F., Ben Abbes, S., Usoro Usip, P., & Hantach, I. (Eds.). (2023). *Semantic AI in Knowledge Graphs*. Routledge. DOI: 10.1201/9781003313267

Tiwari, S., Ortiz-Rodríguez, F., & Jabbar, M. A. (2022). Semantic modeling for healthcare applications: An introduction. In *Semantic Models in IoT and eHealth Applications* (pp. 1–17). Academic Press., DOI: 10.1016/B978-0-32-391773-5.00007-8

Vakaj, E., Tiwari, S., Mihindukulasooriya, N., Ortiz-Rodríguez, F., & Mcgranaghan, R. 2023. NLP4KGC: Natural Language Processing for Knowledge Graph Construction. In Companion Proceedings of the ACM Web Conference 2023 (WWW '23 Companion). Association for Computing Machinery, New York, NY, USA, 1111. DOI: 10.1145/3543873.3589746

Valencia Sandoval, K., Duana Avila, D.: Los c´ıtricos en m´exico: an´alisis de eficiencia t´ecnica. An´alisis econ´omico **34**(87), 269–283 (2019)

Van Eck, N. J., & Waltman, L. (2010). Software survey: VOSviewer, a computer program for bibliometric mapping. *Scientometrics*, *84*(2), 523–538. DOI: 10.1007/s11192-009-0146-3 PMID: 20585380

Vartiainen, H., Tedre, M., Jormanainen, I.: Co-creating digital art with generative ai in k-9 education: Socio-material insights. International Journal of education through art **19**(3), 405–423 (2023)

Vaswani, A., Shazeer, N., Parmar, N., Uszkoreit, J., Jones, L., Gomez, A. N., & Polosukhin, I. (2017). Attention is all you need. *Advances in Neural Information Processing Systems*, •••, 30.

Villazón-Terrazas, B., Ortiz-Rodriguez, F., Tiwari, S., & Shandilya, S. (2020). Knowledge Graphs and Semantic Web : Second Iberoamerican Conference and First Indo-American Conference, KGSWC 2020, Mérida, Mexico, November 26–27, 2020, Proceedings (1st ed. 2020.). Springer International Publishing. DOI: 10.1007/978-3-030-65384-2

Villazón-Terrazas, B., Ortiz-Rodríguez, F., Tiwari, S., Goyal, A., & Jabbar, M. A. (Eds.). (2021). *Knowledge Graphs and Semantic Web: Third Iberoamerican Conference, KGSWC 2021, Kingsville, TX, USA, November 22–24, 2021, Proceedings*. Springer Nature.

Villazón-Terrazas, B., Ortiz-Rodríguez, F., Tiwari, S., Riechert, T., & Marx, E. (Eds.). (2025). *Knowledge Graphs and Semantic Web: 7th International Conference, KGSWC 2025, Leipzig, Germany, November 26–28, 2025, Proceedings*. Springer Nature.

Villazón-Terrazas, B., Ortiz-Rodríguez, F., Tiwari, S., Sicilia, M. A., & Martín-Moncunill, D. (Eds.). (2022). *Knowledge Graphs and Semantic Web: 4th Iberoamerican Conference, KGSWC 2022, Madrid, Spain, November 21–23, 2022, Proceedings*. Springer Nature.

Vilone, G., & Longo, L. (2020). "Explainable artificial intelligence: A systematic review." *arXiv preprint arXiv:2006.00093*.

Waikhom, L., & Patgiri, R. (2021). Graph neural networks: Methods, applications, and opportunities. *arXiv preprint arXiv:2108.10733*.

Wang, B., Wang, A., Chen, F., Wang, Y., & Kuo, C. C. J. (2019). Evaluating word embedding models: Methods and experimental results. *APSIPA Transactions on Signal and Information Processing*, *8*(1), e19. DOI: 10.1017/ATSIP.2019.12

Wang, J., Wang, X., Ma, C., & Kou, L. (2021). A survey on the development status and application prospects of knowledge graph in smart grids. *IET Generation, Transmission & Distribution, 15*(3), 383–407. DOI: 10.1049/gtd2.12040

Wang, S., Wang, F., Zhu, Z., Wang, J., Tran, T., & Du, Z. (2024). Artificial intelligence in education: A systematic literature review. *Expert Systems with Applications, 252*, 124167. DOI: 10.1016/j.eswa.2024.124167

Wang, S., Xu, D., Liang, H., Bai, Y., Li, X., Zhou, J., Su, C., & Wei, W. (2025). Advances in deep learning applications for plant disease and pest detection: A review. *Remote Sensing (Basel), 17*(4), 698. DOI: 10.3390/rs17040698

Waqas, M., Naseem, A., Humphries, U.W., Hlaing, P.T., Dechpichai, P., Wang- wongchai, A.: Applications of machine learning and deep learning in agriculture: A comprehensive review. Green Technologies and Sustainability, 100199 (2025)

Wei, X., Wang, S., Zhang, D., Bhatia, P., & Arnold, A. (2021). Knowledge enhanced pretrained language models: A compreshensive survey. *arXiv preprint arXiv:2110.08455.*

Winaitham, W. The scientific review of ai functions of enhancement english learning and teaching. In: 2022 13th International Conference on Information and Communication Technology Convergence (ICTC), pp. 148–152 (2022). IEEE DOI: 10.1109/ICTC55196.2022.9952632

Wolf, T., Debut, L., Sanh, V., Chaumond, J., Delangue, C., Moi, A., Cistac, P., Rault, T., Louf, R., Funtowicz, M., Davison, J., Shleifer, S., von Platen, P., Ma, C., Jernite, Y., Plu, J., Xu, C., Le Scao, T., Gugger, S., & Rush, A. M. (2020). Transformers: State-of-the-art natural language processing. In *Proceedings of the 2020 Conference on Empirical Methods in Natural Language Processing: System Demonstrations* (pp. 38-45). ACL. https://arxiv.org/abs/1910.03771

Wu, J., Zhu, J., Qi, Y., Chen, J., Xu, M., Menolascina, F., & Grau, V. (2024). Medical graph RAG: Towards safe medical large language model via graph retrieval-augmented generation. arXiv preprint arXiv:2408.04187.

Xiao, Y., Zheng, S., Shi, J., Du, X., & Hong, J. (2023). Knowledge graph-based manufacturing process planning: A state-of-the-art review. *Journal of Manufacturing Systems*, *70*, 417–435. DOI: 10.1016/j.jmsy.2023.08.006

Xu, M. (2021). Understanding graph embedding methods and their applications. *SIAM Review*, *63*(4), 825–853. DOI: 10.1137/20M1386062

Yang, L., Chen, H., Li, Z., Ding, X., & Wu, X. (2024). Give us the Facts: Enhancing Large Language Models With Knowledge Graphs for Fact-Aware Language Modeling. *IEEE Transactions on Knowledge and Data Engineering*, *36*(7), 3091–3110. Advancc onlinc publication. DOI: 10.1109/TKDE.2024.3360454

Yang, Y., Sun, W., Sun, D., & Salas-Pilco, S. Z. (2024). Navigating the ai-enhanced stem education landscape: A decade of insights, trends, and opportunities. *Research in Science & Technological Education*, 1–25.

Yang, Z., Yuan, S., Shao, Z., Li, W., & Liu, R. (2025). A review on synergizing knowledge graphs and large language models. *Computing*, *107*(143), 143. Advance online publication. DOI: 10.1007/s00607-025-01499-8

Yates, B. (2002). *Modelos de recuperación de información*. Addison-Wesley.

Ye, Z., Kumar, Y. J., Sing, G. O., Song, F., & Wang, J. (2022). A comprehensive survey of graph neural networks for knowledge graphs. *IEEE Access : Practical Innovations, Open Solutions*, *10*, 75729–75741. DOI: 10.1109/ACCESS.2022.3191784

Zhai, X., Chu, X., Chai, C. S., Jong, M. S. Y., Istenic, A., Spector, M., Liu, J.-B., Yuan, J., & Li, Y. (2021). A review of artificial intelligence (ai) in education from 2010 to 2020. *Complexity*, *2021*(1), 8812542. DOI: 10.1155/2021/8812542

Zhang, H., Jiang, Y., Li, M., Yuan, H., & Yang, W.-Y. (2024). pEBR: A probabilistic approach to embedding-based retrieval. arXiv preprint arXiv:2410.19349.

Zhang, W., Chen, J., Li, J., Xu, Z., Pan, J. Z., & Chen, H. (2022). Knowledge graph reasoning with logics and embeddings: Survey and perspective. *arXiv preprint arXiv:2202.07412.*

Zhang, W., Paudel, B., Zhang, W., Bernstein, A., & Chen, H. (2019, January). Interaction embeddings for prediction and explanation in knowledge graphs. In *Proceedings of the twelfth ACM international conference on web search and data mining* (pp. 96-104). DOI: 10.1145/3289600.3291014

Zhao, H.-G., Li, X.-Z., & Kang, X. (2024). Development of an artificial intelligence curricu- lum design for children in taiwan and its impact on learning outcomes. *Humanities & Social Sciences Communications, 11*(1), 1–17. DOI: 10.1057/s41599-024-03839-z

Zheng, Q., Zou, X., Dong, Y., Cen, Y., Yin, D., Xu, J., . . . Tang, J. (2021). Graph robustness benchmark: Benchmarking the adversarial robustness of graph machine learning. *arXiv preprint arXiv:2111.04314.*

Zheng, C., Wong, S., Su, X., Tang, Y., Nawaz, A., & Kassem, M. (2025). Automating construction contract review using knowledge graph-enhanced large language models. *Automation in Construction, 175*, 106179. DOI: 10.1016/j.autcon.2025.106179

Zheng, W., Lu, S., Cai, Z., Wang, R., Wang, L., & Yin, L. (2023). Palbert: An improved question answering model. *Computer Modeling in Engineering & Sciences, 10,* •••.

Zhou, B., Li, X., Liu, T., Xu, K., Liu, W., & Bao, J. (2024). CausalKGPT: Industrial structure causal knowledge-enhanced large language model for cause analysis of quality problems in aerospace product manufacturing. *Advanced Engineering Informatics, 59*, 102333. DOI: 10.1016/j.aei.2023.102333

Zhu, S. (2024). Exploring knowledge graph-based neural-symbolic system from application perspective. *arXiv preprint arXiv:2405.03524.*

Zhu, Y., ... (2023). "Large language models for information retrieval: A survey." *arXiv preprint arXiv:2308.07107.*

Zhu, Y., Wang, X., Chen, J., Qiao, S., Ou, Y., Yao, Y., Deng, S., Chen, H., & Zhang, N. (2024). LLMs for knowledge graph construction and reasoning: Recent capabilities and future opportunities. *World Wide Web (Bussum), 27*(58), 58. Advance online publication. DOI: 10.1007/s11280-024-01297-w

Zupic, I., & Čater, T. (2015). Bibliometric methods in management and organization. *Organizational Research Methods, 18*(3), 429–472. https://doi.org/https://doi.org/10.1177/109442811456262. DOI: 10.1177/1094428114562629

Zytek, A., Pidò, S., & Veeramachaneni, K. (2024). LLMs for XAI: Future directions for explaining explanations. arXiv preprint arXiv:2405.06064.

About the Contributors

Fernando Ortiz-Rodriguez is a Full Professor and Head of the Artificial Intelligence and Innovation Lab at Tamaulipas Autonomous University. He was the Executive Director at the International Institute of Studies (IIES). He created the First Business School in Tamaulipas, Mexico. He worked as the Information Technology Manager at Emerson Electric, where he developed more than 40 pieces of software, some of them used globally in Emerson, and, achieved technology convergence by implementing the first efforts on IoT and Industry 4.0. Fernando is a member of National Systems Researchers (SNI) Level 1 of the National Council of Science and Technology (CONACYT) and INDEX IT Advisor

Amed Abel Leiva Mederos. Degree in Information Sciences from the Central University of Las Villas. Master in Information Sciences. PhD in Information Sciences at the University of Granada and the University of Havana. Head of the semantic web research group. Diploma in Intelligent Systems at the UGR. He specializes in IoT, semantic web, and interoperability

Jose L. Martinez-Rodriguez received his Ph.D. in Computer Science from Cinvestav Tamaulipas, Mexico (2018). He is an Associate Professor in the Faculty of Engineering and Science at the Autonomous University of Tamaulipas. His research interests include Semantic Web representation, Data Mining, Information Extraction, and Cloud Computing.

Deepali R Vora was the Professor & Head of Department, Information Technology in Vidyalankar Institute of Technology, Mumbai and has completed her PhD in Computer Science and Engineering from Amity University, Mumbai. She is currently associated with Symbiosis Institute of Technology, Pune as associate professor. She has more than 20 years of experience in total in teaching, research and Industry. She has published more than 50 research papers in reputed national, international conferences and journals. She has co-authored three books and 2 book chapters and delivered various talks in Data Science and Machine learning. She has conducted hands-on session in Data Science using Python for students and faculties. She is appointed as a Syllabus Revision Committee member with Mumbai University and developed the course content for B.E. (Information Technology) course. She has received grants from government bodies like AICTE, ISTE as well as Industry for conducting research, organising conference and training courses for faculties. She is acting as a reviewer for many International Conferences and Journals like IEEE Access, IGI Global – Journal of Big Data Analytics, Journal of Intelligent Systems, Inderscience etc. She has organised many value added courses for the benefit of the students. More than 18 students have completed and currently, 3 students are pursuing their post-graduate studies under her guidance.

***

Otmane Azeroual is a leading expert in data science, artificial intelligence, and digital transformation. With a PhD in computer science, specializing in databases, information systems, AI, and digitalization, Dr. Azeroual has made significant contributions to both academia and industry. He holds senior positions in research institutions and the private sector, where he has developed cutting-edge AI solutions. As an educator, Dr. Azeroual teaches AI and data science courses at the University of Hagen, shaping the next generation of experts in the field. His research focuses on big data, data quality management, and the integration of digital technologies. His work has been widely published in prestigious journals and presented at international conferences. Recognized for bridging the gap between academic research and real-world applications, Dr. Azeroual's expertise continues to drive innovation and digital transformation across industries. As a sought-after speaker, he is committed to advancing the global conversation on AI and fostering collaboration in digital innovation.

Yadier Betancourt Martínez is a Computer Science graduate and a dedicated GenAI Engineer with a strong foundation in backend development. Yadier has cultivated a deep passion for learning new technologies, with a particular interest in the transformative field of artificial intelligence. In his role as a GenAI Engineer, Yadier is at the forefront of developing and fine-tuning cutting-edge AI solutions. His work likely involves designing and implementing systems using large language models (LLMs), creating intelligent chatbots, and building automation solutions for enterprise clients. This position requires a blend of technical skills, including proficiency in Python, machine learning algorithms, and neural networks, as well as a focus on ethical AI practices and data security. Beyond his technical work, Yadier demonstrates a commitment to the developer community by actively sharing knowledge and contributing to collective learning. He embodies a proactive approach to professional growth, constantly exploring new techniques and architectures to drive innovation in the fast-evolving landscape of generative AI.

Tania Guerrero Meléndez holds a Ph.D. in Knowledge Management and Knowledge Transfer from the Autonomous University of Tamaulipas, where she is affiliated as a professor and researcher. Her research interests focus on data management and its applications to engineering, as well as on knowledge-based information systems.

Francisco Isaí Morales-Sáenz is a professor-researcher at the Faculty of Commerce and Administration Victoria, Tamaulipas, México. His research line is information technology and strategy.

Index

A

AI 1, 2, 3, 5, 6, 8, 10, 12, 14, 15, 24, 29, 30, 32, 33, 37, 51, 52, 53, 55, 60, 61, 64, 66, 67, 69, 70, 71, 72, 73, 74, 75, 76, 77, 78, 79, 80, 81, 82, 83, 84, 85, 86, 87, 88, 89, 90, 91, 92, 93, 94, 95, 96, 97, 100, 105, 107, 111, 112, 117, 118, 119, 124, 127, 130, 166, 167, 168, 173, 191, 194, 195, 196, 197, 200, 207, 215, 216, 217, 218, 219, 220, 221, 222, 223, 224, 225, 226, 227
Artificial Intelligence 1, 2, 8, 10, 11, 14, 37, 49, 51, 52, 53, 65, 66, 67, 70, 72, 73, 77, 84, 85, 92, 96, 100, 112, 115, 116, 117, 118, 119, 142, 147, 148, 149, 161, 166, 167, 168, 173, 179, 191, 193, 194, 199, 200, 201, 206, 207, 208, 215, 216, 217, 218, 219, 220, 222, 224, 225, 226, 227

B

Bibliometric Analysis 193, 196, 198, 208, 211, 212, 218

C

CamemBERT 99, 101, 107
CEFR 99, 100, 101, 102, 103, 104, 105, 107, 108, 109, 110
CNN 178, 179, 184, 185, 186, 188, 189, 190, 191
Computer Vision 120, 121, 178, 179, 181, 187

D

Data Integration 13, 14, 24, 37
Data Management 10, 21, 32, 72, 97, 117
DBMS 77, 79, 80, 84, 96
Deep Learning 18, 30, 31, 36, 38, 39, 52, 76, 87, 113, 178, 190, 191, 192, 205, 217, 220, 226
Dspace 148, 149, 172, 175

E

e-Learning 215, 216, 218, 219, 222, 224, 225
Embedding 4, 13, 14, 15, 16, 18, 19, 20, 21, 22, 24, 25, 26, 27, 28, 29, 31, 32, 33, 34, 35, 38, 39, 40, 41, 42, 44, 45, 50, 61, 62, 63, 67, 117, 123, 127, 131, 132, 134, 136, 137, 144, 145, 155, 162, 163, 164, 168, 173, 175, 194, 211
End-of-Life Decision-Making 47, 55, 61
Explainable Artificial Intelligence 49, 51, 52, 53, 65, 67
Extensibility 69, 70, 71, 77, 78, 80, 82, 84, 85, 86, 88, 95

F

fine-tuning 5, 99, 101, 103, 104, 105, 107, 122, 184, 185, 187, 188, 189
FLEUR 99, 101, 107, 108, 112
FRACAS 99, 101, 107, 112

G

Generative AI 6, 14, 51, 197, 220, 227
GraphRAG 5, 6, 9, 55, 61, 116, 118, 124, 125, 126, 130, 142

I

Information Retrieval 13, 14, 21, 41, 50, 55, 65, 67, 115, 116, 117, 118, 119, 123, 126, 127, 132, 136, 138, 139, 142, 143, 144, 147, 148, 150, 151, 152, 153, 155, 158, 164, 168, 170, 172, 175
Intelligent Information Retrieval 116, 117, 119, 142, 175

K

Knowledge Extraction 1, 9, 193, 196, 197, 206, 210
Knowledge Graph 4, 12, 33, 34, 36, 37,

38, 39, 40, 41, 48, 50, 55, 57, 60, 61, 64, 99, 100, 102, 107, 109, 116, 117, 118, 124, 127, 130, 132, 135, 136, 138, 139, 140, 142, 143, 148, 162, 173, 194, 197, 202, 205, 210, 211, 212, 213, 214
Knowledge Graphs 1, 2, 3, 4, 5, 10, 11, 12, 13, 34, 37, 38, 39, 41, 47, 48, 49, 51, 60, 61, 65, 67, 99, 100, 101, 110, 111, 112, 116, 117, 118, 124, 125, 126, 130, 136, 137, 141, 142, 143, 147, 148, 193, 194, 195, 196, 197, 198, 202, 203, 205, 206, 208, 210, 211, 212, 213, 214
Knowledge Representation 4, 14, 31, 33, 38, 194, 195, 199, 204

L

Language Models 1, 2, 4, 5, 10, 11, 14, 33, 36, 38, 39, 41, 48, 61, 67, 99, 100, 107, 116, 118, 121, 122, 125, 126, 127, 130, 142, 144, 147, 155, 193, 194, 196, 197, 198, 202, 205, 206, 208, 210, 211, 212, 213, 214
Large Language Models 1, 2, 4, 10, 11, 36, 38, 39, 48, 67, 118, 121, 122, 130, 144, 193, 196, 197, 198, 202, 205, 206, 208, 210, 211, 212, 213, 214
LLM 5, 6, 7, 8, 9, 55, 61, 62, 63, 66, 103, 104, 106, 107, 109, 121, 122, 124, 130, 131, 132, 135, 136, 138, 139, 140, 141, 143, 194, 195, 197, 206, 207

M

Metaverse 69, 70, 71, 72, 73, 75, 76, 77, 78, 79, 80, 81, 82, 83, 84, 85, 86, 87, 88, 89, 91, 92, 93, 94, 95, 97, 226
MobileNetV2 178, 179, 180, 184, 185, 186, 187, 188, 189, 190
MongoDB 69, 71, 73, 74, 75, 76, 77, 79, 80, 81, 82, 83, 84, 85, 97
MySQL 69, 71, 73, 74, 75, 77, 78, 80, 81, 83, 85, 97

N

Neural Networks 18, 22, 23, 30, 37, 38, 39, 41, 47, 48, 49, 53, 64, 65, 66, 118, 119, 120, 121, 143, 154, 179, 180, 190, 205
NLP 6, 13, 20, 32, 39, 50, 51, 67, 86, 92, 112, 120, 123, 126, 154, 155, 221

O

Observatory 115, 117, 125, 126, 127, 130, 137, 142
Ontologies 4, 7, 9, 17, 38, 39, 48, 49, 54, 161, 207, 208
Ontology 2, 3, 4, 7, 9, 11, 48, 49, 50, 55, 57, 66, 116, 118, 125, 126, 127, 147, 160, 161, 162, 204, 206, 207
Open-Source Tools 70
Oracle 69, 71, 77, 79, 80, 81, 82, 84, 85

P

Performance 13, 14, 15, 19, 21, 23, 24, 25, 26, 27, 28, 29, 30, 32, 38, 50, 54, 64, 69, 70, 71, 72, 73, 74, 75, 77, 78, 79, 80, 81, 84, 85, 86, 87, 88, 89, 90, 91, 92, 95, 108, 110, 113, 121, 122, 138, 140, 144, 167, 170, 171, 178, 183, 186, 187, 188, 189, 201, 207, 220
Pest Detection 179, 187, 191, 192
PostgreSQL 69, 70, 71, 72, 73, 74, 75, 76, 77, 78, 79, 80, 81, 82, 83, 84, 85, 86, 87, 88, 89, 90, 91, 92, 93, 94, 95, 96, 97
Precision Agriculture 178

R

Real-Time Applications 9, 69, 70, 72, 73, 74, 75, 80, 81, 83, 91, 92
ResNet50 178, 179, 180, 184, 185, 186, 187, 188, 189

S

Scalability 9, 10, 24, 28, 29, 32, 69, 70, 71, 73, 74, 75, 76, 77, 79, 80, 81, 84, 85, 86, 89, 92, 94, 95, 111, 117, 121,

126, 223
Semantic Information 14, 17, 18, 31, 41, 147, 168
Semantics 7, 29, 57, 125, 127, 150, 151, 152, 155, 170, 204, 205, 225
Semantic Search Engine 115, 117, 125, 126, 137, 142, 149, 160, 168
Semantic Web 1, 2, 3, 4, 5, 7, 10, 11, 12, 37, 40, 161, 193, 194, 196, 197, 206, 212, 213
Spatial Data 70, 82, 84, 85, 86, 88, 95
SQL Server 69, 71, 77, 79, 80, 81, 84, 85

www.ingramcontent.com/pod-product-compliance
Lightning Source LLC
LaVergne TN
LVHW081520300926
849161LV00006B/1239